Dyer Straits

All Those Years Ago in Dorchester, MA

Mary A. Dyer

Cover: Mary on Easter Sunday in 1974, walking towards Dorchester Ave. to Sunday Mass at St. Ambrose Parish.

Page Breaks: Chapter section breaks depict a "Dorchester" cross with hashmarks, a spade, and a dot, honoring the tattoos of her late brothers, John, Bob, and Bill.

Mary A. Dyer

ISBN: 979-8-9941293-0-2

First Print: 2026

Format: Paperback

Publisher: BOSBeat Books

For Dot Rats everywhere

Preface

This is a family story about growing up with addiction, mental illness, poverty, domestic violence, and racial divides, and finding a way through by bonding over music, humor, and love. It's about holding both the dark and the light, honoring with compassion the complicated parents who raised us, celebrating those who were part of those years, and remembering, through shared recollections, the parts of childhood worth keeping and learning from.

Set in Boston's Dorchester neighborhood during the social and political upheavals of the 1960s and '70s and the early '80s, this memoir traces my family's endurance through adversity.

Dorchester was a tough but fun place to grow up, where brotherhoods and sisterhoods—by blood and by bond—came with a lasting sense of pride. Being "O.F.D."—Originally from Dorchester —is a bit of a badge of honor, but it also carried struggles, poor choices, and the weight of untimely losses; loved ones who should have had more time.

It's a tribute to my mother, who raised eight children with resilience and resourcefulness under difficult circumstances, and to the seven siblings who helped raise, protect, and guide me. It remembers my father, a mentally ill man who did what he knew how, challenged by forces larger than himself. In addition, it honors O.F.D.ers everywhere, whose comical adventures, misadventures, and hard-earned grit forged bonds that remain part of who we are today. We know you. We see you. We are cut from the same cloth.

I've tried to portray this period as faithfully as possible, based on what was lived and witnessed. Some offensive dialogue appears as it was spoken, reflecting the language used at the time rather than an endorsement of it. Certain names and identifying details have been changed to protect privacy. Any resemblance to other persons, living or deceased, is coincidental.

This book contains profanity and scenes of violence, addiction, and references to death.

Author's Note
The Beatles Are in My Ears and in My Eyes

As a young child, I remember singing with my siblings to the world around us. My earliest memory goes back to age four, swinging alongside my nine-year-old sister Margie and eight-year-old brother Billy on our metal, three-seater swing set in the backyard. We lived on the corner of Hancock and Glendale Streets in a Dorchester triple-decker, Boston's trademark three-family home with one apartment per floor. The three of us swung back and forth in unison, our voices rising and falling as we sang. Each time we soared up, the red-and-white candy-striped legs lifted out of the cement footing, then slammed back down as we descended. It was a bumpy ride, but one full of simple joy.

Margie sang, "Help me if you can; I'm feeling down."

Billy joined in, "And I do appreciate you being 'round."

Then we all sang with gusto, "Help me get my feet back on the ground. Won't you please, please help me."

As a preschooler, I sang along to Beatles songs like this without knowing who the band was—only knowing that singing them with my family made me happy, and they connected us in a way nothing else did. I've long thought of their music as the soundtrack of my life, first as a band, and later as solo artists. Their lyrics and musicality speak to me like no other.

This connection grew as I got older and I began paying closer attention to the records themselves. When I was young, I studied Margie's albums the way other kids read cereal boxes. I searched for hidden meanings in the photos, artwork, and lyrics. I examined the tiny print on the record labels to see who wrote each song and learned some of Ringo's songs were covers of country tunes by Carl Perkins and Buck Owens—the same records my father used to play.

I remember vividly the night John Lennon died on December 8, 1980. I was fourteen, drifting off to sleep to rock music playing on WBCN. On the radio, *somebody spoke, and I went into a dream.* Then, Margie burst into my room and snapped the ceiling light on.

"Mary, wake up! Did you hear what happened?"

I must have heard the breaking news in my half-dream state because I already knew something.

"Yeah, Paul was shot, right?" I asked, still half-asleep, shielding my eyes from the blinding light.

"No, John was shot dead. It's on the news now."

My haze cleared and I ran after Margie to the parlor. We sat together in disbelief, watching the eleven o'clock news replay the story over and over. The anchor's voice sent chills through me. It felt as though one of my big brothers had died.

That night, I cried myself to sleep, listening to the DJ play "Imagine" and other Lennon songs—quiet tears for one of my heroes.

The next morning, on the school bus to Boston's English High, I pulled out my notebook and, blinking back tears, scrawled "RIP Forever, John" across the top of a blank page. I wrote a poem about how John inspired peace and love worldwide. It was published in the school newspaper, and the following year, I won a contest at the JFK Library for writing a moving essay about John as my hero.

In my life, the Beatles continue to be a source of comfort and identification. When things don't go as planned, when *it's all too much*—or when life is going well, and *I feel fine*—I hear the Beatles, and things feel familiar, like I'm back on Hancock or Bloomfield Street. I feel my family's presence, especially my siblings who are no longer with us.

For that reason, you'll see Beatles sentiments scattered throughout these pages. Think of them as breadcrumbs—little guideposts carrying the mood and meaning of each story, the way only the Beatles' music can for me.

1975

Quincy, MA,
   Age 9

"Get outta the car, ya fuckin' punk!" Dad sputtered at the driver, standing at his window. I sat paralyzed on the rear bench seat as we idled at the red light by the Clam Box. Through Dad's open vent window, cigarette smoke and choking leaded exhaust drifted in from the car idling behind us. The driver stared straight ahead, hands fixed on the wheel, as if my father weren't there.

Dad stormed back and flung his glasses onto the dash. He reached under the front seat and pulled out the Louisville Slugger he kept there for "emergencies." "Stay in the car!" he barked, slamming the door.

My stomach twisted. He taunted the guy, bat raised, calling him a pussy, daring him to get out—like a street psycho from *The Warriors.*

"Come on! Let's dance!"

When the driver didn't engage, Dad smashed his back window. Glass exploded inward. The guy scrambled out.

Fights and shouting matches on Dorchester streets didn't faze anyone, but the sound of breaking glass in quieter Quincy turned heads.

The guy wrenched the bat from Dad's hands and shoved him off balance. He ran to the back of our car and smashed the tailgate window with three savage swings. Glass rained into the back seat —into my hair and down the collar of my plaid smock shirt. I screamed and ducked, shielding my face.

He bolted back to his car, Dad lumbering after him, screaming, "I'll kill you, cocksuckah!" The bat clattered to the pavement as he dropped it and threw himself inside, slamming the door. He backed up, cut over the yellow line, and sped past us, flipping us off, his voice trailing, "Muthafuckah!"

Dad stood in the middle of Quincy Shore Drive, shouting, "That's right, I'm a muthafuckah! That's why ya mutha's shoes are under my bed! I got ya plate numbah, asshole!"

He flung the bat onto the front passenger floor, shoved his glasses back on, and tore down the boulevard after the guy—but he was long gone.

A sudden brake at the East Squantum Street light slammed me into the musty vinyl seat. I cried as more glass spilled forward onto my hair and clothes.

This was Dyer Straits.

Chapter 1

I Heard the News Today

January 1999

It was an unseasonably mild January day in Boston, the deceptive kind that tricks you into thinking winter might ease up a little early. At the office where I worked in the South Station district, colleagues and I gathered at the reception area television to watch Paul Cellucci's inauguration as Massachusetts' new governor. The day felt routine—a blur of emails, ringing phones, and news anchor commentaries in the background.

After a few minutes, I headed back to my work cubicle. The blinking red voicemail light on my desk phone caught my eye. The call log showed it wasn't from an internal work extension but an external 617 number. I tapped play, thinking it must be the caterer calling about a large lunch order for a group of executives I supported.

"Mary, it's Kathy Hanley," the message began. Kathy was a coworker from my previous bank office job. Her voice was gentle and hushed, instead of collegial. I knew right away this call was about something serious. "I'm so sorry for calling you at your new job. An attorney named George Sanchez called here to reach you. He left his number. It sounds like your father may be dying."

I was caught off guard. As I listened, I grabbed a pen and jotted the phone number on a sticky note, my hurried scribble illegible to anyone but me. I hung up and took a long, heavy breath. It froze in my lungs, my body snapping into fight-or-flight mode. It had been twelve years since I last saw my estranged father. It was a fleeting encounter on Broadway in South Boston when he was homeless.

I immediately dialed George.

"Hi, Mr. Sanchez, this is Mary Dyer—Richard Dyer's daughter—returning your call." I paused, giving myself a second to find the right words. Bad news always seemed to leave me sounding scatterbrained and tongue-tied.

"Hi, Mary. Thanks for getting back to me. I'm glad I found you. I'd only heard your father mention you and a few of your siblings once, so I searched a state database and started trying names."

"Your father has been a ward of the court for quite some time. He stated he didn't have contact with next of kin when the V.A. admitted him years ago, so I became his state-appointed legal guardian. He's been dealing with health problems for a long time— I'm sure you're well aware—alcoholism, mental illness, homelessness. And... well... they've finally taken their toll."

They've finally taken their toll. George's words repeated in my mind. My heart rate kicked up a few beats per minute—another jolt of fight-or-flight.

"Oh... That's unfortunate," I said, unsure how else to respond. "But sadly, it's not surprising. I'd always assumed he'd passed away in a homeless shelter by now—or, at best, was still living in one. What's his status?"

George replied, "He's at the Lemuel Shattuck Hospital. I was fairly sure he hadn't talked to any of you in years, but I thought you'd want to know... He's dying from advanced cirrhosis."

George paused. I could hear him shuffling papers on his desk as the news sank in. "The Shattuck" was one of the places people went when options were limited.

"Mm-hmm. I see." I kept my tone even and my voice low, mindful of the open office around me. I don't recall noticing much emotion. Then, as now, my default response was to focus on facts and solutions.

George provided more context. "I saw him earlier today. He's awake and talking some, but the doctors give him a day at best."

"Thanks, George... I... um... I'll reach out to my brothers and sister to see what we can do to get over there."

I hung up the phone, the conversation still settling in my mind. My lizard brain—the ancient survival instinct wired into all humans—took over as it always does in crisis situations, prioritizing logic over emotion. I ran through a mental checklist: phone calls, funeral arrangements, work coverage.

Moments earlier, I hadn't given my father a thought in years. Now I was preparing to say goodbye to a man I hadn't spent any real time with since I was a kid.

Chapter 2

Hello, Goodbye

SINCE MY PARENTS' divorce when I was eleven, my siblings and I had only caught glimpses of my father, homeless on the streets of Dorchester and "Southie," the nickname for South Boston—the area featured in films like *Good Will Hunting, Gone Baby Gone, and The Departed.*

Somehow, he'd made it to nearly seventy, defying all odds. With the news of his impending death, my mind churned.

What condition will we find him in?

Will he even recognize us?

After years of decline, what will be left of him and his mind?

I thought back to the last few times I'd seen him—once in the summer of 1987, when my sister Margie and I, along with her toddler son, Eric, ran into Dad. He was homeless, living on the streets of Southie. We said hello and let him meet his grandson, but it was brief. I saw him again in the fall, and he was pleading for a place to stay. I lied and told him I still lived at home with Ma and her husband Charlie, so I couldn't help him. It was all I could come up with to divert further questions—I needed to get on my way to my morning college class. I felt like a heel for lying. I hadn't seen or heard anything about him again until this call from George twelve years later.

From my cubicle, I called my sister Margie first to share the news about "Dad," "Dickie," "Dick," or "the old man," depending on the memory or story tied to him. Most often, he was called the old man, as if he were a stranger or someone else's relative.

Several phone calls and about an hour later, I finally hung up with Margie again. She had just gotten off the phone with our oldest brother, Bob, who had moved to Florida years ago.

All of my siblings made plans to visit our father—except him, which no one faulted. Bob had taken his share of abuse and had spent years watching our mother endure brutality. His response was no surprise.

"Even if I still lived there, I wouldn't go see him. I'd spit on his grave. Good riddance to that asshole."

I called my mother, Doris, with the news as a courtesy, but she understandably had the most reason not to care. She'd buried the pain and trauma of her twenty-four-year marriage to Dickie Dyer deep in the past, where she intended it to stay.

My second-oldest brother, Johnny, was the outlier in our family, the one Dad bullied and brutalized more than any of us, and who lost his footing along the way. He had no reason to visit or say a last goodbye. But, sentimental and generous by nature, he wanted to pay his respects. To his credit, a less forgiving man wouldn't have.

I spent the next hour tying up loose ends at work, though my mind kept spiraling with questions about what to say and how it would feel to see him after so many years.

Johnny and I got to the hospital first. When we entered Dad's room, a surge of pity came over me. A lump formed in my throat when I saw the state my father was in. His jaundiced eyes and skin reminded me of an overripe banana peel. Now a smaller, feeble sixty-nine-year-old, he was no longer the hulking, six-foot-tall, 300-pound angry giant who'd ruled our childhoods with his iron fist.

I nervously approached his bedside, unsure what I was going to say, the same as I always felt around him when I was young. Only this time it wasn't a feeling of nervousness because of fear, but unfamiliarity.

He said, "Hey, John." Johnny nodded hello and lowered himself into a chair.

"Hi," I said with a nervous, unsure smile.

"Hello, *Marry*."

I never knew why he pronounced my name that way. It wasn't some quirky Boston inflection, but the way he heard and said words, slightly askew. Small talk followed. He took a rattly, shallow breath. The voice that followed was nothing like the bull-horn that used to send me running when I was little. "Are you married? Kids?" This time, unlike when I ran into him in 1987, I shared freely—There was no reason to evade him anymore. "Nope, not married, no kids yet. I went to college and became an elementary school teacher. I taught for a few years, but now I'm a secretary."

"Oh, that's good," he responded flatly.

I added some light banter. "Teachers don't make much."

He paused as if to let it all register. "A teacher, huh?" he rasped. He appeared genuinely pleased with a slight nod of his head.

We kept it light, sharing a few pleasantries. I couldn't think of much to say. I surmised Johnny felt a little awkward too, by how quiet he was, seated in a chair at the foot of the bed. He sat silently, observing. He was dealing with his own alcohol-related health battles.

I wondered how many of us Dad remembered. "Bobby lives in Florida now. He moved there years ago."

The corner of his mouth lifted. "Still a tough bastard? Not taking anyone's crap?"

"He's the same, just a little older."

He nodded toward the window at the dirty snowbanks from last week's storm. "He's not shoveling any of that stuff down there."

"You can say that again. He's probably on a sunny beach right now."

I tried to reconnect our roots and also get a sense of his level of cognition, so I probed, "A lot's changed in Dot since the old days, huh? More stores are owned by Vietnamese and Chinese people now. They're keeping Fields Corner in business."

"Dot" is what everyone calls Dorchester—Dot Ave., Dot High, Dot Day Parade, you name it.

He nodded, seeming a little lost in thought.

"A schoolteacher, you say?" He added a little humor. "Did you keep them in line?"

"Yeah, they hated me."

Johnny cracked a small smile. "Someone had to crack the whip, right?"

Soon, my other brothers and my sister drifted in. I was surprised at how easily Dad seemed with everyone, calling some of us by name as we talked, as if no time had passed. Names were never fixed in my family—we interchange childhood names and grown names, sometimes both, depending on the moment:

Dan (Danny) was outspoken and always eager to share old family stories.

Jim (Jimmy) developed a nervous stutter around Dad early on, later offset by a quick-witted, fun-loving sense of humor.

Marj (Margie)—my only sister, five years older—was patient and wise, someone I've always thought of as a second mother.

Bill (Billy)—was restless and sharp-tongued; his nervous stammer later masked by raunchy, Don Rickles–style comebacks.

Thom (Tommy)—was the youngest brother, sports-minded like Bobby, and pretty laid-back while the rest of us carried on during debates.

And then there was me, the baby of the family, who challenged everyone and everything.

As I watched Dad address us so easily, I couldn't help but wonder if he remembered the violence he'd inflicted on us growing up.

Johnny perked up when Dad asked if he'd been at Whitey's, a bar in Southie. During the '80s and '90s, they occasionally crossed paths there—or at the Pine Street Inn, a homeless shelter where they both drifted in and out.

"Nah, I don't go to bars anymore."

John still drank, but mostly alone at a rundown rooming house in Southie. His lifelong heavy drinking and smoking were taking their toll. He looked older than his forty-three years and his health had been worsening.

Dad nodded, his gaze drifting somewhere far off. I wasn't sure if he was wandering through old memories or just losing his place in the moment.

I noticed we all kept things upbeat for Dad; a small gesture of compassion on such an awkward visit. It's a trait we got from Ma. In a quick aside to me, Thom said he wanted to see if he could jog a memory for Dad. He turned to him and asked, "Remember when we used to go out on the boat?"

In the '70s, we spent countless summer days barreling out to the Boston Harbor islands in Dad's prized sixteen-foot aluminum motorboat. But Dad just looked at Thom, as if not following. Dan, fond of his Dorchester childhood and early outings with Johnny and Bobby—back when Dad could sometimes pass as a "normal" father—shifted the conversation. He had a way of pulling up old, forgotten stories.

"Remember the go-karts in New Hampshire?" Dan asked with enthusiasm.

A faint smile of recognition crossed Dad's face. "Oh, yeah."

He seemed as if he was going through the motions, his attention drifting in and out. I watched my siblings' exchanges for a while and wondered if Dad knew how close he was to the end.

During my visit, I'd hoped to glimpse a little of the real Dickie Dyer—a sober, mellowed one—not the violent alcoholic I grew up with. I don't remember any meaningful talks with him from my childhood. The few memories of conversations I had have faded with time. I vaguely recall him giving me fifty cents for my honor roll report cards—saying, "Keep up the good work—don't be a flunkie."

As we stood around his bedside, I thought about how the older kids had endured my father's violent outbursts through their late teens. But they'd also seen his laid-back side during brief stretches of sobriety after his many jail stints. His recidivism rate was high, and those stretches never lasted long.

In movies, the dying often express regrets or reveal insights, but there was nothing for me to learn about Dad. I'd hoped the visit would leave me feeling I knew him better. Instead, it felt neutral and flat, as if he were an acquaintance or a distant uncle. Our conversations stayed shallow, leaving me searching for something—anything—to give me an adult's understanding of my father, not the view I'd carried as a petrified child.

I AWOKE the next morning to a voicemail from the overnight doctor. Surprisingly, Dad made it through the night, but it was only a matter of time. He'd declined, as they had predicted. I knew what I had to do. I called my manager at work to say I would be late, then drove alone to the hospital to see my father again. I still wanted to catch a glimpse—just a scintilla—of the Dickie Dyer beneath it all before he passed, hoping that understanding him might help me understand myself, the way an adopted child seeks to know their biological parent.

When I entered his room, he was on oxygen, his breathing labored. He mumbled, disoriented and agitated. I couldn't tell if he knew who I was. The end was near. I felt for him as I would for any sentient being in pain—compassion and relief that this tortured soul, who happened to be my father, would soon be released from the misery which had followed him since at least his late teens. As an adult, he had fleeting moments of decency, happy moods, and generosity, usually before too many bottles of wine set in.

Some who knew our family's history have called my father evil. I reserve that term for tyrants like Hitler and Bin Laden, who showed no remorse for their brutality. My father didn't fit the same mold as them. There was no pride in what he did or in his inability—or unwillingness—to change. His actions were often uncon-scionable, but at his core, he was an average Joe, trapped in a mind spiraling beyond his control. His life—manic, violent, and fueled by addiction—was nearing its pitiful end. There was nothing more for me to see there, so I muttered something about needing to get to a meeting and left.

On my Red Line train ride into work, I wondered what it felt like for him, knowing most of his kids were there in his last hours. I hoped, in some small way, it eased the loneliness which had defined his twenty-two years on the streets.

Later in the day, the attorney, George, let me know my father had passed away. I didn't know how to feel. Grief felt unfamiliar, as though it belonged to someone I barely knew. Instead, I slipped into my usual distraction: "doing" mode. With my sister Marj, I focused on hiring a funeral home, writing an obituary, and arranging the practicalities of his burial. We all chipped in to buy a burial plot for Dad at Cedar Grove Cemetery in Dorchester, where most of our extended family is buried.

The following Monday, on a freezing gray day, a priest, my siblings, and a couple of close family friends gathered for a graveside service. My mother understandably didn't attend. A priest from nearby St. Gregory's Parish said a few prayers with us as the orange Mattapan/Milton trolley clattered by. Its rhythmic sound highlighted the unique charm of it being the only cemetery in the nation with a train running through it.

I went through the motions of the service, but I didn't feel much. His passing didn't register as a loss, just a sad end-of-life circumstance. Mostly, I was grateful Dad was finally out of his misery. All I thought was, *Okay, rest in peace, Dad,* as we gathered up to leave.

Since we were already at the cemetery, a few of us drove over to the other side of the grounds to visit the gravesite of Dad's parents, Alma and Robert. After a lengthy search for the plot, Marj cleared the snow from the round, three-inch marker stone with her shoe tip. There was no headstone to mark the grave. As we paid our respects, we couldn't help but think about Dad's intellectually disabled older brother.

I wondered aloud. "Whatever happened to Uncle Bob? Is he still alive?"

"I was just thinking the same thing," Marj said. I never heard anything about him passing away. I'll make some phone calls and find out.

A couple of years before our parents' divorce, Uncle Bob had faded from our lives so quietly, it was as if he'd been erased. Our family hadn't seen him since the early '70s, when he used to join us for Sunday dinners. But now, standing under the bare weeping willow, the thought of him lingered, filling me with a mix of urgency and guilt that we'd lost touch with him.

Marj and I agreed our next order of business after the funeral was to find out if dear Uncle Bob was still alive, and if so, let him know he still had extended family.

Driving out through the weathered stone arch framed by the open wrought iron cemetery gates, I felt relieved Dickie Dyer was finally free of his tumultuous, self-destructive, and lonely life. But what did that mean for the rest of us—if anything? I hoped wherever he was, he'd found his way back to who he might have been before he lost his mind.

Chapter 3

Dot Rat

To UNDERSTAND my father and the complexity of his role in my family history, it helps to know some background about him and the area we called home.

Dorchester, one of the twenty-three neighborhoods of the City of Boston, has a rich history. It is home to landmarks like the Mather School, America's first public elementary school, and Donna Summer's alma mater, Jeremiah E. Burke High School. Famous figures like Ray Bolger (the Scarecrow from *The Wizard of Oz*) and the singing group New Kids on the Block also have roots there. But for Dad, Dorchester wasn't about fame. It was about survival and the blue-collar community that came with it. It wasn't just a neighborhood—it was the backdrop to our family story.

Richard "Dickie" Dyer was born in 1929 to Alma and Robert Dyer in Dorchester's Fields Corner area, where making do was second nature. As the third of four children born at the onset of the Great Depression, Dad learned early how to navigate a working-class life marked by scarcity and survival.

Growing up, Grandma Dyer told Ma and my older siblings that Dad had a kind heart, a boy who gave his last nickel if someone else needed it more. Admiring his own father, Dad learned how to tinker, building things or fixing whatever mechanical item needed repair. They scavenged the neighborhood dump for anything with potential—a bent wheel here, a rusty handlebar there—and pieced together a bike sturdy enough for Dad to ride.

In the winter, they built a soapbox car from old boards and bits of rope. After school, Dad slung a canvas bag over his shoulder, delivering newspapers in the wagon to help ease the family's financial burden.

When Robert's health declined from renal heart disease, it pushed the family deeper into poverty. Dad dropped out of seventh grade to take on more work fixing bikes, running errands, and repairing neighbors' cars. Grandma used to say, "When your grandfather was too weak to walk even a block, your father perched him on his bicycle handlebars, riding him all around Fields Corner."

They rode to the post office or the store together on the bike, occasionally stopping by Lucky Strike Bowling Alley, where Robert kept score for Dad and his friends. Some kids in the neighborhood taunted Dad for this awkward spectacle and coined an unsavory nickname for him.

"Hey, Dyer-rhea!" the kids teased. "What's-a-matter? Your old man can't afford a bike of his own? Haha!"

But Dad cherished his father and did anything to help or spend time with him, even if it meant being the butt of mean-spirited jokes.

When Robert died in 1945, it was a heavy blow to sixteen-year-old Dickie, but he pushed on, taking whatever work he could get to support his widowed mother. He got a job manually setting up bowling pins at Lucky Strike, the way it was done before automation. There, his friend and co-worker, Kenny, a fellow "Dot Rat," often talked about the two of them joining the Army together when they were old enough. Dot Rat was the nickname scrappy

Dorchester kids gave each other, a badge of toughness and resilience that usually came with a reputation for mischief or troublemaking.

A year later, Dad was still too young to enlist; however, he was determined to support his mother financially, so he came up with a plan. He started hanging around the National Guard Armory on Victory Road, blending in with the uniformed guardsmen, practicing marching drills in his street clothes, and palling around with the guys. Determined to get in, he used his Dot Rat sensibilities to work the system. With his mother's help, he filled out the Army application, lying about his age. Recognizing his mechanical skills were being wasted in low-paying jobs, Alma turned a blind eye. The following week, Dad got a *ticket to ride* to the Army, leaving Dorchester behind, eager to prove himself and be all he could be as he set out to build a better future.

Chapter 4

Nowhere Man

After Dad's burial service, my siblings and I met back at my apartment for a post-burial luncheon. We leaned into what has always bonded us: music—starting with the Beatles' *White Album*, comfort food, and a steady stream of outrageous stories about Dad and our lives growing up in Dorchester. Since my parents' divorce in 1977, every holiday gathering had turned into a marathon of war stories about our estranged father, and on the day of his burial, lunch was no different. We swapped memories about the hellion we'd grown up with, including who got a beating from him and for what absurd reason, and the extent of his public outbursts. Some accounts made us laugh, others made us cringe, but most were steeped in the chaos we'd endured together.

Dan and his childhood friend Ted were bringing the Chinese food. As we waited for them to arrive, the first thing anyone mentioned was Dad's cemetery plot. Since he was currently the only occupant, there was plenty of room to bury other family members there in the future. The question arose whether any of us would want to be buried with him when our time came. After all, we'd already paid dearly for the plot.

Johnny straightened up on the couch, suddenly more animated. "I don't wanna be buried with Dickie Dyer. Keep me far away from him. I said it before—when I croak, I want my ashes scattered in the Zone."

Johnny was looking more worn lately. In the '80s and early '90s, he worked in Boston's red-light adult entertainment district, the Combat Zone—a place with a long reputation for violence and crime. Long nights came with the territory, as did heavy drinking, but for him, it was a place where he was known and seen.

Through the mid-and late '90s, he'd had a few surgeries related to worsening cirrhosis. His clothes hung more loosely on him, his movements less steady. Years of hard living had slowed Johnny's reflexes and thrown off his balance, and he was falling more often, including a bad escalator fall in the South Station subway a few months before.

Bill tossed out one of his typical hare-brained ideas for his own end-of-life arrangements. "Just cremate me and feed me to the fish in Dorchester."

Marj shook her head and gently clued him in. "Fish don't eat bones, Bill." She leaned closer to her husband. "I'll be buried with Dale, so I'm all set."

Dale smirked. "Damn right you are. I'm not living with any of you crazy Dyers, even when I'm dead." His usual smart-ass delivery, with the right amount of playful sarcasm, lifted the energy in the room a bit.

"I already bought a plot a few years ago," Jim said. "So I'm all set."

The rest of us hadn't planned that far ahead yet, and though Dad's grave was spacious enough for a few more occupants, so far no one volunteered to share it down the road. Dan hadn't arrived yet to ask, but I remembered he did say once: "Cremate me and scatter me around Dorchester."

I looked at Marj, the one who knew my chronic dating woes

best, and raised my brows in mock optimism. "With any luck, by the time I'm dead I'll have someone halfway decent to share a grave with. I'll pass on Dad's grave."

With little to show for my choices in men at thirty-three, I blamed luck, invoking Albert King's lament: "If it wasn't for bad luck, I wouldn't have no luck at all." I chased fixer-upper musicians and bad boys, never considering my choices were the problem.

So it was agreed. Dad would stay alone in his grave. On a practical level, it seemed a shame because cemetery plots are so expensive. But we all respected everyone's choice. Our father played the role of "Dad" only in rare moments when his inner turmoil hadn't consumed him. Those glimpses were fleeting, overshadowed by the trauma and violence he'd inflicted. In the end, it seemed fitting he remained the sole occupant. And so, like Eleanor Rigby, when Dickie Dyer died, he was buried along with his name, with no one to keep him company in death.

A few of our brothers chatted back and forth between the open living room and dining room, while Marj and I started clearing space at the table for the lunch order.

Johnny craned his neck through the kitchen doorway. "Margie, remember when you and Mary saw the old man that time in Southie... Eric was about a year old?"

"Yeah, he wanted to pick him up, but there was no way that was happening."

I said, "Yeah, he probably would have dropped him."

The sighting he was asking us about happened in 1987, when I was a junior in college. Marj came to visit me at my apartment in Southie. We were walking down West Broadway, enjoying a Saturday stroll with Marj's infant son in the stroller. We stopped briefly in a hardware store, and just as we set off again, we saw our homeless father approaching. Aside from a brief sighting Marj and Dale had in the early-'80s, we hadn't seen him since around '76 or

'77, after he served time for splitting Ma's head open with a fire extinguisher.

"Marj, that's Dad. What should we do?" I whispered sharply.

As always, she was calm and level-headed. "Well, I guess he should know he has a grandson. Let's say a quick hello but I don't want him holding him."

Dad approached in an oversized windbreaker and sneakers. I had never seen him dressed in anything but work clothes and heavy black shoes. Recognition crossed his face when he saw us, and when he noticed the baby, his face lit up.

We said hello and Marj motioned toward the carriage. "This is my son, Eric."

"Can I hold him?"

Marj made up a quick diversion. "He's just getting over a cold. I don't want you to get sick. I'll hold him up to you. You can see him that way."

Hesitantly, she reached down and started to unbuckle Eric. But the universe conspired with her, causing the stroller buckle to jam, so he stayed put.

"Ya got a hallway or cohn-nuh your old man can sleep in? I got nowhere to go," he pleaded in his thick Boston accent. "I'm clean; I get a shower every day."

Marj didn't lie. "Sorry, I don't live anywhere near here."

My apartment was around the corner, but I didn't let on. "I'm still living at home with Ma. Sorry."

It felt cruel to lie and turn him down, but he was too much of a safety risk. To get moving on our way, I fibbed again, "Okay, we gotta run to an appointment."

He looked sad and lost as we watched him walk toward East Broadway and disappear. I felt a wave of sorrow at his condition and his isolation.

Johnny followed us into the dining room, jumping back into the story.

"Marj, remember I called you because I saw him at the bar? He was talking crazy about Eric's head?"

"Oh, yeah, that was bizarre."

Johnny glanced at Billy and repeated the story from years ago. "I says, 'Hey, check this out. I ran into the old man at Triple O's.'"

He stopped mid-sentence. "By the way, don't ever go there, Marj. Trust me, it's a total dive bar."

Bill jokingly mocked Johnny's judgment. "Whaddya think, she's hanging out in Southie bars now? She don't even live around here." He shook his head.

"True. Okay, lemme finish... So, when I saw the old man at the bar, he told me he ran into Margie and Mary with Eric. And get this..." Johnny sipped his blackberry brandy, letting the moment hang.

"He goes—why's the side of Margie's baby's head all bashed in? I said—what crazy shit are you smoking? Eric's fine..."

I remembered it. "Yeah, that was crazy."

Marj, Johnny, and I recognized Dad's bizarre, distorted perception might have been some warped flashback—his mind confusing his grandson with a memory of something he'd done to his own kids, especially Johnny, whom he'd tormented all of his life. I reflected on how reckless drinking and mental illness had taken Dad long before that sighting in 1987. I pictured him that day we saw him, leaving me in that moment with the quiet reckoning I'd never known him and I never would.

Chapter 5

He Blew His Mind Out in His Car

Dan and his friend Ted arrived at my apartment with shopping bags full of Chinese food from a restaurant Bill mockingly called Cafe Pathetic. He had a clever nickname for every restaurant he deemed mediocre or horrible. We dove into the bags, pulling out white boxes of fried rice, butterfly shrimp, and chicken fingers.

"At least it's not from Yuck Yuck," he cackled, poking fun at Yum Yum, the Chinese takeout spot popular among patrons spilling out of bars like Cunningham's, the Blarney Stone, and the Irish Rover.

Some of us gathered at the dining table, while others settled in the adjoining living room, balancing plates on their laps as the *White Album* played. Between bites of food, we shared snippets about my father's erratic, unpredictable behavior, reflecting on the chaos he'd incited but also making light of it. It was one way we all handled the awkward topic of him.

Dan brought up how he used to run into Dad occasionally years earlier.

"I used to see the old man when I worked at Lappen Auto in

the '80s. He'd wander down Dot Ave. and sometimes drift into the store because he knew I worked there. Same question every time: 'Ya got a spare couch or hallway I can sleep in? I have nowhere to go.' One time when he came in begging for a bed, I told him, 'No, Dad, I'm married now. If I let you stay, you'd probably hit my wife, and then I'd have to kill you. Sorry.' I gave him twenty bucks so he could get something to eat."

As Dan spoke, a similar moment came back to me.

"I ran into him in Southie in the fall of '87, a couple of months after Marj and I saw him that time with Eric. I was heading out for a morning college class when I noticed him standing right in front of my apartment. He didn't know I lived there."

"Oh, yeah," Bill cut in. "Back when you had the silver '75 Monarch I gave you. That car ran good for a Ford."

"Right... Anyway, he asked me the same thing: 'Ya got a hallway or a corner I can sleep in for the night?'"

"So wha'ja say?" Dan asked.

"I lied and said, 'No, I don't live around here; I'm just visiting a friend.'"

It was never easy to see my father begging for shelter. Lying to him and turning him away felt cruel, but his mental state had deteriorated, and his history of violence made him a risk. There was nothing we could have done to change his situation. As hard as it was, he was on his own.

Johnny sank into the couch with a plate of food and a pint of brandy.

"So, the old man finally kicked the bucket... I can't believe he lasted this long. That asshole kicked my butt all over Dot..."

He sipped his brandy. "Sometimes I deserved it, but most of the time? Not even close."

Dan pointed his fork toward Johnny in jest, chuckling, his Boston accent slipping through. "You just always got caught. You weren't cafful. Bobby and I nevah got caught for all the crazy shit we did."

"Nah, not true. He always had it out for me 'cause I looked like Grandpa. He hated him and took it out on me. I was just an innocent little kid. Fuckin' maniac..."

We all knew the truth in Johnny's words. Ma always said as a toddler, Johnny looked just like her father—the man Dad despised. That resemblance, and whatever drove Dad's daily rage, defined Johnny's childhood from the start and followed him all his life.

Johnny bit into an egg roll, chewing. "I've always wondered... When did the old man start losing his mind? I mean... Was he ever normal, or was he always a ticking bomb with a defective fuse? 'Cause all I ever remember was craziness, from day one."

"No," Dan said. "He wasn't always like that. Not according to Grandma Dyer."

Johnny paused for a moment, muttering aloud to himself. "Hard to believe... And didn't someone say his grandmother was a nut or something? Do we even know anything about any aunts? Uncles? Grandparents?"

Dad's mom, Alma, was an exceptionally patient, kind woman. We never knew Dad's father since he died way before our time. We'd been told bits about Dad's paternal grandmother being bitter and combative—not unlike him.

"From what I'd heard, his grandmother was the type to throw a bucket of dirty mop water at you if you so much as looked at her the wrong way," Marj said.

For various reasons, we had no Dyer relatives we could ask, and Ma rarely shared details about our father or his family. Who would fault her after twenty-four years of hell with him? We could only wonder about Dad's family traits. Whether mental illness "ran" in his family was anyone's guess. Even if it did, who's to say how much it played a part? Siblings can grow up in the same home and turn out completely differently.

"Grandma Dyer always said Dad was a good kid... he'd do anything for anybody," Dan said.

Marj nodded. "Yeah, Uncle Billy said the same thing, that he changed after the Army."

"Wait a second," Bill interjected. "Who's Uncle Billy?"

Marj explained, "He was Grandma Dyer's brother. Dad's uncle on her side, not on the Dyer side. A really nice guy. Dad looked just like him. I have a picture of him somewhere I can dig up."

"Huh... So maybe they named me after him?" Bill asked.

"Probably." Dan said, then thought a moment. "Well, actually, they named you after Ma's first Billy—the baby who died of crib death. He was born after Johnny, before me. But yeah, they probably named that baby after Dad's Uncle Billy first."

"Naming me after a dead baby. Now, that's morbid..." Bill broke into an Alice Cooper chorus, snarling, "Dead babies can take care of themselves."

Like my siblings, I often wondered about Dad's mental decline. Did he go into the Army "normal," and come back "changed"? What had he witnessed or endured in his time in Japan during the Korean War? We didn't know. The timeline of his military service and when he first became violent was never clear.

Discussing it that day, we only had fragments, bits of hearsay, and old stories to go by. Ma had mentioned through the years a terrible car accident in 1956. The details were fuzzy, pieced together by her distant recollection of what the police told her, and what she remembered about her hospital visit to him.

I said, "I remember Ma saying years ago that Dad was never the same after a bad crash and head injury. She always said that— and of course, the drinking—made him worse than he already was."

Johnny: "Yeah, that's what I always heard her say, too. An accident waiting to happen."

In the winter of 1956, Dad was twenty-six and Ma twenty-one, with Bobby and Johnny still babies. I don't know for certain what my parents' life pressures looked like day to day, but supporting a young, growing family on factory wages couldn't have been easy. I can imagine it was a factor in Dad's drinking.

Ma had shared what started as an occasional after-work escape for Dad turned into a nightly habit in Dot Ave. bars, like Mallow's Café or Dad's favorite, Foley's Tavern. As the drinks flowed, so did his recklessness. Most nights, he cautiously navigated Dorchester's familiar streets, but over time, his judgment would slip. His late-night drives, fueled by too many highballs and drunken overconfidence, were risks that would eventually end badly.

One of Dad's drinking buddies described to Ma what happened at the bar right before Dad had the accident.

Dad had been drinking at a bar six miles from home in Quincy. The type of place thick with cigarette smoke, the jukebox humming Fats Domino and Hank Williams. Despite it being a work night, he stayed until closing, knocking back highballs with Schlitz chasers, one after another. He leaned on the bar, betting and boasting with another regular over whose driving prowess would get them from Quincy to Dorchester the fastest on the icy roads.

When the blinding ceiling lights signaled last call, the bartender, Sam, cut the power on the jukebox and settled up Dad's tab. "Hey, Dickie, lemme call you a cab. The streets are a mess and you've had quite a few."

Dad waved him off, slurring, "Freeport Street's only a couple exits up, Sam. I can drive."

He stumbled out to his '45 Roadmaster, its four bald,

mismatched tires ill-suited to the messy roads. After defrosting the windshield, he gave it too much gas, slamming into the car behind him. He wrestled the Buick free from a snowbank and headed north onto I-93 toward Dorchester. He never made it home that night.

The police surmised he may have hit a slippery patch of fresh snow near the Freeport Street off-ramp. Fresh tire tracks suggested the car spun out before crashing into a large tree on Victory Road. Like most drivers back then, Dad wasn't wearing a seatbelt. The impact was brutal. His chest slammed into the steering wheel, and his head shattered the windshield. Emergency responders found him unconscious in the wreckage. He was rushed to Boston City Hospital, where doctors treated him for a traumatic brain injury and skull fracture.

I remember Ma saying when she visited him in the hospital, Dad couldn't remember who people were or what year it was. She'd brought Bobby and Johnny in to see him, and the sight of him took her aback. Swathed in head bandages, he was barely recognizable because of his massive, swollen head. I could picture her, mustering an upbeat Edith Bunker-like tone, announcing, "We're here, Dick."

He slowly lifted his bandaged head off the pillow.

"Oh, hey, Dot," he said weakly, using his nickname for Ma.

She motioned toward the boys. "Daddy, look who's here to see you."

He glanced at Johnny in Ma's arms and down at Bobby, huddled close to her. He narrowed his eyes with a look of confusion, as if searching his memory for who they were.

She brought them closer. "See? It's Bobby and Johnny."

Ten-month-old Johnny shrank back and whined when he saw the mummy figure in the bed. Two-year-old Bobby pulled away, afraid to get any closer.

Dad forced a small smile, his eyes lingering on the boys. "Oh, yeah, Bobby and Johnny." The uncertainty in his voice and face was undeniable.

Ma adjusted his bed pillows and pulled up a chair to make small talk. "How's the food? Anything good on TV? Let me see if I can find that Groucho Marx show for you."

Holding Johnny, she crossed the room to turn the dial. Bobby hurried after her, clinging to her legs, afraid she might leave him. The TV flickered as each black-and-white channel clicked past and Ma settled on *The Art Linkletter Show*.

When she returned to Dad's bedside, his expression brightened, and he quietly spoke. "Hey, Dot, my old man's in a room upstairs here. My Ma's up there visiting him. You should go up there and say hello."

"Dick, your father died eleven years ago when you were sixteen. This is 1956."

He blinked, dazed. "Oh, I must be thinking of someone else."

Ma's heart sank as the full extent of Dad's brain injury became clear. Clinging to the hope his confusion was temporary, she spent the rest of her visit gently grounding him in the present.

Dad spent two weeks recovering in the hospital. On the morning of his discharge, the surgeon who had performed the skull repair gave him strict orders, with Ma present for reinforcement.

"Mr. Dyer, you've sustained a very serious brain injury. A metal cranial plate is stabilizing a skull fracture. You're fortunate to even be walking out of here today. Drinking alcohol, even in small amounts, will most certainly lead to irreversible cognitive damage—permanent brain injury." He looked between Ma and Dad, making sure they both understood. "It's critical that when you go home today, you rest and stop drinking entirely. You need to heal up and change your lifestyle."

He jotted down a name and number on a prescription pad and tore off the page. "Here's someone who can help with this sort of thing. Give him a call. He can point you to a men's meeting group."

Despite the stern warning, Dad went home and carried on as though nothing had happened. A few days later, he bought another jalopy and went back to his nightly drinking. While his physical injuries eventually healed, the lingering impact, worsened by alcohol and the painkiller Darvon, seemed to feed his volatility.

Chapter 6

———

Southie Girl

THE LIVING ROOM air hung thick with the smell of fried rice and greasy chicken fingers. I picked at my chop suey, wondering how Ma must have felt then—caught between dysfunction and the rose-tinted hope that things would get better.

"I think Ma really thought he'd quit drinking. Course it only got worse," I said.

Johnny shrugged. "Woulda, coulda, shoulda. She had no idea it would get as bad as it did. Back then, women took a lot of crap. Not like now." He looked from me to Marj. "You two wouldn't have put up with a guy like that. You'd've kicked his ass to the curb long before."

I laughed at how Johnny put it. "You got that right. But back then, she already had you and Bobby and she was pregnant with that first Billy who died. Who was gonna support her? I know Grandma and Grandpa offered help a few times, but she didn't take it."

"It's not like she could move back into the projects with them," Dan reasoned. "Not with Bobby and Johnny. Grandma had her hands full with her own kids. Don't forget, Ma had a sister just a few years older than Bobby."

Mention of our grandparents brought back fragments of stories Ma had shared over the years—tidbits about growing up in the Southie projects with her parents and sisters.

"Ma always said Grandma Peters was kind of strict," Johnny said. "Plus, Ma and her five sisters were probably all crammed into one tiny bedroom in the projects. I bet she couldn't wait to get out on her own."

"Same as us boys," Dan pointed out. "We had six boys in one room. No different."

"Yeah, but I think Ma wanted her freedom," Johnny went on. "Maybe she thought a better life was waiting, but if so, she went from the frying pan into the fire."

Talk of Ma's possible need for independence shifted to how her parents didn't approve of Dad early on. Margie shared what she knew.

"Ma said Grandma Peters didn't like Dad from the beginning. She had his number early on. Like, she knew something was off about him. She wanted Ma to date some other kid named Bobby, but Ma liked Dad more."

"I'm sure the old man laid on the charm thick," Johnny said. "Ma was so young, just a kid still."

"Easy prey," I said. "He could talk the talk and charm her."

"Yeah." Johnny's voice dropped. "She just didn't know any better."

"Well, at least she has Charlie now, and she won't grow old alone." Marj's voice carried a trace of gratitude.

"Charlie... he won't go on *Jeopardy!* because of stage fright," Bill grumbled, shaking his head. "He coulda been a millionaire already!"

Charlie, a Mensa member our mother married in the late '80s, regularly read five-hundred-page novels in one sitting. He moved through life on a different intellectual plane, yet their marriage worked on many levels.

Our conversation circled back to the beginning of Ma's life—her childhood, and eventually how she came to marry our father.

MY MOTHER, Doris Peters, was born in 1934 in South Boston. Her mother, Kay, had emigrated from Sicily to Boston as a young girl. Doris' father, Ralph, worked as a leather tanner in the Leather District of Boston. The family lived in the Old Harbor housing project during the first half of the Peters' marriage. Kay, a practicing Catholic, ensured her six daughters attended Mass and Sunday school at St. Monica's Church, where they received their First Holy Communions and Confirmations.

Doris, the eldest of the six girls, differed from most of her sisters. While most did well in school and built stable lives, her path was less steady. At times, she trusted too easily, which left her vulnerable to others' influence, and academics never came easily for her. Where she faltered in school, Doris excelled at domesticity. She could whip up elaborate meals and sew homemade dresses and matching outfits, and she shared household duties with Kay, acting as a second mother to her five younger sisters. Frustrated in eighth grade, she approached her parents about quitting school.

She waited for an opportunity when her father was around, knowing she would have a sympathetic ear. "I don't like school," she said to her parents. "I hate being there. The other kids are way ahead of me. I'm always falling behind." She sweetened her plea bargain. "If you let me quit, I can help you around the house more. And I'm old enough to work. Maybe I can get a job at a store in town."

Kay, the no-nonsense matriarch, shut the idea down.

"You're only fifteen. You're not going to loaf around here or get mixed up with project hoodlums."

Ralph, Doris' more reserved and easy-going parent, expressed his concerns gently.

"Doris, we just want you to have a better future than we did, dear. You need to stay in school."

But Doris' struggles were hard for Ralph to ignore. He hated seeing her defeated. After a quiet discussion with Kay, he convinced her to let Doris quit school and find a job. They were barely scraping by, so Doris' extra income would make all the difference.

The following week, Doris boarded the Red Line train in Andrew Square and rode into the city to Washington Station. She filled out applications at department stores like Jordan Marsh and Gilchrist's. Jordan Marsh hired her as a salesclerk, paying about thirty dollars a week. Her parents kept most of her earnings, leaving her with carfare and pocket change. Still, that sliver of money she could call her own. And the feeling of working downtown gave her a sense of independence.

After work, she pitched in at home, cooking meals and scrubbing laundry on the sink's washboard. On summer days, she took her little sisters to the Boston Public Garden, treating them to Swan Boat rides and letting them splash in the Frog Pond fountain. These outings gave her a taste of motherhood—a full-time role that, unbeknownst to her, was waiting just around the corner.

At eighteen, Doris ran into Blanche, another girl from the projects.

"Hi, Doris. Say, are you still seeing that Bobby Stimpson fella?"

"Not really. We've been to the movies and got a hotdog once at the Woolworth's lunch counter."

"Well, how about a double date Friday at Blinstrub's with me and Kenny? You can meet his friend, Dickie Dyer."

"I don't think so... My mother is pretty strict."

Blanche leaned in. "He's a real looker. Tall with wavy hair. He even has a car."

The lure of Blinstrub's Village—"Blinnie's"—Southie's hottest night spot, hosting acts like Jimmy Durante and Connie Francis—sealed the deal.

To slip out for the night, Doris told her parents a half-truth—that she was meeting Blanche at the Broadway Theatre to see a movie. That evening, she boarded the #10 bus to West Broadway.

When she met Dickie, his good looks and swagger swept her off her feet. He called her Dot, for short, which made her feel special. Plus, it was the same name locals called Dorchester, where he was from. He leaned closer. "Growing up everyone called me Dickie. But you can call me Dick." Five years her senior and a former Army guy, he seemed worldly and confident—a man able to handle himself. Knowing how much she loved Perry Como, I imagine she floated home that night, humming "Some Enchanted Evening."

The two grew close fast, spending nights bowling and going to the movies. While Doris felt like the luckiest girl in the projects, her parents had doubts. When they met Dick, his cocky attitude and flippant demeanor set them on edge from the start. Kay's disapproval deepened when she noticed his crude Army tattoos. On one arm he sported a full-length, nude pin-up holding a cigarette. A large, coiled snake with a forked tongue lashing out covered the other forearm.

Doris brushed off her parents' concerns about Dick, but their worries grew when on a couple of occasions, they noticed bruises on her arms that looked like hand marks. She laughed it off, blaming her poor eyesight or clumsiness.

"I tripped. You know me—Mr. Magoo," she joked. But her parents weren't convinced, especially Kay, who never minced her words or held back her strong opinions. They grew increasingly concerned for her well-being.

"Doris," Kay pressed her one night, "what are you doing with this guy? He's a hoodlum, and he's too old for you. He's got nothing to offer. Bobby Stimpson is a much nicer fella. Plus, he's your age. Dick's five years older than you. What's he dating you for? Can't he find someone his own age? Is he just looking for a good time?"

Seeing Dick through rose-colored glasses, Doris dismissed her parents' worries. "I like him," she insisted. "He takes me out, we have fun. And he's even got a car. Bobby doesn't have a car."

One evening, as Dick and Doris were heading out for a bite at Henry's Hamburgers, Kay cornered Dick in the hallway and delivered a few choice words while Doris was busy looking for her coat.

"You have no business dating Doris. You know full well she's young and innocent. Why don't you date someone your own age? I know what you're all about. Leave her alone."

The couple went on their way. What the Peters didn't know was it was already too late. Doris was pregnant. How to break the news to her parents was agonizing for Doris. She rehearsed a dozen approaches in her mind, settling on telling them when they were in a good mood.

One Monday after supper, Ralph and Kay were in the parlor listening to their usual AM 850 on their tube radio. The Andrews Sisters sang about a sunny side of the street. Sensing their light mood, Doris took her opportunity to join them on the couch. Her voice trembled. "I'm pregnant with Dick's baby."

Kay put down her mending, her face a mix of disbelief, as if she hadn't heard correctly. "You're what?" She rose to her feet, hands on her hips. "How far along are you?"

Doris looked down at her feet, mumbling, "Two months. I'm due in the fall."

Ralph turned off the radio and set his cherry tobacco pipe into the big glass ashtray, his expression grim. "How could you let this happen, Doris?" he asked, his voice heavy with disappointment.

Kay's voice rose in anger. "I knew that bastard would take advantage of her! Now what? This is a disgrace."

"Well, Doris," her father asked, "is he going to do the right thing and marry you, or—"

Kay cut him off. "Or just leave you high and dry?"

Doris explained the couple had already applied for a marriage license, and Dick's mother Alma had offered to let her move in with the family on Dorchester Ave. once they were married.

Ralph sighed. "Get Dick over here tomorrow. We need to settle this."

When Dick arrived the following day, he assured Ralph and Kay he was capable of taking good care of Doris and the baby. He explained he had a steady job as a machinist at Boston Gear Works. "I can manage things," he insisted.

With reluctance, they consented to the marriage, and Kay delivered one final message to the couple. "You made your bed, now sleep in it. Both of you."

Ralph reinforced the message. "You'd better follow through, young man, or you'll be answering to me."

Up to this point, Dick had lived a carefree bachelor life, drinking with his buddies after work and hitting the bottle harder in the years following his Army discharge. Now he was about to have a rude awakening with the responsibilities that came with being a new husband and father.

Despite their limited funds, in April, Kay scraped together enough money to host a modest wedding party for the newlyweds. Doris' sisters decorated the apartment, and Kay spared no effort. She bought a beautiful Italian wedding cake from a North End bakery and prepared homemade Sicilian meatballs and sauce, along with a platter of imported Italian delicacies.

Doris Peters became Doris Dyer in a clerk ceremony at Boston City Hall. However, there would be no wedding celebration with her family after. At the last minute, Dick instead drove Doris to

New Hampshire for a spur-of-the-moment "elopement" honeymoon. Her parents were furious, left with the crushing expense of food and decorations they couldn't afford, and a roomful of guests waiting for a celebration that never came.

Although the newlyweds had known each other only a brief time, they were eager to begin their new life together. Dick moved Doris into his mother's already cramped apartment, where he lived with two other siblings, as Doris awaited the arrival of her baby.

Living under the same roof, Alma noticed the way Dick treated Doris—his impatience with her, the edge in his voice. She said he wasn't the same since the Army and, gently but firmly, urged Doris not to tolerate his growing disrespect.

Doris' parents shared similar misgivings. As they spent more time around him, they sensed a marked moodiness. When asked why his Army service ended after only two years, he said it was due to a back injury from a Jeep rollover. That was the extent of it.

By late September, Dick found a tiny two-room studio apartment up the street from Alma on Dot Ave, and the newlyweds moved in. Bobby was born in late October. Doris was nineteen; Dick was twenty-four. Despite their reservations, Doris' parents did their best to support the young couple, passing along household items and baby clothes from her younger sister.

For Doris, life felt full of promise. A new wife and young mother, surrounded by family on both sides willing to help, she pushed aside any unease there may have been and focused on the fresh start that lay ahead. Little did she know, within months her world would begin to turn *helter skelter*.

Chapter 7

The Junk in The Yard

My living room buzzed with conversation and the clink of forks. Thom got up to take his plate to the kitchen, leaving my favorite rocking chair by the front windows vacant. I quickly confiscated it, just like when we were kids.

"Would'ja jump in my grave that quick?" he teased.

I peeked through the curtains and noticed a family moving into the apartment across the street. Two teens looked miserable carrying huge boxes inside.

"Ugh, glad I'm not out there moving today," I said, crossing my arms against the cold. "Moving in the ice and snow is the worst."

"We did it all the time growing up." Dan crowed. "The old man didn't care. We moved in blizzards, heatwaves. Didn't matter."

We stayed in many apartments a year or less, with one upset or another always driving Dad to move. Whether another tenant parked in what he thought was "his" spot or a landlord like Westerdorf didn't fix something quickly enough, Dad spiraled into a rage. He called Westerdorf a Dorchester "slumlord," saying he owned half the rundown triple-deckers there and railed about repairs that took forever to get done if they were done at all.

With repairs dragging on, Dad's temper always boiled over. Arguments with landlords escalated into threats of physical harm. Evictions and broken leases were the norm. The older kids would get settled into a school and neighborhood, and in a year or so, Dad would announce, "Pack it up, Dot. We're leaving this shithole."

Dan retold a story that always made Ma recoil in disgust—the time he was showering in one of our awful apartments, and Dad had to deal with a filthy intruder—one who, for once, ended up on the receiving end of an eviction notice instead of Dad.

In the early '60s, my father moved the family to Houghs Neck in Quincy. After two years in a dumpy apartment there, he decided to move the family back home to Dot. His options were limited to tiny, cramped apartments in rough condition. The household budget was already strained by his increasing drinking, which narrowed the choices even more. After a long search, he settled on a run-down third-floor apartment in a Beach Street triple-decker. Ma and Dan always described it as dim, cramped, and worn, with peeling paint and shoddy plumbing—but it was all Dad could afford.

On their first night in the apartment, Ma shrieked and shuddered when she opened a kitchen cupboard and found cockroaches scurrying over the dishes and Gerber cereal boxes. She did her best to transform the grim space into something resembling a home, adding a tablecloth from Goodwill and sewing up some cheerful yellow curtains. But there was no escaping that the apartment was a nightmare. The Ashmont train tracks ran parallel to the street, and every eight to twelve minutes until late at night, trains rumbled through, shaking the apartment like a 3.5-magnitude earthquake. The stress pushed Dad's already frayed nerves to the edge.

Out back, the view was even worse—a vacant lot turned neighborhood dumping ground, littered with shopping carts, rusted bikes, old couches, bald tires, urine-stained mattresses, and garbage bags that drew vermin.

Dan recalled one summer day when he was five. The tiny bathroom in the apartment had only a toilet, and a cramped, half-size shower stall, with no drywall over the shower walls, just exposed rock and water pipes jutting out like an outdoor garden spigot. He was enjoying his weekly Sunday night shower, the cool water running down his head as he daydreamed about riding Bobby's bike with its chrome fenders and shiny chain guard.

He reached for the red bar of Lifebuoy and closed his eyes, working up a lather on his wiffle—the military-style haircut Dad made the boys get every summer from Al Farina, the neighborhood barber. As he raised his face to rinse off, Danny froze. A small gray nose and black whiskers twitched from the open shower head above him. Paralyzed, he squinted, his eyes stinging from the soap. Next, two black eyes appeared, and yellow teeth glinted. The rat sniffed the air below, considering Danny, as if sizing up whether he was meal-worthy. Frozen with fear, Danny felt warm urine trickle down his leg, mixing with the thin water stream sputtering from the blocked showerhead. He wiped his eyes to clear his vision. The sewer rat squeezed through the tiny shower head and plopped onto the shower floor with a heavy thud, drenched. The frantic, water-logged rat darted in circles around Danny's feet, its tail smacking against his ankles.

Danny screeched in a loud shrill. "Ma-aahh!"

"What's wrong, Danny? What's wrong?" Ma rushed in.

"A rat!" was all that escaped his panicked voice.

Ma whipped open the shower curtain and froze, her eyes locking on the disoriented rat darting around Danny's feet. Dan described how Ma shoved him aside and started kicking at the rat, doing a frantic version of the Mexican hat dance. She was wearing pointy, black pumps—the kind women wore back then, even when doing housework or lounging at home. She tried to stomp on the rat, but it kept slipping away, making her movements look like something straight out of *The Three Stooges*. Ma bolted out of the bathroom with Danny in tow. She slammed the door behind her, leaving the rat in the closed-off space.

"Dick! There's a huge rat in the bathroom!"

"What the...? Move!" He shoved Ma aside.

Ma grabbed a towel and hoisted naked, soaking-wet Danny up to the sink, rinsing soap from his hair and burning eyes, leaving Dad to deal with the rat.

Dad wasn't afraid of anyone or anything, human or otherwise. He relished a good fight and loved an easy win. He grabbed Ma's old, rusty dustpan from the pantry and ripped the rubber strip off the top edge as if it were nothing more than a piece of Scotch tape. In the bathroom, he cornered the rat, pinning it with his work boot. With a swift move, he used the ragged edge of the dustpan to deliver a quick blow, severing the rat's head. He marched through the kitchen, proudly holding the dustpan aloft, showing Ma and Danny the grisly remains.

"There. You don't have to worry about that anymore."

Ma and Danny screamed, "Argh! Get it away!"

Dad didn't need to show them his bloody prize but, of course, his judgment was often clouded. He took the dustpan with its vile contents and descended the back hallway's three narrow flights of stairs. Ma and Danny watched from the kitchen window as Dad, with a satisfied grunt, tossed the rat's severed remains into the growing pile of raw garbage out back, muttering, "Filthy son of a bitch. Take that!"

At this time, Billy, about a year old, was still bottle-feeding. Besides the apartment being infested with roaches, and now rats, Ma worried the constant presence of milk and formula would draw more rats to Billy's makeshift bureau-drawer crib. And so, as the story went, the family set out to find yet another place to live.

Chapter 8

Sky of Blue and Sea of Green

Marj and I cleared away the empty Chinese food boxes in the kitchen while our brothers' voices carried in from the dining room, a loud mix of stories and scattered flashbacks involving Dad.

Thom's voice rose above the din. "When we were at the hospital the other day, I asked the old man if he remembered taking us out on the boat. He didn't know what I was talking about. That tells ya how bad off he was."

"I remember the boat," I called out from the kitchen. I joined my siblings in the living room doorway and shared my memory. "Those boat trips were fun. We got to see all the Boston Harbor islands and swim all day. Back before the harbor got too polluted."

Jim mentioned Ma cooking burgers and dogs on the firepit and how we could smell the charcoal for hours drifting over the beach.

This pulled me back—the charcoal smoke rising into the sea breeze, the scents of the salt air, food cooking, suntan lotion, and the sounds of laughter from those carefree summer days spent with my siblings. Smiling at the thought, I wiped my hands on a dish towel and took a long sip of Chardonnay, making my way to an empty seat on the couch next to Thom.

I said, "I remember when Dad bought that boat. It was around 1974. He was bragging to Ma about how he got it dirt cheap."

"Oh, you mean, how he conned someone?" Bill's exaggerated laugh echoed through the apartment.

I shared what I'd heard Dad tell Ma the day he bought the boat—how he'd gotten such a deal.

Around some of Fields Corner's barrooms, Dad was the go-to backyard mechanic. If your shitbox needed cheap fixing, you brought it to him. One day, he strolled into his favorite dimly lit watering hole, Foley's, where the walls were plastered with posters of the era's voluptuous sex symbols: Sophia Loren, Elizabeth Taylor, and Jayne Mansfield.

When Dad approached Vinny to collect on a clutch repair, he didn't have the money. Hoping to gain some fraternal sympathy, he blamed his wife. "Dickie, the old lady went hog-wild buying goddamn lobsters and steamers at Capitol Market. All I got's a sawbuck."

Not a good answer, considering who my father was. Everyone in the bar knew that unless he was in a jovial mood, he was a hair-trigger away from snapping, maybe punching someone out. I could picture his face going red, arms crossed, jaw set as he said, "That's not my problem, jackass."

"I know, Dickie, I know." Vinny paused, searching to conjure up a better offer.

"How about I sell you my boat for two hundred bucks? You liked it that time we caught all those bluefish out by Boston Light."

Dad didn't suffer fools, and Vinny was desperate. He upped the offer before Dad had a chance to lash out.

"Tell ya what, Dickie. I'll throw in the trailer and outboard motor. The whole shebang."

Dad had his eye on a used Honda motorcycle but wasn't about to pass up a steal. His car already had a ball hitch. It was too easy. The motorcycle would come later.

"I'll take it all for a C note and a case of Schlitz. And write that I paid twenty on the bill of sale, so I don't get screwed by Taxachusetts."

Vinny knew better than to argue. Dad drove to Vinny's house and left with a sixteen-foot motorboat. As he hauled it away, he yelled back, "Don't ask me to fix your shitbox again, jamoke. And it better not be a lemon. I know where you live."

Over time, Dad realized just how valuable that boat was. It gave our family memorable summer outings and gave him a sense of pride—especially in a neighborhood where few could afford such luxuries. Least of all, a welfare case. He loved taking the family out to the Harbor Islands, cramming us into the tiny boat with mounds of gear and coolers full of food and beer. We'd all pile into the Falcon wagon, Tommy, Billy, and I waving peace signs at cars on Morrissey Boulevard as we rode to Rainbow Park at the Dorchester gas tanks, where Dad launched the boat.

Once out of Dorchester Bay, Dad gunned the motor. He paid no mind to the harbor speed limit, flying over the wakes of much larger boats. We were scared and laughing all at once, soaring up and down over the waves like a carnival ride. All the while, Dad grinned with a Narragansett in hand as the bow pounded the water and the spray drenched us. It's a wonder one of us didn't bounce out or the boat didn't capsize while he played Evel Knievel on the water.

Each time we went to a new island—Thompson, Georges, Rainsford, Lovells. We spent hours swimming, beachcombing the shore for shells and exploring Civil War forts. Dad was usually content, guzzling cold beer all day and eating Ma's cookout food. Those were rare moments when it was fun to be around him. If only for a day, we traded our *pools of sorrow* for *waves of joy*—times when Dad put the "fun" in dysfunction, until something set him off once we got home and wiped out any enjoyment we'd just had.

Dan hardly remembered those outings.

"I didn't go on the boat much. I was out doing my own thing by that age. But I remember he used to take us to New Hampshire... Bella Vista Beach, remember?"

Marj lit up. "Yeah, the place with the huge water slide."

Dan's face warmed. "Remember when Dad would make a human totem pole with us older kids in the lake? We'd all sit on each other's shoulders until we toppled over into the water."

I remembered Billy, Tommy, and me laughing from the shore as they all fell over.

Dan turned to Ted. "Remember my old man taking us to that go-kart place? I think it was Epping, New Hampshire. Me, you, Bobby, and Johnny?"

"Yeah, he was good about taking us places, except for all the yelling. He was just never happy with anyone or anything. But I still liked hanging out at your house over mine. Even with your old man around, it was still pretty fun, at least for me. Of course, I never got hit by him, so...."

I couldn't make sense of that.

"How was our house more fun than yours?"

"My father didn't like us playing inside, making all kinds of noise. Your old man let us hang out most of the time. So, your house was more fun, right, Hook?"

As a kid, Dan earned the nickname "Hook" because neighborhood girls seemed to gravitate toward him.

"Oh, yeah," Dan said. "Until he snapped. Then, look out."

Ted remembered well. "But he wasn't so bad when he was in a good mood. We used to camp out on your back porch on summer nights, remember that? And the Blue Hills. We had a friggin' blast." Johnny and Dan agreed.

"Dad had his good moments," I said. "He used to sing me the chorus from that old Italian song." I quietly sang— "Lazy Mary, you better get up, we need the sheets for the table."

"And when I was seven, I wanted to ride a regular bike like you older kids. Dad took off my training wheels, which was great, but instead of explaining, he just shoved me down steep Bloomfield Street, saying 'balance the bike!' I had no idea what to do. I crashed so hard." I lifted my pant leg. "I still have a scar on my knee from it."

I headed toward the kitchen for more refreshments, thinking about those rare moments when we were kids, pushing aside Dad's anger and its cost. For a while here or there, everything felt forgiven—until the next day, and the one after that.

Chapter 9

Living is Better With Eyes Closed

When I returned to the living room, Jim was deep into sharing a teenage memory. "Speaking of the boat... Here's one for you. As we all know, you couldn't disagree with the old man. If you did, you got your ass kicked."

Some of us gave small nods, a few murmuring, "Ya, no kidding."

"Well, I don't know if you all remember this, but the old man thought the moon and the sun were the same thing."

This was something I didn't recall, but it was believable.

"Fuckin' Moron," Johnny muttered to himself.

"More off than on," Bill cackled, throwing in one of his made-up phrases.

Jim pressed on through the interruption. "So, this one time, we were all out on the boat. I was looking up at the clear Boston skyline. I noticed a sliver of the moon was still glowing next to the sun. So, I'm looking up at them, and I wanted so badly to point it out to him." Jim's voice took on a belittling tone. "Are the moon and the sun the same thing now, Dad? But I didn't dare say a damn word. You know he woulda kicked my ass."

The risk of being tossed overboard into fifty feet of ocean water wasn't something you could ignore. Pointing out a mistake could earn you a swift backhand—enough to give you a nosebleed. For Johnny, it meant something far more brutal, like a broken nose, a theme that played out again and again through the years.

Dad's self-righteous naïveté was comical now, but back then, there was nothing funny about it. I leaned against the living room door frame, listening to my siblings talk about my father's crazy notions and examples of how out of touch he was.

Johnny cut in with a memory.

"Dan, when you were just a little tyke—like two or three—you used to bawl your eyes out every night when the old man came through the door after work. You'd run straight to Ma, looking for protection. He'd yell, 'Why's Danny always crying when I come through the goddamned door?' Ma risked a beating, but she told the truth—"

Johnny pitched his tone up, channeling Ma's voice. "Because he's scared to death of you, Dick. All the kids are."

"It was right in front of his face every night. For the life of him, he didn't get why you were so petrified of him. We all were. Fuckin' nut-case..."

My siblings' memories weren't just stories. They were windows into the lives they'd lived under my father's reign of terror. The day of his burial, I felt like a fly on the wall in my apartment, picking up pieces of stories I was too young to remember—or hadn't been born yet.

Dan spoke, cutting through my thoughts.

"There were so many things the old man never knew about the crazy stuff we did. And don't forget, Ma covered up for some of the dumb shit we did so we wouldn't get a beating. But there were things he didn't see that were plain as day."

I added an example of my own. "He didn't even know Marj had pierced ears. One time, he came into our room and picked up her earring tree with a bunch of pierced earrings hanging on it. He thought they were clip-ons! He would've murdered her if he knew she had pierced ears. I'll never forget that."

Dan's voice picked up, his expression animated. "And he was clueless about what really happened that time when Jackie Lambert got killed crossing the expressway. "And even with the whole neighborhood talking about me being there, he never found out I crossed. If he knew, I would've ended up in the hospital from a beating."

It was one of Dan's go-to stories, one Ma usually filled in with extra details because she had been part of it. But she wasn't with us that day, so Dan told it himself.

Dan's story illustrates how my brothers, and plenty of other Dot kids, carved out small victories in a childhood where defiance and risk were fairly common. But some of those risks, as we came to learn, carried a heavy price.

Chapter 10

Little Willow

Summers on Glendale Street in the late '60s and early '70s were like an all-day schoolyard recess. Legions of kids poured into the street each day to play games of tag, dodgeball, Relievio, Red Light-Green Light, and Billy-Billy Buck-Buck. Sidewalks were cluttered with Clackers, bikes, jump ropes, pimple balls, hula hoops, and jacks, along with a few dogs and cats running loose. Kids playing kept an ear and eye out for cars and, after supper, watched for the streetlights to flicker on—a signal it was time to head in. Some kids cried when it was time to come in, not ready for the fun to end. By preschool age, parents like our father had drilled a rule into our heads. To us younger kids: "Hold an adult's hand." And to all of us: "Always look both ways before crossing, even when you're with an adult." By age seven or eight, many kids crossed the busiest Dorchester streets without supervision, whether adults were aware or not.

For the many big families of kids tearing around Dorchester back then, shortcuts weren't just time-savers—they were acts of rebellion.

Kids played outside more than in, so we knew every nook and

cranny of the neighborhoods we lived in. We knew which fences squeaked, which cellar doors we could sneak into, and which dead ends you didn't walk alone on. Boys darted through alleyways, scaled fences, and cut through backyards with snarling dogs just to shave off a block or two. Every new shortcut was a victory, a way to buck the system.

In the summer hustle, kids swarmed through endless rows of triple-deckers like armies of ants. Ma, like many mothers of the time, cycled through several of her kids' names before landing on the right one—because we all looked so much alike and were so close in age. In fact, all my life, Ma called me "Ma-Mary," thinking of Margie's name first. She did the same with our brothers: "John-Jim—I mean, Bill—oh, whoever you are, take the trash out."

Parents mixing up kids' names was usually comical and harmless. But one summer day, when two young boys' names got crossed, it wasn't.

It was late June in 1969, and eleven-year-old Danny was hanging out with two neighborhood boys, Jackie Lambert and Davie Finn. Mrs. Peluso from Glendale Street offered to drive a group of boys to a city pool. At the last minute, Danny, Jackie and Davie decided to skip the pool and swim at Malibu Beach instead, about a mile and a half away. Their parents had no idea they had changed plans.

Since Ma took us to adjoining Savin Hill and Malibu Beach regularly, Danny knew the walking route well.

"It's easy," Danny said with authority. "Once we get to Savin Hill, we walk over the train station bridge and then take the right on Playstead Road."

The boys separated from the pool group and set off to the beach, happy to be doing their own thing. After twenty minutes of walking, they approached the Savin Hill area. Jackie slowed. "Hey, guys, wait. I know a shortcut to the beach."

Eager to get there faster, Danny and Davie followed. But instead of walking to the Savin Hill pedestrian overpass, Jackie led them on a detour toward the Savin Hill train tracks that run parallel to the six lanes of I-93. Danny glanced around, uneasy. He knew he wasn't supposed to be anywhere near the expressway.

"This doesn't seem like a shortcut to me."

The old man's stern voice echoed in his head: *"Don't you kids ever go near that expressway, you hear me? I'll break your goddamned legs, and you'll spend your life in a wheelchair."* But Danny followed along.

At the tracks, the boys reached a chain-link fence with an MBTA sign—"NO TRESPASSING ALLOWED"—its first seven letters scratched out, leaving "ASSING ALLOWED."

Davie howled when he read it.

Those funny signs were nothing new to Danny: "I see that on the train all the time. And there's another one—*No Assing Rough.* Kids always scratch that into *No Passing Through* on all the train doors."

Jackie scaled the fence first, then Davie and Danny followed. They crossed the train tracks and ducked through a narrow gap in a second chain-link fence where years of kids had worn a path. On the other side, they stepped onto the southbound shoulder of I-93 and waited until traffic cleared.

"Massholes"—notorious, speeding Boston drivers—barreled past at 75 to 80 mph, the wind from cars and trucks blasting the boys off balance. Danny knew how to cross busy streets like Dot Ave., Bowdoin Street, and Hancock Street. He looked left, and when the coast was clear, he yelled to the boys, "Go!" They all ran across to the median. There, they waited on the northbound side.

Danny checked right to see that Davie was safely waiting for traffic to break. He glanced left to make sure Jackie was doing the same—but it was too late. Jackie was already sprinting across I-93. In that split second, a car struck him, hurling him into the air. Just as he hit the ground, a large delivery truck hit him.

Danny and Davie stood frozen on the median, eyes wide, unable to move or speak. They'd just watched the unthinkable unfold. Danny didn't want to look, but he did. Jackie lay on the asphalt, blood pooling beneath his small body. Panic rose in Danny's chest, his mind screaming for what to do next. His breaths came short and heavy as tears slid down his cheeks, silent. His hands shook; his body wouldn't move. Sirens wailed in the distance, and beside him, Davie cried softly, murmuring words Danny couldn't make out in his shock.

Danny heard the old man's voice bellowing in his head again: *Stay away from that goddamned expressway!*

I'm dead meat, flashed through Danny's paralyzed mind.

Traffic ground to a halt, backing up quickly as emergency vehicles arrived. Danny looked up at the mob forming on the Savin Hill overpass. He was too far away to make out what anyone was saying—just a low hum. Speculation and murmurs about the boys' identities swirled amongst the crowd.

They'd seen his face before:

"Hey, I know that kid from the Boys Club."

"Isn't that Stevie Finn's little brother?"

"I think that other kid goes to the Mather."

Pointing to the motionless boy being lifted into the ambulance, a mother from the crowd exclaimed, "That's one of the Dyer boys." Covering her mouth, she added, "That's Danny Dyer on the stretcher." The wrong name passed through the crowd and reached the police: Danny Dyer had been killed on the Southeast Expressway. Fifteen feet below, on the expressway, Danny had no idea he had been misidentified.

A Boston Police detective ushered Danny and Davie behind a firetruck on the shoulder of I-93, shielding them from the gruesome scene and to speak with them quietly about what happened. The detective, pencil and pad in hand, addressed Danny first.

"It's okay, Jackie. We're just going to get some details on what happened—slow and calm."

"You're Jackie Lambert," the officer said to Danny, then turned to the other boy. "And you're Davie Finn?"

Danny shook his head, crying. "No. I'm Danny Dyer. Jackie Lambert's the one who got hit."

A second officer seated the boys in a cruiser. "I'll give you boys a ride home. Sit tight—it's okay."

A lump formed in Danny's throat; his mouth went dry. He knew what awaited him if the old man found out he'd been on the expressway. Unbeknownst to him, their names were still mixed up on the police report.

Back home, Dad was fixing a busted tailpipe at the house of one of his drinking buddies. Ma was getting Billy and Tommy ready for a birthday party, wiping Tommy's snot-crusted face with a facecloth when the phone rang.

"Mrs. Dyer, this is Detective Kelly from the Boston Police Department."

Ma's heart sank. *Which kid's causing trouble now?*

"Yes?"

His tone turned somber. "We'd like you to come to the city morgue on Albany Street and identify the body of a boy who lost his life on the expressway a little while ago. The deceased boy may be your son, Daniel."

Ma stopped wiping Tommy's face and silently motioned for him to get in the other room.

Unfortunately, after sixteen years of coping with Dad's violent outbursts and tending to her own injuries and those of her eight children, Ma had become adept at handling crises.

In disbelief, she kept her composure, her focus laser sharp as she asked one critical question a wise mother knew to ask.

"What was the boy wearing?"

"A white T-shirt and red shorts," the officer replied.

"No, my Danny is wearing blue dungaree cutoffs and a red Monkees T-shirt today. And anyway, he's at Turtle Pond Pool today. It's not my son." She exhaled an enormous sigh of relief, both for Danny's safety and her own, had it gone differently.

"I'm sure you're right, but we still need you to come down, just in case."

"I just told you, those aren't the clothes my son is wearing. You have the wrong boy."

"It won't take long, Mrs. Dyer. We'll pick you up in ten minutes."

Ma lowered her voice to a whisper. "Okay—but pick me up out front, not on Glendale Street. I don't want any kids to see me leaving."

Ma, now understandably nervous, quickly changed out of her house dress and with a shaky hand, dabbed on scarlet lipstick—the only makeup Dad allowed her to wear. She handed the younger kids off to Bobby and Johnny and made up a quick line about leaving.

"Kids, I ran out of flour. If your father comes back, tell him I took a cab to Elm Farm market. Bobby, take the boys to the birthday party. Johnny, stay here and watch the girls."

When Ma arrived at the morgue, she braced herself. The coroner led the detective and her into a viewing room and lowered the sheet covering the boy. She turned away, overcome with nausea—and relief. It wasn't Danny.

"That's not my son. I told you," she said, stifling a sob. "I don't know who this poor kid is."

On the ride home, Ma choked back tears and tensed as the

cruiser neared our block. The panic eased when she saw Dad's car wasn't out front yet.

When she got inside, Danny was in the boys' bedroom, sobbing on the bottom bunk bed. Ma sat down next to him and hugged him, relieved he was ok. Shaking, Danny sat up and recounted what happened. "It was this kid, Jackie Lambert, Ma. He's gone. The cops mixed up our names. They thought I was him."

Tears slid down Danny's face as he thought of Jackie, then of the old man. "I don't want to get in trouble."

Ma reassured him with a side hug. "You won't." Then, in a stern voice, for his own safety from our father, she said, "Don't ever tell anyone you crossed the expressway, you hear me? Not a word. If your father finds out you crossed, he'll explode. Go wash up. It'll be okay."

Danny nodded, feeling somewhat reassured. "Okay, Ma."

As he headed to the bathroom, he turned and wiped tears away. "Ma, can I sleep over at Davie's? We could use each other's company."

Ma saw an opportunity to keep Danny off Dad's radar. "Sure. Go pack a bag before your father gets home. I'll call Davie's mother. Hurry, now."

Davie's mom picked Danny up just in time because Dad came home five minutes later.

"Dot, what's going on? Kids on Payson Ave. are saying some kid got hit on the expressway. Was Danny there?"

Ma, nervous he would see through her, kept her voice steady. Lying by omission, she didn't specify whether Danny had crossed the expressway or not.

"A kid named Jackie was killed crossing the expressway today," she said. "Danny and that kid, Davie Finn saw it happen, but Danny's fine."

Dad barely reacted. He filled in the rest himself. "Cripes. Well, at least Danny didn't cross. Where is he?"

"He's at Davie's, the other boy's house. I told him he could sleep over."

Dad turned to leave, but then stopped and looked back at Ma. Her stomach twisted with fear, bracing for an interrogation. She thought he'd caught on.

"See?" Dad said. "What do I always tell the kids? 'Stay away from that expressway.' That poor kid."

Ma's mouth tightened. "I know."

Satisfied with Ma's account, Dad left. The tightness in Ma's stomach eased.

That night, Danny lay awake in the lower bunk at Davie's, the day's scenes looping in his head—the screech of tires, Jackie motionless on the expressway. He kept hearing Dad's warnings about the expressway and imagined what would happen if he found out. Danny cried himself to sleep.

For two days, while Danny was at Davie's, the rumor made its way throughout Uphams Corner that Danny Dyer was the boy who was killed.

When Danny arrived home, a young neighbor boy, Markie Devlin, looked at Danny, aghast in disbelief. He bolted away crying, convinced he'd glimpsed an apparition. The downstairs mother, Mary Walsh, hugged him. "Danny! You're okay. They all said you were dead."

When Danny walked in the door, Dad sat him down. Unsure of how much he knew, Danny braced himself for the worst.

"I heard what happened to that kid. See what happens? But you listened, didn't you? You didn't cross the expressway 'cause you knew what woulda happened if you did, right?"

Danny perked up. *He doesn't know.*

"That's right, Dad. I didn't cross. I'd never go on the expressway. You always tell me not to."

"Good. Now go out and play with your friends. They're all acting like it was you who died."

Through tears, he laced up his cheap "Bobo" sneakers—the no-name knockoffs poor kids wore while other kids wore Chuck Taylor Converses. The only relief Danny felt was in knowing there would be no beating from the old man. It dulled the pain, if only slightly, of witnessing Jackie's tragic death, but nothing softened the fact that his friend was gone.

Chapter 11

Drive My Car

AFTER HEARING Dan's expressway story once again, Johnny shook his head in disbelief. "Whew. Man, I remember that kid, Jackie. I remember the whole thing. All the kids around Uphams Corner and Ronan Park were talking about it, asking me and Bobby if you were dead. I still can't believe the old man bought it that you didn't cross. You're lucky he didn't piece it together... He woulda kicked your ass worse than he ever did me."

"I know," Dan agreed. "He was probably wrapped up in whatever trouble someone else was getting into."

Then, in a teasing tone, he added, "Probably you, Worm." Johnny had been nick-named "Worm" since childhood because of all the trouble he got into.

Johnny straightened up, quick to defend himself. "Or maybe he was too drunk and clueless to catch on, as usual."

We all agreed how tragic it was that the boy died... and both Ma and Danny had dodged a major bullet with Dad.

Dan broke the tension by segueing out of the story with another oblivious Dickie-ism. "Johnny, remember when the old man used to tell us: 'You can smoke pot, but stay away from that marijuana.'"

"Yeah, he was oblivious, man," Johnny smirked. "I think he confused a line he heard from a Dragnet episode about teenagers smoking pot. We'd say, 'Yeah, okay, Dad. We won't touch any marijuana—whatever you say.'"

Bill cut in. "Speaking of which..." He caught Thom's eye and lifted his brows as an invite. "I'll be going for a 'ride' soon to smoke some horrible marijuana—err, I mean pot."

Bill's mention of the car took me back to Dad again. I brought up how he used to rant at drivers from the front porch.

"I remember in the summer, Dad used to sit on the front porch in his undershirt, a bottle of Boone's Farm in one hand and his shotgun in the other. He'd wave the gun around, shouting racial slurs and threats at random drivers. I don't know if the gun was loaded. I don't remember him ever using it. But I remember he wanted the neighborhood to know one thing—don't fuck with Dickie Dyer."

Dan sipped his beer and stubbed out his cigarette. At that time, I hadn't banned indoor smoking yet. He tilted his head up, thinking back. "Well, he had bullets for the shotgun, so it could have been loaded. He mostly yelled at speeding drivers to keep all the kids safe. There were so many kids running around back then, not to mention us. It's just... the way he went about it was wrong. Threatening people with a gun out in the open like that. But he didn't care."

I shook my head. "I'm surprised someone didn't seriously hurt him."

I thought back to all the times he hollered racial slurs at drivers going by, calling them spics, wetbacks, and coons, like he was begging for a fight. Then, another thought occurred to me.

"I wonder if some of them sped up on purpose in front of him, just to get his goat. Because if they were going a little over the speed limit, he'd holler, 'Slow down to fifty, asshole! Next time, I'll blow your effen head off!'"

Thom lit a smoke and chased it with a big gulp of Meister Brau. "They all knew he was crazy. They just flipped him the bird and kept driving."

"Yeah, and he was the most notorious rule-breaker himself," Jim said, his voice picking up with an edge of annoyance. "Remember how he'd dodge the red light at Park Street and Dot Ave.? He'd cut through the MBTA bus terminal every time to beat the light. Signs were posted everywhere, but the rules didn't apply to him." He threw up his hands, shaking his head at the hypocrisy of it.

"Do as I say, not as I do," Jim added for emphasis.

I brought up the time someone torched Dad's car, but most of my siblings didn't recall it.

In the winter of 1975, Dad had lost his driveway privileges for some reason, and a woman across the street used to let him park in her empty driveway. At dusk on an icy Sunday, Dad's Ford Falcon suddenly went up in flames there. I'll never forget the sickening sound of the horn dying as the flames burned the car to a crisp. The fire department arrived just in time to keep the blaze from spreading to the woman's house.

When the fire was out, Dad called Lennie, his "Maine-iac" cousin. Their love-hate relationship rose and fell with however much booze they drank on a regular basis.

"You and your fuckin' delinquent son set fire to my car. I know it was the two of you cocksuckahs!"

I heard his son, Stephen, in the background through the phone, "No, Dickie, it wasn't us. For real, we were out food shopping all afternoon."

Dad threatened them with revenge, of course, but I'd forgotten how it ended until now, years later, when Thom reminded me.

"No, they didn't do it. It was that kid, Rico, who set the fire. Remember him?"

I paused to think. "Oh, wow. I remember him, but I never knew he did it. Or, maybe I just forgot."

Thom said word on the street back then was that Rico, a notorious teenage troublemaker, and his two older brothers had fire-bombed Dad's car in a drive-by—payback for the many times he screamed *spics* or worse at them as they tore down Bloomfield Street in their '64 Impala with a loud, leaky muffler. It seemed they'd finally gotten their revenge for his racist insults.

Dad replaced the Falcon wagon with another just like it. He never had proof that Lennie set fire to his car, but he wasn't about to apologize, so the family feud dragged on.

Just another day in Dot paradise...

Sharing car stories with my siblings, Lennon's disorienting "Revolution 9" droned on the stereo. Bill announced, "Enough of Mr. Ono's gibberish." He crouched down and ejected the CD. "Time for some bass malfeasance." He gave me a sly grin, pleased with how he'd used our newly discovered word. He swapped out The White Album for The Who's *Quadrophenia*.

The piano intro of "5:15" kicked in, and Dan gave a satisfied nod. "Good choice."

We all settled back into our conversations.

Talking about cars reminded me of Dan's teen driving days. "Dan, I remember when you had that gas-guzzler station wagon during the gas crisis. I think that must've been, what... '74?"

"Oh, yeah, my '67 Vista Cruiser. The old man helped me find that car when my first car, the Falcon, shit the bed." Dan paused, picturing the Oldsmobile in his mind. "It had a 350 rocket with a turbo tranny and a posi rear-end. A beast! I loved that car, man."

"Remember the long gas pump lines during the gas shortage?" I asked. "We'd wait in line behind fifteen cars to get gas on Morrissey Boulevard, near the Puritan Mall. If I recall correctly, there was a limit, so you couldn't even get a full tank."

Thom remembered. "People ran out of gas idling in line to fill up." He turned to Dan. "After idling for like, forty-five minutes, you'd get half a tank of gas and take us all to Nantasket Beach on Sundays."

Dan nodded along. "Yep. Just needed to get in the gas line before the church crowd."

Dan and Bill had inherited their love of American cars from the old man. He showed Dan how to fix them, and Dan, in turn, taught Bill. But when the talk turned to Fords—especially Dad's Falcons—it always sparked a debate between the two brothers. Bill never understood why Dad swore by them.

"The old man's the reason my first car was a Falcon," Dan said. "Plus, they were so friggin' easy to work on. That's why he loved them so much."

"I don't care. Fords suck. I'll take a '72 Bonneville any day."

Their back-and-forth brought me back to another of Dad's car battles, in 1975, when his road rage was on full display.

"Marj, remember when Dad smashed that guy's car window in? And then he smashed ours? Glass fell all over us..."

It came right back to her. "Oh yeah. In Quincy. Coming home from roller skating in Houghs Neck."

"Right. On Wollaston Beach, near the Clam Box."

"Yeah," she shook her head. "That was insane."

Dale wandered into the conversation with a facetious grin.

"Another Dickie baseball bat story? Who'd your old man think he was, Nomar?" I giggled.

Marj and Dale drifted into a conversation about phoning home to check on their young boys who were with an aunt for the day. I slipped back into the memory, to that road rage when I was nine—Dad's fury etched clearly in my mind.

On Sundays in the '70s, Dad often drove Margie and a friend to DiMarzio's roller skating rink in Quincy, picking them up a few hours later—a cool, normal "dad" thing for him to do.

Going skating gave Margie a break from me, her pesky younger sister, always tagging along. At fourteen, she had her own friends and interests. At the rink, she talked to boys, hung out with her girlfriends, and felt like a normal teenager. She did things Dad forbade—chewed gum, wore makeup, and wore pierced earrings, her long hair concealing her pierced lobes. Before picking her back up, she'd wipe off the makeup and slip the earrings into her pocket. From what we could tell, he never suspected a thing.

One late Sunday afternoon, with darkness settling in, I went along with Dad to pick the girls up from the rink. On those car rides, I hung on their every word. To me, Margie and her friends were adults, and for that half hour in the back seat, I felt a little grown-up too.

Dad had the worst road rage I'd ever seen. He became incensed if another driver didn't use a blinker or cut him off. That day, with three girls in the car, his fury peaked when a guy behind us on Quincy Shore Drive kept tailgating him—the worst offense. Dad kept hitting the brakes to send the message for him to back off.

At a red light by the Clam Box, Dad cranked his window down and hollered backward, "Get the fuck off my ass, moron!"

"I wasn't on your ass, loser!" the driver hollered back. A KISS song blasted from the car—one I knew from Jimmy's records. He rolled his window up, probably thinking that was the end of it.

But Dad leaned farther out his window, craning his neck back. "You talkin' to me, asshole?"

Oh, boy. Here we go.

Margie, her friend, and I exchanged nervous glances. Her friend had never seen anything like this.

The guy unrolled his window and threw up a middle finger. "Yeah, whatever, old man!"

"Oh, yeah?" Dad yelled, the light still red. "Get outta the car, cocksuckah!"

"Come and get me out, old man!"—the guy clearly underestimated the maniac he'd just pissed off.

Dad slammed his Ford-O-Matic shifter into "P." He whipped off his horn-rimmed glasses and tossed them on the dash, a clear signal he was about to fight. He reached under the front seat and grabbed the Louisville Slugger he kept there for "emergencies".

"Stay in the car," he commanded us.

He stepped out and slammed his door shut, storming back to the other car, bat in hand. He yelled through the guy's window, "Old man, huh? Watch this old man beat your ass, you fuckin' maggot!" Dad was forty-six.

We sat stiff as boards, too scared to breathe. My eyes welled up with tears. I knew this was going to be ugly. Dad stood at the guy's window, bat raised like a street psycho from *The Warriors*, yelling, "Get outta the car, ya fuckin' punk!"

The driver rolled his window back up, hands clamped on the wheel, eyes straight ahead, ignoring Dad.

Dad ranted obscenities, every other word an F-bomb. The guy stayed silent, fueling Dad's temper. My side clenched with a sharp ache, a familiar sign of things about to spiral. Dad pressed on, hurling one insult after another, trying to engage him.

"Come on! Let's dance!" Dad sputtered.

Through Dad's open vent window, cigarette smoke and choking leaded exhaust drifted in from the beat-up Nova idling behind us. The driver stared straight ahead, hands fixed on the wheel, as if my father weren't there.

When the guy refused to get out, Dad ran to the back of his car, drew back, and swung at the rear window—once... then again —like he was settling a score, Tony Soprano style. The window shattered and glass exploded inward onto the back seat.

Fights and shouting matches on Dorchester streets didn't faze anyone. But the sound of breaking glass in quieter Quincy turned heads. Nearby drivers slowed. Beach walkers stopped, craning their necks over the sea wall. Inside the car, we sat frozen as the scene played out around us.

The guy jumped out of his car, ready to assert his dominance. "Now you're gonna get it, muthafuckah." He tore the bat from Dad's hands, knocking him off balance, then ran to the rear of our car and hit the tailgate window three times until it smashed. Did he even notice there were young girls in back seat, or did he just not care? I'll never know.

Shards of glass rained onto our hair and clothes, down the front of my plaid smock shirt. We shrieked and ducked. I raised my arms to shield my face.

The bat clattered as the guy dropped it and flung himself into his car, slamming the door. He backed up, then cut over the yellow line and shot past us. He flipped his middle finger out the window, his voice trailing off as he yelled, "Muthafuckah!"

Dad stood in the middle of the road, shouting, "That's right, I'm a muthafuckah! That's why ya mutha's shoes are under my bed! I got ya plate numbah, asshole!"

He snatched up the bat and flung it onto the front passenger floor. Behind the wheel, he shoved his glasses back on and steered one-handed. He tore down the boulevard after the guy, but he was long gone.

A sudden brake at the East Squantum Street light slammed us back into the musty-smelling vinyl bench seat. I cried as more glass spilled forward onto our hair and clothes.

I can't remember what happened after that, but I think it was the last time I saw Margie's friend.

Chapter 12

Dickie's Bloody Hammer

PULLING myself out of my windshield memory, my attention shifted back to my siblings' conversations. A few of them were revisiting the earlier topic of when my father's mental illness might have started.

Marj's tone turned subdued.

"I remember when I first realized something was off about Dad." She thought back. "It was on Lyon Street, so I was about... four or so..."

The room quieted. Everyone was attentive except for Johnny, who was inserting another disc of *The White Album* into the CD player.

Billy interjected. "Hey, put my *Quadrophenia* back on."

"Shhh," Johnny quietly cut him off. "Let Margie tell her story," he muttered, fumbling to lower the volume knob.

Marj went on.

"Anyway, when you older boys were at school, I loved my time alone with Ma. In the morning, I'd watch *Captain Kangaroo* and *Romper Room*. Then after lunch I'd sit with Ma and we'd watch *General Hospital*—you know how she loved her soap operas. One day, she took me to the Five and Ten on Bowdoin Street and bought me some hair bows and pink nail polish, and when we got home, she painted my nails. I was so happy. I felt like a little princess."

She paused, the memory heavy. "Well, you know how Dad was about makeup—all hell broke loose when he got home and saw my nails."

Margie was too young to understand his words as he struck Ma repeatedly. "She looks like a goddamned painted lady!" Margie didn't know what a painted lady was, only that her best day ever ended with Ma getting a beating and everything good about the day disappearing. Hearing Ma being struck over and over frightened young Margie, and she felt it was all her fault.

We shook our heads, not so much in disbelief, but in a shared understanding of how these incidents with Dad always played out.

Marj relayed another frightening story.

"I remember another time when I was the same age. Dad got into a hammer fight with the guy downstairs. I don't know whose blood it was, but I'll never forget the blood all over Dad's white undershirt."

I'd heard this story long ago, but hearing it again, I pictured it all through a four-year-old's eyes, like a scene from a bad nightmare.

In 1965, Margie was playing with her friend Jenny at Grandma Dyer's apartment on nearby Tovar Street. She loved prancing around in Jenny's dainty white dress gloves, edged with lace and tiny embroidered roses.

A few weeks later, Jenny's mom gave Ma a shopping bag of Jenny's hand-me-downs for Margie and inside were the coveted white gloves. Margie's face lit up. "Yay, those are mine?"

"Yes, Margie. We have to take good care of these. These will match the pretty yellow Easter dress I'm making for you. I'll wash them so they're nice and clean."

A few days later, a late-March snowstorm dropped half a foot on Boston's cars and streets. Lyon Street off Dot Ave. was as tight as Salem Street in the North End, a labyrinth of narrow alleyways making parking a nightmare, even in summer. In the parlor, Margie watched *Huckleberry Hound* while Ma cooked supper and the boys played in their shared bedroom. Dad passed by and headed out the front door.

The sudden thud of Dad's sledgehammer fist on the downstairs tenant's door made Margie jump, dropping her Betsy Wetsy doll. On the first-floor landing, Dad stood in his white undershirt and oil-stained blue work pants, yelling at Jerry—a young guy Dad dismissed as a "faggot hippie" for wearing his hair past his ears.

Dad's voice echoed in the front hallway. "It took me an hour to shovel that spot out with my bad back. I had a friggin' barrel holding it. You just come along and take my spot? How fuckin' ignorant are you?"

Jerry pushed back. "I was only *paahked* there for five minutes, man."

Dad shot back, mocking him. "Yeah, well, I had to park down on Dot Ave., *man*. And I walked up here in the goddamned sleet. What the hell's wrong with you, huh? Ya think you'd've learned some respect getting your ass kicked in those Southie projects you crawled in from. Why don't you learn some fuckin' manners, huh?"

After more shouting and obscenities, Dad stormed back upstairs and grabbed his old, rusty hammer. He flung his eyeglasses on a metal tray table in the parlor and stomped back out, slamming the door behind him hard enough to rattle the frame, and Margie.

The hallway echoed with more muffled shouting. "What the frig, man. Calm down! I didn't know you shoveled out that spot."

"Who the fuck'ja think shoveled it? The goddamned Easter Bunny?"

"It's a public street! You don't own it!"

Dad's yelling intensified. "Oh, yeah? You maggot."

A body slammed into the stairwell wall, and the parlor floor shook. Frightened, Margie ran to Ma in the kitchen. A minute later, Dad reappeared, looking disheveled, his white T-shirt streaked with fresh blood. Margie had no idea whose blood it was, but the sight stopped her cold, and she began to cry.

Ma ushered her to the boys' bedroom. "Jimmy, Danny, play Candy Land with your sister." She shut the door behind her and tended to Dad in the kitchen. She poured him a glass of Wild Irish Rose and scrubbed the bloody undershirt in bleach water at the sink. They had no back porch to hang clothes out to dry, nor a clothes dryer, so in those early days, Ma hung the family's wet clothes over kitchen curtain rods or on a makeshift clothesline. Dad had rigged one from the back doorframe to a thick metal eye hook driven into the ornate molding of the triple-decker—damage he left behind in every place we lived.

The next day, Margie walked into the kitchen and froze. The hair on the back of her neck stood up. Her white gloves hung on the clothesline beside Dad's rusty colored, blood-stained under-shirt. The gloves were ruined for her by hanging so close to something so icky, something that carried such a horrifying memory with it.

In that moment of reckoning, four-year-old Margie sensed something wasn't right about Dad.

Chapter 13

Beware of Darkness

As the three youngest, Me, Tommy, and Billy hadn't spent much time around Johnny when he was a teenager. Much of what we knew of those years came later, through stories we heard. I'm relieved I didn't witness our father tormenting him in those early years. But distance has its downside. Maybe if I'd seen it up close, I wouldn't have judged Johnny's life choices as harshly as I sometimes did.

The day of Dad's funeral, some of those stories began to surface. Standing in a loose circle in my kitchen, we revisited an incident involving the same baseball bat Jim would later use to stop Dad. But in this encounter, Johnny was the undeserving target.

"Didn't the old man pull some kind of sneak attack on you with a bat once?" Thom asked Johnny, his voice uncertain.

"Sneak attack? More like a fuckin' ambush! He tried to smash my head in with the baseball bat just because I had to work late!"

Jim interrupted in John's defense, "I remember that. The thing is, Johnny, you did everything right that night, and the old man still tried to kill you."

Johnny took over the story.

It was January 1973, around ten o'clock at night, when the phone rang at our house. Johnny was seventeen and working second shift as a security guard at a Boston warehouse. He called from the freezing guard shack to say he'd be working late. Most of the house, including Ma, was already asleep. Dad was in the parlor, drinking. By that time, he would've been on his fifth or sixth bottle of Boone's Farm, the TV glowing as *M*A*S*H* transported him back to his army days at the start of the Korean War.

Johnny held his breath as the line rang once, twice, then a third time. Each ring stretched longer than the last, thick with anxiety as he silently willed Ma to answer. *Come on, Ma. Pick up.* When Dad's voice came on the line, Johnny forced his calmest tone.

"Dad, it's Johnny. I, uh—have to stay a little late at work. The guy taking over my shift had car trouble, but he's on his way. I should be home closer to twelve thirty. I've got my house key, but can you leave the storm door unlatched? I don't want to wake everyone, ringing the doorbell late."

Making that call was the courteous, responsible thing to do. But courtesy never counted for much with Dad when it came to Johnny.

"Fine," Dad said surly, and hung up.

But Johnny knew it definitely wasn't fine.

A little before twelve thirty, Dad shut off the TV, along with the porch and foyer lights. He positioned himself in the dark, wedging himself between the big wooden coat wardrobe and the front door, gripping the bat.

He waited.

Johnny continued. "When I came home, the house was completely dark. I turned the deadbolt, pushed the heavy front door partway open, and for some reason I stopped. I couldn't see anything, but I just knew. I had this gut feeling, like a sixth sense, telling me something wasn't right. I knew someone—probably the old man—was hiding behind the door."

Johnny said he stepped inside cautiously, instinctively reaching his hand upward into the dark. The bat came crashing down on his outstretched hand, knocking him off balance before it could reach his head.

"What the hell are you doing?" Johnny shouted, shoving Dad back with the bat. His hand stung from deflecting the bat. "What the fuck's wrong with you?"

Dad lunged at him, grabbing him by the neck.

"You son of a bitch! Don't you come waltzing into my house at twelve thirty in the morning! This is my goddamned house, you hear me, you loser punk?"

Johnny struggled to get his words out. "I called and told you I was gonna be late! I even asked you to unlock the storm door so I wouldn't wake everyone. I did what I was supposed to do!"

But nothing Johnny ever did or said was enough.

Dad backhanded him in the dark, sending Johnny reeling. Blood poured from his nose, still healing from a "lesson" Dad had delivered a few weeks earlier.

"I ran into the bathroom. It took so friggin' long to get my nose to stop bleeding. It didn't help that my hand was all numb and shit from the bat—luckily, it wasn't broken. And the old man just went off to bed like nothing happened."

We all shook our heads.

"Man, I forgot all about that one," Dan said.

Johnny stood up straighter. "But the bat wasn't the only time," he said. "Remember that same year, Hook? When he pulled the gun on me?"

"That one I remember," Dan said. Jim said he also remembered it and they told the story.

· · ·

A FEW MONTHS after the bat attack, Dad was deep into one of his usual late-night moods—a dangerous mix of booze and simmering hatred. Ma was fast asleep in the master bedroom when Dad slipped in, eased his shotgun from the bedroom closet along with a box of shells, and tiptoed back out to the parlor.

I pictured him slouched on the couch, the shotgun against his leg, a bottle of apple wine in his hand, watching *Dragnet* as he loaded the gun, building a case in his mind over some imagined slight. Maybe someone forgot to wring out a drippy washcloth in the tub, or maybe Ma missed a few crumbs on the kitchen table. Whatever it was, it was usually one of two people who were at fault—Johnny or Ma.

Johnny, still working the night warehouse job, got home at 11:20 p.m. As he opened the door and pressed on the old push-button light switch, the cold steel of a shotgun muzzle was pointed at his face. Johnny didn't flinch. In the harsh foyer light, he threw his arms up in surrender and yelled, "Pull it! Pull the fuckin' trigger! Go on! Just do it!"

Dad didn't pull the trigger. It seemed he wanted the power more than the shot, spewing drunken obscenities about Johnny being late again before storming down the hallway to bed.

Awakened by the commotion, Ma came into the hall in her bathrobe.

"What's going on?"

"Your shit-for-brains son, that's what!" Dad yelled. "He thinks this is a goddamned flop house."

He shoved her back into the bedroom, told her to mind her business, slammed the door, and went to bed.

"The fact that the old man even considered pulling a gun on his own kid shows how friggin' crazy he was," Johnny said. "And for what? Because I looked too much like Grandpa? Because he terrorized me as a little kid so of course, I acted out?"

We all took beatings growing up, but Johnny was singled out—tormented and brutalized in ways the rest of us weren't.

"Yeah," Jim said. "I remember the day after that. You told me and Dan you weren't afraid. You said you wished he'd have just pulled the trigger—once and for all—to end the misery. That it would've been a relief."

Johnny nodded. "It would have been."

Chapter 14

Honey Pie

Marj and I cleared the first stack of lunch dishes as "Ob-La-Di, Ob-La-Da" segued into "Wild Honey Pie." The song sparked a childhood memory with Thom that flooded my brain like a wave at Nantasket Beach, and I sprinted into the living room before the fifty-two-second track ended.

"Hey, Thom, remember the CB radio you got on Bloomfield Street?"

"Yeah, I got it in a skateboard trade from a kid at the Grover," he said, meaning Grover Cleveland Middle School. "My CB handle was Chuckles. Yours was some Beatles song, wasn't it?"

"It was this song playing right now," I said, pointing to the stereo. "This was my handle—'Honey Pie.' That's what made me think of your CB. It reminded me of when things started getting rough in Fields Corner. You got the CB radio to listen for neighborhood crime, right?"

"Yeah, I used it kinda like a police scanner to keep tabs on trouble around Geneva Ave., but really, all of Fields Corner. There were so many B&Es [breaking & entering], people getting jumped. I mean, come on... We were sitting ducks living there.

Same thing at the Grover. That's why I played hooky so much. The old man wasn't gonna move us out. Except for the Camerons and maybe two other White families, we were the only ones left. Everyone else was gone."

His voice trailed off as he took a swig of beer and swiped one of Johnny's unfiltered Camels. He was talking about what people then called Boston's "White flight."

By the early 1970s, Dorchester's demographics were beginning to shift. Black families from the American South were moving to Boston during and after the civil rights era, settling in neighborhoods such as Roxbury, Dorchester, and Mattapan, in search of better economic opportunities and schooling. At the same time, migrants from Puerto Rico and other parts of the Caribbean were establishing communities across the city, followed later by refugees from Southeast Asia, primarily Vietnam.

As Boston's neighborhoods began to integrate, racial tension grew in Dorchester's Uphams Corner and Fields Corner—neighborhoods we bounced between for years. Crime also increased in some areas, and many White families moved farther south to Quincy, Randolph, Braintree, and other nearby towns.

Our brother Bob, who left home at sixteen, later moved from his downtown Boston apartment up to Malden, hoping to put more distance between himself and the unrest.

At an early age, I noticed subtle changes. In kindergarten in 1971, things were carefree and easy. My best friend was a Black boy named Billy. We walked hand in hand to the Mather School with Ma, oblivious to the divisions brewing around us. From first grade on, I played with children of all ethnicities. My three closest playmates on Bloomfield Street were Haitian, Irish, and Black American. On Fridays, our families swam together at the school pool. We rode our bikes together, carved pumpkins together, and played outside until the streetlights came on. Skin color had no bearing on our fun. But in 1974, when I was in third grade, things started changing.

Under the 1965 Massachusetts Racial Imbalance Act, federal judge W. Arthur Garrity Jr. ordered school desegregation, mandating busing between predominantly White and Black schools. Violence erupted across parts of the city as the court-mandated reassignment of students beyond neighborhood lines led to widespread protests and racial unrest in affected areas.

Before busing, my older brothers could safely walk to and from Dorchester High, their neighborhood school. In the first two phases of busing in 1974 and 1975, they were bused to Madison Park High in Roxbury or to Jeremiah Burke in Dorchester, both predominantly Black neighborhoods. Around the school grounds and on the buses, they were pelted with bricks and bottles and spat on. Black students bused into white neighborhoods like South Boston and Charlestown faced the same hostilities.

The situation for my brothers grew so dire that three of them—along with thousands of other Boston students—eventually flunked out, dropped out, or transferred, like so many kids we knew. Some rode school buses into Roxbury under heavy Tactical Patrol Force motorcycle escort while kids lined the bus route, ready to light and throw Molotov cocktails. Before long, families we knew in Dorchester began leaving Boston for safer neighborhoods and schools.

Some parents scraped together tuition for parochial schools to keep their kids out of the Boston Public Schools, often at great personal cost. I remember a father in the neighborhood who died young. I heard adults say he'd "worked himself into an early grave" putting his children through parochial school. At eight, I took that literally and pictured him working in a cemetery. His widow sold the house and moved away, trading school tuition for a safer place to raise her children.

In the first year of busing, I met Cheryl in Mrs. Park's third grade class at the John Marshall Elementary School. We became fast friends, playing together after school, and as racial trouble brewed in the school and the neighborhood, we stayed inseparable for another reason—personal safety. Cheryl lived a seven-minute walk from my street, so we walked to school together every day. Another student made school unbearable for Cheryl. She bullied her almost daily, threatening to "kick her White booty" after school. She was the size of a high schooler and carried herself with an intimidating toughness that left Cheryl petrified.

School had its own challenges for me, though. Girls cornered me, demanding my homework answers, my prized tri-color pen, and sometimes, parts of my lunch. Some threatened to kick my "honkey hiney" after school. I got beat more than enough at home, so I gave in to the bullying and stayed as close to my teachers as possible. Like my sister, they felt like my safe place. I loved school work, but I also did well so I could stay on my teachers' good sides, hoping they might look out for me.

Some days after school, I came home hungry after losing much of my lunch earlier that day. We didn't have much, so I raided the pantry for my father's bland Uneeda Biscuit crackers, slathering margarine on them or sandwiching hot banana pepper rings between them and washing them down with a glass of water. It became my after-school meal, tiding me over until suppertime.

I remember that winter in third grade. Every school day at 7:15 a.m., as we all ate our Cream of Wheat at the kitchen table and watched *Father Knows Best* reruns, the loud ring of the rotary wall phone jolted us out of our sleepy haze. The call was always for me, of all people. Those five seconds were as vital to me as the morning briefing was to Governor Dukakis. It was a daily safety check from Cheryl.

Draping the twisted, stretched-out phone cord fifteen feet across everyone's ducking heads, Ma would ask me the same worn-out question, as if my reply might be different for once.

"Mary, why does she have to call here every morning?"

"She wants to know if I'm going to school."

"Can't she find out when she gets there? Cripes' sake..."

"No, she's scared to go alone, Ma."

I'd grab the phone. "Hello?"

The timid eight-year-old voice on the other end would whisper, "It's me, you going?"

I would reply with a simple yes or no and hang up.

We were scared little kids in a changing neighborhood, and now school was starting to feel unsafe. If I were going to school, Cheryl would go. If I was sick or home nursing the welts from Dad's belt for some minor offense like refusing to eat homemade pea soup—because, what little kid likes pea soup?—Cheryl would feign illness or beg her mother to let her stay home as well. She believed it was her only safe option: safety in numbers, at least theoretically. There were times I also lied to my mother to avoid getting bullied or beat up after school.

"Ma, can I stay home? I'll clean the house." Ma couldn't keep up with the endless housework and she occasionally took me up on my offer, letting me slide, since I was an honor student. I don't recall why I never told her about the bullying; perhaps I feared my father would find out. It made no sense, but that's how things were at our home. Better to keep quiet than bring negative attention to myself.

Even before adolescence, the instinct to stay on guard extended beyond school and our front door, onto MBTA trains and buses. I remember when the Guardian Angels, a volunteer anti-crime group, patrolled Boston's subways and streets. Seeing them in their red berets on Red Line trains and platforms offered a small sense of comfort at a time when the city felt so fractured.

Racial integration and busing, though it paved the way toward a more fair and equal society and expanded school opportunity for all, brought challenges to many parts of Boston. The White population in many parts of Dorchester dwindled during the flight to the suburbs, and those who remained, like us, became a minority and faced harassment and intimidation. It's what prompted Thom to trade for the CB radio, so we could monitor what was happening around our area. My older brothers started carrying knives for protection.

Sometimes on Sundays, I ice skated at the Neponset Skating Rink. I saw mostly White kids there and I wished we lived in Neponset instead of Fields Corner, just two miles away. As a family on welfare, our parents couldn't afford to move, so we dealt with whatever came our way.

Chapter 15

Crippled Inside

WHILE SHARING tidbits about the old neighborhood and the estranged father we'd just buried, Dan revisited the possible onset of Dad's mental illness.

"Johnny, you asked earlier about when the old man started getting worse... Don't forget, by Adams Street, he was taking all kinds of pills..."

"So, like, '63? 'Cause I think I was born there," Thom asked.

We moved so often, it became easier for Ma and us to mark events by which sibling was born in which apartment.

Dan paused to think. "No, Mary was born on Adams Street. So, like, 1966."

He went on. "Anyway, Johnny, remember he had that shoebox full of prescription bottles up in his closet?"

"Course I remember. I'm older than you, man. I used to swipe pills from that box all the time." He chuckled at the memory.

Thom teased, "And his booze too."

Dan thought back. "Yeah, man, he took pills for everything... shoulder bursitis, back pain from the Army Jeep accident, gout..."

Johnny added another. "High blood pressure meds..."

"Right... I forgot about that." Dan rubbed his chin. "I remember him taking diet pills, sleeping pills... He had pills for staying awake, going to sleep, and whatever else he could get from his doctors. Back then, prescriptions were filled anytime. You didn't even need to ask for refills."

"Wait." Bill halted the conversation. "So, he could walk into Murray's Drugs and say, 'I'm all out; I need more.' And they just kept giving him more? A bottomless supply?" In a tone of mock outrage, he asked, "How do I get some of that?"

"Yep, that's how prescriptions were done back then—all the refills you wanted—like the Stones' song, 'Mother's Little Helper.' Same idea."

The list of Dad's pills was long enough to make me think of Elvis Presley and his infamous daily cocktail of pills—only in a triple-decker, not Graceland. Johnny's eyes rolled upward, his head tilting back as if the sheer thought of all the drugs made him dizzy. "Yeah, he was a walking drugstore, man. Along with all the booze... Crazy Dickie didn't know if he was coming or going."

None of us knew much about Dad's medical history, but whatever he struggled with was compounded by a brain injury and years of heavy drinking and pills. All of it had to have compounded his physical issues. An unsettled mind can push the body into overdrive. I can relate. For years, I've had plenty of chronic pain flare-ups from my overactive mind—back pain, limb and joint pain.

Talking with my siblings, I tried to better understand his plight. "So, it's like he had varying degrees of temporary insanity pretty much every night of the week."

Marj answered, "Yeah, pretty much."

Dan gave his take. "Some people are happy drunks. Others get depressed. When the old man drank, he got violent. Some people drink and turn into Mr. Hyde. The old man turned into Crazy Dickie Dyer."

Johnny lit a Camel. "Yeah. He could start off in an okay mood. Then something tiny would set him off, like a grease spot on the stove, and, bam! He'd snap. Crazy Dickie would come out again. He was like a ticking time bomb, man."

Dan shrugged. "He couldn't control his temper. That's why he ended up in the slammer all the time."

The Boston Police knew our family well. Neighbors often called for domestic well-checks when they heard Dad beating the family. From upstairs or downstairs in a triple-decker, they could hear bodies slamming against walls, Ma and us kids crying, and Dad screaming his lungs out. It was impossible to ignore. And anytime Ma hinted at calling the cops herself, he threatened to kill her, promising she would never make it out of the house alive if she reported him.

We watched, or listened from our rooms, petrified, as Dad pinned Ma by the throat in the narrow hallways and cramped kitchens of every apartment we lived in. Most times, when police arrived, she was afraid to press charges. Their hands were tied. Occasionally, with police persuasion and support, she would. The cops would cuff Dad, throw him into the back of a cruiser, and he would spend the night locked up at Police Station 11 in Dorchester or Charles Street Jail in Boston. The following morning, he would appear before a judge at Dorchester District Court for domestic assault and battery. Some judges ordered him to attend AA meetings, while others sentenced him to Deer Island Prison or Bridgewater, a state psychiatric hospital.

The forced sobriety of incarceration temporarily neutralized him. But the mania still simmered beneath the surface, returning in full force once he was released and began drinking again.

When I was seven, I knew we weren't the only family dealing with abuse, because I could see the signs in other mothers. I remember on many walks with Ma through Dorchester, she kept her dark sunglasses on to hide her bruises and I occasionally saw the same pattern in others. Like when Ma and I were standing in the checkout line at Purity Supreme one day and I noticed the woman behind us was wearing a head scarf tied tight around her face with dark sunglasses, her head down, as if studying the floor. I could see a swollen bruise on her cheek and the dark mark of a black eye beneath poorly applied concealer. I stared, recognizing in her the same suffering Ma endured. *Does she have kids my age? Do they suffer beatings too?*

I was pulled from my thoughts as Marj lightened the mood with a funny memory. "Hey, Bill, remember when Dad went to jail on Bowdoin Street? We were so happy he was gone. We were singing that 5th Dimension song."

Bill's brow furrowed. "Huh? I don't remember."

"The time he went to jail for beating up Ma and Johnny, remember?" Marj sang the start of the chorus, "One less bell to answer..."

Recognition flickered across Bill's face. "Oh, yeah. We did the question-answer thing." In an off-key singing voice, he belted out, "One less egg to fry."

Listening to their memory, the reaction felt akin to "Ding Dong, the Wicked Witch is Dead." They said for those few months when Dad was in the clink, Ma's face was free of stress. For a while, everyone felt, *Thank God, he's gone. We're gonna be okay now.*

Johnny shook his head. "Yeah, but then he'd get out of jail and it was like, *tick, tick, tick...*"

His time bomb comment took me back to when I was small, and Dad would explode over the tiniest imperfections. If we left the shower head angled differently from his height preference or forgot to turn off a light, we got the belt. We were nervous little kids, struggling to remember the endless rules we were supposed to follow.

Minor irritations triggered Dad's brutality, reminiscent of Joan

Crawford in her adopted daughter's memoir, *Mommie Dearest*. He would start off happy, enjoying his country records in the parlor over several bottles of wine. Around eleven, he would stumble off to bed. Chaos arose if, on the way, he noticed the kitchen or bathroom wasn't spotless, which they never were. Running a household of ten, Ma had bigger fish to fry. Even on school nights, he would turn on all the lights, rampage through the house, and unleash a torrent of obscenities and demands, dragging us out of bed to clean—especially the boys.

"Get the fuck out of bed now! Doris, get your ass in here and mop the kitchen floor. Jimmy, scrub the stove. Billy, clean the tub and get all the goddamned hair out of the drain."

It all had to be done, or no one was going to bed. Midnight cleanings were followed up with a severe beating. Ma would intervene, but then she got beat too. We would get sent to bed sore, crying, and scared. Sleep was hard to get on those nights.

When Tommy, Billy, and I were young, we bit our fingernails down to nubs because we were so nervous. Sometimes, Dad would line us up for a military-style nail inspection. None of us ever passed, so we got a beating. In school the following day, my butt would be so black and blue I couldn't sit on my chair. I wonder why the teachers never questioned my squirming, bruised body. Maybe it was because I hid my pain and exhaustion so well.

Another regular upheaval was when my father forced the three of us to do sit-ups. It may have been a throwback to his Army mentality—"Stay in shape." We would have to take turns holding each other's ankles for sit-ups so we wouldn't get fat. We were skinny kids. Ma couldn't splurge on Twinkies, potato chips, or Ring Dings. Welfare food and cheap cuts of meat were our staple, and they were far from abundant. Dad's obsession with monitoring our weight was unwarranted.

But they say the road to hell is paved with good intentions. By morning, as we ate our Maypo and nursed our bruises, Dad had sobered up and apologized, full of remorse. It seemed he couldn't grasp the person he'd been the night before.

This was something my young mind could never grasp... *You can beat us up, then say you're sorry.*

To his apology, he added, "If anyone asks you what happened here, you don't know anything." But I did know. It was mind-bogglingly hard to keep his irrational, paranoid rules straight.

To supplement the welfare checks, Dad moonlighted fixing cars at a gas station, and later, he repaired bicycles at a shop on Dot Ave. He told us, "If anyone asks if I work, you say no."

These *mind games* were confusing because we knew where he worked. But we were terrified of physical harm—or of him killing our mother—so we stayed quiet. Witnessing something and being told to deny it was hard to grasp at such an early age. It was a paranoid, secretive way to grow up. Adults have the benefit of experience and reasoning to navigate life's gray areas, but children don't. Those gaslighting mixed messages left me seeing relationships in absolute terms, a habit I carried into friendships and dating. I would learn later in life, the long, hard way, how limiting that was.

I consider myself lucky because as a kid I had Margie to model and teach me and I could observe how other kids with more stable parents behaved. To figure out what "normal" looked like, I watched adults at school and in the community. Some neighborhood parents offered a glimpse of what ordinary family life could look like, though not all of them set the best example. A few Dorchester families seemed solid and steady, while others I knew had their own issues behind closed doors. I heard adults use foul language and tell inappropriate stories, and I knew kids whose parents drank too much. We weren't unique in this regard, just more on display than most because of out of control father.

Chapter 16

Hey, Bulldog

As the afternoon of our father's burial went on, my siblings mingled and cracked open fortune cookies. In the dining room, Bill scoffed as he read his fortune aloud.

"'Good fortune is within your reach.' Yeah, right. Not while I'm collecting unenjoyment."

He cackled at his made-up word. Laid off from pumping gas, Bill always turned hard times into a sarcastic joke, a coping mechanism I sometimes fall back on. He nodded to Thom and the two of them headed for the door, saying they were "going for a quick ride."

In the kitchen, I sponged and dried the counters. Behind my apartment, a dog barked incessantly to be let in. As I rinsed a few more dishes, a flashback hit—how Dad had treated our family dogs.

"Ugh," I muttered to Jim. "Why don't they let the poor dog in already? They always leave him out in the yard for way too long. It's freezing out."

Jim sighed. "People shouldn't have pets if they can't care for them."

It put me right back in those old memories. "Remember how mean Dad was to our dogs?" I said.

"Yeah, no shit, man," Johnny added, strolling into the kitchen to join in on my words. "Even the poor dogs couldn't escape the old man's craziness."

He pulled a kitchen chair out from the table and sat, lighting a Camel. "Yeah, the old man had no heart, man. He never should have had animals."

A painful animal memory surfaced for me. "When I was about seven, I remember Dad bragged at the supper table about how, as a kid, he tied a litter of kittens into a burlap bag and drowned them at Tenean Beach."

Johnny, a sentimental, tender-hearted guy, closed his eyes on the painful image. Jim shook his head at how wrong it was. "Well, I'm not saying it was right, but the old man came from a different time. Back then...in what? The late '30s, early '40s? Boys did stupid shit like that when they were bored. It was wrong, but that's how it was, I guess."

I tsked. "The old adage—'boys will be boys.'" I reflected back. "But he wasn't a kid anymore in the '70s when he was bragging about drowning the kittens. He was in his forties by then. That's just messed up."

"True," Jim said, getting what I meant.

I remember being small, watching my father handle yet another dog he'd "found" somewhere in Dorchester. They came from Rainbow Park, Town Field Park, or a bar along Dot Ave. He trained the dogs like he trained us when he was irritable—with impatience and brute force. Each dog quickly learned to fear him, enduring his temper as we did. A puppy struggling with newspaper potty training, missing the target by an inch, got just as harsh punishment as us kids did. When they couldn't read his mind, he kicked the dog across the floor with work boots on. A rolled-up magazine wasn't just a light tap on the butt, it was a full-force, painful whack on the snout, sending them yelping and cowering in their own puddle of pee. My heart hurt each time I overheard their cries, and I quietly cried for them in my room, knowing I couldn't protect them. I sat with them whenever I could, hoping my presence might bring some comfort, some minor relief from the fear we all shared.

One dog, a young German shepherd named Sam, shivered whenever I approached him after an outburst, his head and tail tucked low, afraid to trust. Late at night, I would hear Sam crying from the pantry, where Dad locked him up as a lesson, though I couldn't fathom what lesson he thought an innocent dog could understand.

Some dogs only lived with us for a couple weeks, some a few months. When Dad decided a dog was no longer worth his time, he would "drive it out to the country," and we would never see it again. One winter day, he tied one of our dogs to a pole outside a Purity Supreme and drove off. I cried when I overheard him talking about it later that day.

Those impressions stayed with me, and as an adult I helped animals where I could. I fostered abandoned and abused shelter cats, each one a small way of making peace with the times I couldn't intervene as a child.

Chapter 17

Picture Yourself on a Train at Park Street Station

LUNCH MIGHT HAVE BEEN OVER, but the day was young. The stories rolled on, drifting from the kitchen to the living room. Bill and Thom came back in from their "ride," the skunky smell of pot trailing behind them.

Jim's nose caught the lingering smell. "You're still smoking that crap?"

"Who said I ever stopped?" Bill, glazed, headed for the CD player to queue up Alice Cooper's *Killer* CD.

"Anyway," Jim said, "here's one for you about the old man—from my Dot High days. Do you guys remember when I played hooky and slept at Park Street train station?"

A few of us exchanged glances, but no one seemed to recall.

"I was too scared to go home and face the old man, so I slept overnight at the station."

The room quieted and Jim filled in the rest.

In September 1974, when busing began, Jimmy started his freshman year at Dorchester High. He was an excellent student, but like many kids back then, he found it hard to focus on schoolwork amid the busing chaos. Around the school, mounted police patrolled the sidewalks, bracing for riots as buses pulled up and students poured out—some throwing punches or spitting in each other's faces before the first bell even rang. Inside, you kept your head down and your senses sharp, never sure when a fist or a knife might find you in the hallway or bathroom. After lunch, the buses rolled up again. This time, they carried students across the city to a technical high school in Roxbury for afternoon shop classes. The rides were tense; getting there meant bracing for more assaults along the way.

Jimmy wasn't mechanically inclined and hated shop. He and a couple of friends dreaded going so much they began skipping the afternoon sessions altogether, choosing instead to ride the subway and hang around downtown Boston. To pass the time, they boarded the Red Line at Washington station and rode it to Harvard Square, back when it was the last stop on the line. They repeated the round trip several times, crossing under the pedestrian tunnels to the opposite track so they paid just one fare to ride all afternoon.

After missing five continuous afternoons of woodworking class, Jimmy's homeroom teacher pulled him into the school office. "All right, Mr. Dyer. What's your phone number? I have to call your parents about your absences."

Jimmy reluctantly rattled off our phone number, his voice dropping lower until it was almost a whisper.

From the corridor, he heard the teacher dialing the rotary phone. When the line engaged, the teacher asked, "Hello, Mr. Dyer?" Dad had picked up.

Jimmy's heart sank because now the old man would be the first to learn about him playing hooky, instead of Ma, who probably would have covered for him. The thought of the beating which awaited him brought instant panic.

Jimmy chose the path of avoidance. Instead of going to shop class that day, he took the train into downtown Boston, wandering, stressing about his fate at home. He killed time at his favorite haunt, Little Jack Horner Joke Shop, where he liked to buy whoopie cushions, fake vomit, fake dog poop, hand buzzers, and the toy which always cracked me up, the Laugh Bag. When that lost its appeal, he strolled through the Combat Zone and Chinatown. From there, he walked through Boston Common toward Newbury Street, where he flipped through hundreds of albums at used record shops. He ended up in Copley Square, where he roamed around some more.

At 11:00 p.m., he made his way back to Park Street Station to catch the last train home. Pacing nervously near the end of the concourse, he noticed a hidden nook in the corner and settled down, exhausted. He slept there for the night, undiscovered by MBTA police.

The next morning, hunger pangs woke Jimmy. He had a small savings account at Shawmut Bank, so he withdrew five dollars to buy a couple of train tokens and a donut at Mug 'N Muffin and wandered around Tremont and Boylston Streets again.

Before the school day started, Ma and Dad went to Dot High, asking staff and kids in the yard if they'd seen Jimmy since the day before, but no one had. Worried sick, Ma asked any kid who knew Jimmy to please tell him to come home—or at least call—if they saw him. "Tell him he can come home. We'll work it out, whatever's going on," Dad said, more worried than mad at that point. They then filed a missing person report at Police Station 11.

Dad checked with the bank's Fields Corner branch to see if Jimmy had made any withdrawals, hoping it might offer a clue to his whereabouts or activity. The bank manager, however, couldn't share Jimmy's private information.

Jimmy spent a tense morning strolling downtown, putting off facing the old man's wrath. Around one o'clock, about the time the boys would start playing hooky again, his friend Mike caught up with him on the Boston Common. Jimmy was exhausted and disheveled but relieved to see a familiar face.

"Hey, Jim, your parents have been looking for you, man. Your mom is real worried. Your old man said to tell you whatever's going on, he wants you to come home and figure it out."

Figure it out? Jimmy thought. There was never any "figuring things out" with the old man. Maybe on *Leave It to Beaver* or *Father Knows Best*, but not in our house.

Around three o'clock, Jimmy reluctantly returned home, petrified. When Dad questioned him about his whereabouts and why he hadn't been in school, he nervously confessed. "W-Wh-whenever I take the afternoon bus to R-Roxbury, the White kids get hassled around the school. I don't like shop classes, either. I d-didn't know what to do, so I skipped school and slept in P-Park Street Station."

In a rare display of fatherly concern, Dad surprised Jimmy with compassion. "Jimmy, you can always come to us if things aren't working out. The thing is, you put your mother through hell worrying about you."

None of us would have ever considered talking things out with Dad, but with Ma, always. Jimmy knew he was damned if he did, damned if he didn't. With Dad, we never knew which way the cookie would crumble, but it rarely crumbled our way.

Jimmy paid for Ma's worry that night. Dad's earlier reassurances meant nothing once his mood turned sour, and he gave Jimmy a beating.

In the fall, Jimmy was transferred from Dorchester High to the Jeremiah Burke school, a full-day academic school in a mostly Black section of Dorchester. There, amid the ongoing busing chaos, he kept his head down, stayed focused, and did his best to get along with kids of all races. He persevered and became the only Dyer boy out of six to graduate high school. Given the stress at home and the dangers in the surrounding neighborhood, his accomplishment was nothing short of miraculous.

Chapter 18

Aunt Sally Blues

BILL STEPPED out of the room, and I slunk over to my CD player. As much as I loved early Alice Cooper, it was time for more Beatles. I shot a knowing look at my fellow Beatles devotees Marj and Johnny, and popped in *Abbey Road*, John's signature vocal repeating the "Shhh" opening of "Come Together."

Johnny pointed to the stereo. "You know what he's saying right there?"

I shrugged. "Shhhh?"

"No. He's saying, 'Shoot me,' as in, *shoot me up*." He mimicked sticking a needle into his arm. He took a pull of brandy and muttered, "Mary, start the song over."

Dubious, I restarted the song. "Oh, ya, I think I hear it faintly now."

"Told ya. The Beatles had tons of hidden drug messages in their songs. Especially Lennon." I'd already heard and read those rumors long before. But Johnny enjoyed being the knowing older brother, so I let him have the authority.

We all chatted some more, and the conversation turned to how we'd grown up poor on welfare. Memories unfolded like old family photos, each with a story of how Ma took care of us, no matter how tight things got. Feeding and clothing eight kids on nothing but welfare money and hand-me-downs wasn't easy, but Ma made sure we got three squares a day and clothes suitable for Boston's harsh winters and scorching summers.

"Every Labor Day weekend, Ma had us boys go through all our clothes," Dan said. He leaned back, as if he could see those piles in front of him. "She'd say, 'Danny, give Jimmy those dungarees I patched for you last year,' and we'd just pass 'em on down to the next kid in line. I was like, 'But Ma, the fly's ripped, and the knee patches fell off.' She'd say, 'I'll sew the patches back on and sew in a new zipper. And give me all your ripped socks to sew. Billy and Tommy need socks for school.'"

"Good ole Aunt Sally hand-me-downs." A thin smile crossed Johnny's face.

Handouts from the Salvation Army—clothes, food, even summer camp—were jokingly dubbed "Aunt Sally" by the boys, in her honor.

"But we did all right." Johnny looked toward Dan and Jim. "I hated getting Bobby's clothes when he was done with them." He paused to take a haul off a Camel. "I mean, he was already six-two in middle school, and Ma had to sew six-inch hems on the bottom cuffs of his dungarees so I could wear them. I looked like a clown at school."

Jim walked in adding, "Better than wearing sleeve floods. Most of you and Dan's shirts fell three inches above my wrists."

Toughskins made their rounds, moving from one boy to the next until they were worn beyond repair.

"By the time they got to me, there were more patches than pants," Thom joked. We all had a good laugh.

A memory from kindergarten came to me.

"One day, Ma sent me to school in Dad's white tube socks

because I didn't have any of my own. The heel was halfway up my calf."

Fortunately, most of my clothes were Margie's hand-me-downs, always in decent condition, since she was the only girl ahead of me. Ma also saved money by sewing matching outfits for Margie and me from the same sewing pattern. Whether it was a goofy set of plaid pant suits or pastel dresses for spring, they looked as nice as store-bought. Matching Margie's outfits made me feel special because I got to look like my big sister's twin. It was Ma's way of making something unique just for us and affordable for her.

Thinking about how poor we were brought back memories of my gum obsession. Candy was a luxury we couldn't afford, and Dad had banned chewing gum, even if it was sugarless. Margie occasionally slipped me a half-piece of Juicy Fruit, which she hid at the bottom of her jewelry box. But when I needed my gum fix, my supplier was the sidewalk in front of our house.

Kids on Glendale Street always had gum from baseball cards and from Batman or Wacky Packages trading cards they picked up on penny-candy runs to Mighty Midget. The variety store on Bowdoin Street was every kid's favorite destination, packed with candy and toys, with just enough milk, eggs, and bread to call it a grocery.

I regularly scanned the sidewalk for discarded gum, as if I were searching for a hidden treasure.

I confessed my gross habit to my siblings. "Did you know I used to eat chewed-up gum off the sidewalk on Glendale Street?"

Jim recoiled, sticking out his tongue. "Blech! That's nasty, girl." He paused, weighing it against other childhood atrocities. "Then again, I guess it's no worse than kids eating their boogers."

"Exactly. I'd scour the pavement for a blob of spit-out gum—sneaker tread marks and all. I'd peel it off the sizzling hot sidewalk in gooey, stringy pieces, pop it in my mouth, and start chewing."

I mimicked a *crunch, crunch* sound. "The rocks and dirt didn't bother me. And hey, it was free."

The gum sometimes held onto a faint hint of mint or fruit flavor, enough for me to practice blowing bubbles. I thought of the colorful Fruit Stripe gum wrappers scattered on the ground and smiled. I probably ingested traces of *E. coli*, thanks to all the unleashed dogs pooping around the neighborhood. But discarded gum felt brand new to me—and even better because it was forbidden. Thinking back, it makes me gag. But who knows? I'm confident that chewing gum off the dirty streets of Dorchester helped build up my cast-iron immunity. Aside from your garden-variety common cold, I rarely get sick. With all my family went through, none of us has ever had cancer, allergies, or other diseases, thank God. Aside from how we've lived at times, we're a hearty bunch of survivors. I like to tell people, "My family's like cockroaches—you can't kill us."

Besides government-issued "welly" (welfare) food, Ma and Dad received AFDC, Aid to Families with Dependent Children, the infamous welfare check, along with food stamps.

I tried to get Bill and Thom's attention. "You guys remember Welfare Check Saturdays?" They didn't respond, caught up in a debate over who was the better bass player—Geddy Lee of Rush or Mel Schacher of Grand Funk Railroad. Seeing my question fell on deaf ears, I drifted into my own quiet recollections.

On Welfare Check Saturdays, Dad started his day the same as most others. First, he dulled the edge of a hangover with Bromo-Seltzer. I remember him pouring two big capfuls into a glass of water like a mad scientist, the fizzy essence popping up out of the glass. He transferred it back and forth between two glasses until it dissolved, then knocked it back with one gulp before digging into his breakfast of powdered scrambled eggs and a margarine-soaked English muffin.

"All right, kids, let's go." He would call for the three youngest

—Tommy, Billy, and me. Many a time, we piled into the Falcon station wagon, ready for the routine.

First stop: Foley's Tavern on Dot Ave. to cash the welfare check. Ma would wait in the car, and sometimes Dad would let us go inside with him. I hung on every interaction among the bar patrons, quietly eavesdropping on adult conversations laced with profanity, nosy about what they were discussing, while Dad handed the signed welfare check to Jack, the bartender.

Jack counted out the bills to Dad's open, baseball mitt-sized hand, then Dad would slide a ten back to Jack. "Here's the sawbuck I owe you from last week's tab. Pour me a highball, will ya, Jack? I'll be right back."

Dad always pocketed a wad of cash for "gas and car repairs" but a large share of it funded his booze budget. By the early to mid-'70s, that meant six full bottles of wine per night and a few cases of beer for the week.

Back in the car, we dropped Ma off at Purity Supreme, where she did the grocery shopping and picked up Dad's booze at Supreme Liquors next door. Then it was back to Foley's for us. Ma's shopping kept her busy for a couple of hours, giving Dad plenty of time to tie a good buzz on.

Inside the smoky barroom, Dad bought us a round of potato chips and tonics, Boston-speak for soda in those days. We sat at the same wobbly table, sticky with beer spills and coffee-brandy Sombrero rings left by the crowd the night before. He handed us the bags of chips and our icy glasses of Coke, then slid a few quarters onto the table. "Here, kids. Enjoy your snacks. You can play the bowling game. Just keep it down."

We happily ate our snacks and played a few rounds on the worn-out Shuffle-Puck bowling game in the corner. The bar was lit by a few dim overhead bulbs and a sliver of sunlight sneaking through the heavy, red curtains. But we loved being there, part of the grown-up world. The guys at the bar didn't care about us being there. They were too busy drinking and talking ragtime toughness. The stories were usually the same: about fights, someone ripping someone off, or cars.

"I kicked Sully's ass," Lefty bragged to the guy beside him. "He tried charging my kid an extra C-note for the shitbox Corvair he bought off him."

"You didn't kick nobody's ass," Dad cut in from two stools down.

"Speaking of shitboxes," Vinny said, leaning back. "Dickie, you gotta adjust my clutch. It's slippin' in second gear on friggin' Pope's Hill."

"Wha'ja buy that piece of shit for? For fuck's sake," Dad snapped. "I kept tellin' ya, you dumb Polack—buy the Galaxie. The farthest the old lady drove was to church on Sundays."

"Here we go," someone muttered.

"But no," Dad went on, "You shot your mouth off to your old lady, and now you're driving a Valiant. Stupid Bastard... See what happens when you let a woman pick your car?"

"She didn't—"

"Aw, stop your belly-achin', I'll fix your shit-kicker clutch."

Two hours later, when it was time to pick up Ma, we'd step outside, squinting in the bright daylight. Our eyes, red and stinging from the cigarette and cigar smoke, didn't bother us. For a couple hours, it felt like Dad cared, like he was taking care of us—letting us have fun. It wasn't much, but it was something special to us.

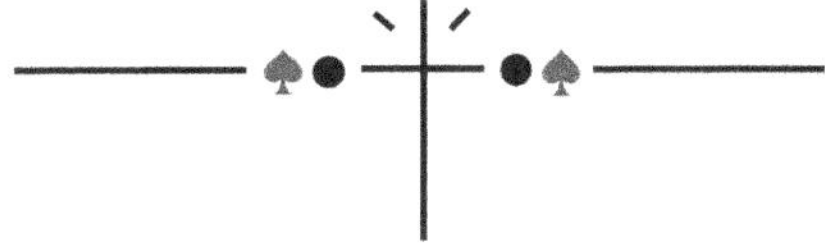

Marj passed around plates of cheesecake, Ma's dessert tradition once we could afford it after her divorce. Dan brought up our infamous family camping trip when Jimmy and I became the target of harassment on a school bus.

He painted a comic picture.

"When Jim was little, he had the dirtiest face... Dirt and snots smudged all over."

"Very true," Johnny added with a grin.

Over the years, hearing about Jimmy's dirty face always made me picture him as Pig-Pen from *Peanuts*.

"That's what started all the trouble on the bus ride home from that awful camping trip," Johnny said.

Dan told the camping story, with Johnny's bits along the way.

Every summer, Ma sent us kids to the free overnight camp run by the Salvation Army, which the boys jokingly called "Sally Camp." In the summer of '69, she changed it up and signed the whole family up for a Sally Camp weekend, along with Baxter, a neighbor kid.

The older boys looked forward to escaping the old man for the weekend to soak in the New Hampshire woods and fresh air—things Dorchester didn't offer. The excitement fizzled when Dad dropped Ma and the nine of us at Aunt Sally's Boston headquarters. Bobby, fifteen, frowned in disbelief, looking out at a sea of Black families waiting to board the bus.

"Ma, what are we doing here?" he whispered. "We're the only White family. We're gonna get killed!"

Johnny groaned, throwing out his favorite ten-dollar word. "Ma, this ain't copacetic."

Lately, around Fields Corner train station and on the Kane Square bus, the boys were running into tense encounters, getting hassled.

Ma, on the other hand, was comfortable going. She let out a heavy sigh, offering them the only two choices she could. "Well, we can go on this camping trip or go back home and be stuck with your father all weekend."

Groans of "No way!" and "Uh-uh!" arose. We all boarded the bus.

Halfway to New Hampshire, it started raining. By the time the bus pulled into the campground parking lot, it was pouring out and all the families had to walk a quarter mile in the drenching rain to reach the campsites. A family in a car stopped alongside us. A kind woman rolled down her window and asked Ma, "Do you want us to take the baby for you?"

Everyone was growing weary from taking turns carrying their chunky three-and-a-half-year-old sister through the mud.

"Oh, yes, that would be great." Ma handed me off like a sack of groceries.

In a tone reflecting concern and authority beyond her eight years, Margie whispered, "Ma, what are you doing? We don't know them."

"Oh, she'll be fine."

I cried for my mother and siblings as the dark strangers put me in their car. I'm told I was handed back to Ma unharmed when we arrived at camp.

The weekend was a soggy mess, and the boys and Baxter were picked on the whole time. They holed up in the wet tent, slipping out only for meals instead of joining the other families in the mess hall for games and activities.

By Sunday, everyone was grateful to leave the drenched campground behind. It was the first time all weekend that the boys felt relaxed. Then came the bus ride back to Boston.

A teenager pointed at Jimmy's filthy, snot-smeared face and jeered. "He's so dirty, he looks Black instead of White." The whole bus erupted, the laughter aimed squarely at Jimmy. Humiliated and scared, he sank into his seat, his eyes welling up with tears.

Seldom one to filter her thoughts, Ma defensively blurted out, "You're so Black, you can't tell if you're dirty."

Jeers and vocalizations grew. Murmurs echoed through the bus.

"Oooooh."

"Oh, sweat!"

"She just capped on you, man!"

Ma had stepped over the line. Bobby and Johnny tensed, worried they were going to have to fight.

I was on Ma's lap, with Danny and Margie on the end. A man in front of us turned, hocking a huge loogie onto my face to give Ma the message, she'd best be quiet. I have a vague memory of being startled by the force of the spit hitting me and I cried. Margie tried to soothe me, cooing, "It's okay, Mary. Don't cry," while Ma searched for a napkin to wipe my face.

A man sitting across from us intervened, sucking his teeth. "Hey, man, let it go. Look at 'em. They're just ignorant white trash."

Ma shut her mouth, and the rest of the ride to Boston was tense but uneventful. Back home in Dorchester, everyone trudged inside, damp and exhausted. Bobby, still brooding, muttered, "Being home with the old man would've been better than that hell-hole camping trip." For once in a blue moon, everyone agreed, it felt good to be home.

Chapter 19

Wonder How She Managed to Feed the Rest

"MAN, that was some good cheesecake! Almost as good as Ma Dyer's home cooking," Ted said, as we traded stories stretching back decades.

Growing up, that sentiment about Ma's cooking was shared by just about every neighborhood kid wherever we lived. Ma was always in the kitchen, wearing her well-worn apron and hair net, cooking delicious meals from supermarket dented cans and marked-down ready-to-expire meats. Whether it was an everyday supper, holiday meals, or homemade birthday cakes, her kitchen was everyone's favorite place.

I brought up the infamous welfare food with my siblings. "Remember Dad used to pull up in the station wagon, loaded with all those boxes of welly food? I was so embarrassed every time."

"Yeah," Jim snickered. "Ma called it 'surplus food.' I guess it didn't sound as bad that way."

Kids playing outside teased us whenever the "Dyer Mobile" pulled up, full of crates of government food. "Dyer-rhea, cha-cha-cha! Sounds kinda funny, but it's really wet and runny!" they chanted.

The free food we received included large blocks of orange "processed cheese food product." Another staple was large silver cans of fatty meat in gravy, stamped with the black letters, "USDA" and an emblem of a pig, cow, or chicken. Ma always served it over white rice or on slices of stale, toasted bread. We also received powdered eggs and powdered milk in plain white boxes. From the cheese, Ma made delicious grilled cheese sandwiches and baked macaroni and cheese which tasted divine. She could make powdered eggs and English muffins taste like a diner breakfast by adding cheese to the eggs, like an omelet. She knew how to cook something out of nothing.

Marj wrinkled her nose. "Bobby hated the powdered milk. He'd say, 'Ma, this isn't milk, it's water! Why do we have to drink this crap?' Ma would say, 'Don't like it? Lump it.'"

My young taste buds didn't know the difference, but I did recall it. "She mixed half powdered milk with half whole milk to stretch it out, right? That was pretty smart, actually."

Marj knew the dilemma. "Ma went through ten gallons of milk a week with us kids. We were lucky we got that."

Besides us ten, Ma generously fed neighborhood kids. Friends often ate over because they loved her cooking. Ma never said, "We don't have enough." She'd just put out another plate and stretch the meal with more ingredients. Friends didn't mind eating our "welly" food because it was far superior to the bland meals their mothers served. One night when Billy's friend Stewie ate over for spaghetti and meatballs, he said, "My mom's idea of Italian food is dumping a can of tomato soup over spaghetti. It's nothing like this."

Ma could make the cheapest cut roast from Rump 'n Round market taste like a five-star meal from the poshest European restaurants. Her chicken cacciatore was legendary. Stale, expired bread from the Sunbeam bread factory made great French toast and bread pudding. Sunday's boiled, smoked shoulder dinner carried us through the week. The ham bone became Monday's split pea soup, and by Tuesday, the boiled-dinner leftovers were pan-fried into a crunchy medley. Hate liver? Not the Dyer kids. We liked Ma's delicious calves' liver and caramelized onions. She cooked it tender, not tough like shoe leather. We devoured it with the powdered mashed potatoes and gravy she whipped up. On Sundays, her pancake syrup made from corn syrup and maple extract stretched far enough to feed all her hungry kids pancakes.

Ma was a traditional New England cook in every sense. Thom recalled our Saturday night suppers of hot dogs and beans. "We used to call Ma's homemade baked beans 'bullets.'"

"Yep. Tasty for sure, but big and hard," Dan laughed.

Every Friday during the winter, Ma soaked pinto beans in water overnight. On Saturday morning, she simmered them in the crock pot. The scent of molasses, fatty bacon scraps, onions, and brown sugar filled house all day until suppertime, warming the kitchen. She served the beans with broken, misshapen Maple Leaf hot dogs—rejects she bought for half price from a Dorchester meat plant. Warm, canned B&M brown bread rounded out the meal, making our Saturday night suppers a cherished weekly tradition. I'm glad I didn't have to share a bunk in the boys' bedroom!

When birthdays came around, sometimes two in a month, Ma outdid herself with beautifully decorated cakes made from scratch, whipping up colorful homemade frosting. Her first stop at the grocery store was always the day-old rack for dented cans. She bought bruised and overripe apples and turned them into a warm baked dessert for Sunday, filling the cored middles with brown sugar, cinnamon, and raisins. One cooking memory still returns to me every Christmas, reminding me of her resilience and cheer, while living with my father's insanity.

In the kitchen, her off-key Edith Bunker voice blended with Nat King Cole and Burl Ives as she made Christmas cookies in her flour-spattered apron. She lost herself in the cheerful music for a few hours while she baked. The good feelings carried over to me as I helped cut enormous gingerbread men with an antique aluminum cookie cutter and pressed M&M buttons into their chests. I remember thinking, *If she can sing and feel okay, then we'll all be okay*, and my mood was joyful as I anticipated the arrival of Christmas.

When there was money for it, Ma's Sicilian dinners were divine. Her meatballs and spicy Italian sausages simmered in homemade sauce all day in her army-size aluminum pot. As you entered the first-floor hallway in any of our triple-deckers, the aroma of tomato, meatballs, and garlicky fennel sausages intensified with each flight you ascended, so tantalizing, all our friends begged to eat over. I would ask Ma for a meatball sandwich to tide me over until supper. "Meat's too expensive," she'd say. As a consolation, she would make me a spaghetti sauce sandwich on fresh Scali bread from nearby Bombardieri's bakery.

Ma stretched every dollar until it screamed "Uncle." She made vats of ZaRex brand fruit punch and filled gallon milk jugs with cheap iced tea. She handed out ice-cold drinks in paper cups to neighborhood kids on sweltering summer days. There was always enough to go around. "Share and share alike," she always said. She made homemade orange juice popsicles and served us generic, store-brand ice cream in sugar cones topped with walnuts, jimmies, and chocolate syrup or a maraschino cherry on top.

When the ice cream truck approached our street, blaring its shrill, looping carnival tune, kids stood under their triple-decker windows, shouting up, "Maa-aaah! Throw me down a quattah! The ice cream man's coming! Hurry up!"

We ate our "welfare" cones alongside the other kids, while they licked their Bomb Pops and Fudgesicles. But Ma made ours with love, something we couldn't buy from the ice cream man.

Chapter 20

Here, There, and Everywhere with Ma

Growing up, we watched shows like *Good Times*, *Happy Days*, *The Waltons*, and *The Brady Bunch*, where parents told their kids they loved them. But in our house, Ma showed her love by making sure we were fed, clothed, schooled, and equally important, entertained. Dad showed it by teaching the boys how to fix cars, taking the family on fun outings, and giving us rides with our friends.

Despite the chaos at home, Ma made sure we had fun and got us out whenever she could, out of Dickie's line of fire. She found ways to give us nurturing experiences, exposing us to healthy and age-appropriate social situations. For brief periods, we were far removed from our father's insanity.

Ma took us every Monday to dollar movie night at the "Paaahk" (Park) Theatre in Fields Corner. She would pop a huge pot of popcorn, divvying it up for each of us into brown lunch bags along with chilled cans of tonic. We looked like we were packing for a picnic, not heading to the movies.

Once we settled in our seats, *Snap!* Our cans cracked open in unison, probably making the theater staff wish we'd at least sprung for a small popcorn. But Ma couldn't afford it. Sometimes, she threw in a stale box of Milk Duds or Junior Mints bought on clearance after Halloween or Easter. For us, it was a feast. If people around us thought we were obnoxious, we never noticed.

Fridays nights were for family swim at the John Marshall School pool, where me, Tommy and Billy learned to swim. There were no blow dryers back then, so walking home in the winter air, my long hair would freeze into haircicles under my hat. We practically ran home, eager for the delicious treat Ma would make once we got there—homemade English muffin pizzas piled high with cheddar cheese, peppers, onions, and on occasion when she could afford it, pepperoni. We washed them down with her homemade root beer, made from carbonated water and a Hires powdered root beer mix.

Summer was a season of small escapes, which felt like big adventures. "Free Friday Flicks" on the Charles River Hatch Shell was a highlight. Again, Ma would pack up homemade snacks and drinks. We rode the Red Line train to Cambridge, and spread out on blankets surrounded by pot-smoking hippies, watching classics like *The Wizard of Oz* or *King Kong*. Those nights felt carefree—a brief respite from our father, with Ma getting a few hours to relax and a taste of childhood freedom for the rest of us.

Even mundane errands became adventures with Ma. I remember her taking me on the bus to Elm Farm Market while everyone else was in school. Every time, she bought me a red box of Barnum's Animal Crackers with the white string handle. I carried it around like a purse, nibbling on the animals one body part at a time, feeling special and loved.

Long summer days at Savin Hill or Malibu Beach in Dorchester were another favorite. Ma didn't drive, so we took the train, spending hours splashing in the waves and eating Fluffernutter sandwiches on the beach.

Revere Beach was much farther away and took two train line switches. We'd swim all day, then hit Wonderland Amusement

Park at night for a couple games of Skee-Ball. My older siblings all had part-time jobs, so they generously paid for us younger kids and shared their winnings, making sure I left with a prize—a Magic 8 Ball, Slinky, or a stuffed animal. They were always so generous with me. They still are. Those outings gave us formative experiences, allowing us to be normal kids for a while.

Some trips took more time, but they were worth every minute. In the summer, Ma sometimes took us by train to Quincy Center, then we took a long bus ride to Nantasket Beach in Hull—nearly two hours each way. We would spend hours in the huge waves and picnic on the sand. If Ma managed to slip some of the welfare money past Dad, we'd go on rides at Paragon Park, our skin tan and salty from being on the beach for hours. The boys loved the roller coaster, while Ma, Margie, and I rode the teacups and saucers or the Kooky Castle ride. When I finally hit the height requirement at age ten, Jimmy took me on the roller coaster ten times—once for each year. I never wanted it to end.

Chapter 21

So, This Is Christmas

Thom grabbed his hoodie from my front hall and, coming back in, he pointed to the dried-up Christmas wreath on the door.

"You keeping that up 'til Easter, or what?"

"Oh. I forgot all about it." I lifted it off the nail, my mind recalling Christmases when we were kids. I glanced at Thom and Bill to pull them in with me.

"You guys remember Globe Santa toys every year?"

Bill looked up from a *Rolling Stone* Magazine and muttered, "Beastie Boys—White boys tryin'a be rappers. What poseurs…"

Thom seemed interested. "Yeah, we got some okay stuff from them, but a lot of it was misfit throwaway toys."

The *Boston Globe* newspaper, based in Dorchester, ran a charitable Christmas toy drive for low-income families. Every year, Ma applied for assistance, listing the ages and genders of her kids. Around mid-December, the familiar washing machine-sized box would arrive, crammed with toys for her to wrap. Most of the donations were quirky prototypes or leftover stock from unknown manufacturers. There were sewing cards, leather wallet kits, and unfinished wooden toys—similar to the ones the Burgermeister outlawed in the classic cartoon *Santa Claus Is Comin' to Town.* The toys weren't flashy, but I was grateful to have something new to open and play with.

I reached for my glass of Chardonnay, took a long sip, and interrupted Bill's reading again. "You probably don't remember, but I learned about Globe Santa from you."

"Me?" He pointed to himself and scratched his head, not remembering.

"Yeah, one year I got a set of weird, hard plastic Disney figurines. They were one solid neon color, like green or pink, with no eyes or other details. Remember?"

Recognition flickered across his face and he turned to Thom. "Oh, yeah. I used to whip 'em at you and Johnny for keeping me awake on Saturday mornings watching fake wrestling." He gave a short laugh.

Thom shook his head. "Whatever."

I circled back to Bill. "I remember I asked you why those plastic Disney toys from Santa didn't bend like my Barbies. And that's when you told me they were Globe Santa toys, remember?"

"Yeah... I said it was because they were donated welfare toys for poor kids. Something like that." Bill chuckled, proud of himself for telling it like it was, even as a kid.

Ma scrimped and saved every penny for groceries, heating oil, and keeping the lights on. Still, she always set aside a little cash from the monthly welfare checks to get us one special gift from the Sears & Roebuck Christmas Wish Book. My all-time favorite was my Howdy Doody doll when I was nine.

During the nation's energy crisis, Christmas of '74 was lean for families like ours on welfare. That year, Ma accepted used toys from our generous neighbor, Mrs. Dolan, and re-gifted them to me. One was her daughter's old GE "Show 'N Tell" record player, complete with a box of scratched-up story records. The tag read, "To Mary from Santa," but I knew right away where it was from, because I had played with it so many times. The cracked screen in the upper corner was a dead giveaway. The used "luxury" toy still thrilled me. I never questioned it, knowing Santa Ma was doing her best.

Dad's drinking always set the tone for Christmas spirit in the Dyer house. He started the holiday on a high note—highballs early and then a slow slide into chaos for everyone, especially Ma. Talking about Christmases past made me think of Ma's telling of when Tommy was born, right before Christmas—how Dad pulled a "Dickie Dyer" and didn't lift a finger to help her.

A few days before Christmas 1963, Ma gave birth to Thom. On Christmas Eve, Boston City Hospital discharged her with her newborn. At home she had six other kids, all under the age of ten; two were still in diapers. After nine births in ten years—including two babies lost, one stillborn, and another who died at six weeks from SIDS—she was spent. And rest wasn't an option with a drunk, unpredictable husband who refused to help her most of the time.

When Ma and Dad arrived home from the hospital on Christmas Eve, the younger kids were asleep. Bobby and Johnny were still up, but too young to be of much help. Ma introduced them to their new baby brother, Tommy, and then sent them to bed so she could feed him and decorate. Dad's strict but quaint rule was simple: the Christmas tree didn't go up until Christmas Eve, after all of us kids were asleep. When we awoke on Christmas morning, we believed Santa had put the tree up and delivered all the gifts. The scrawny, silver aluminum tree had a rotating color wheel under it, which cast a majestic kaleidoscope of radiant colors across the tree and the otherwise dingy, tired parlor.

"I'm so tired, Dick," Ma murmured while feeding Tommy. "I need to get some sleep. Can you please put the tree up?"

Dad, in his usual foul mood, slammed the aluminum tree into

the stand and plugged in the color wheel. "There, it's up. Now you decorate it."

He settled back on the couch, cracked open a beer, and made himself comfortable.

Exhausted but determined to give her children a proper Christmas, Ma decorated the tree by herself until midnight. While Dad watched Johnny Carson rib Buddy Hackett, she untangled and strung the heavy glass bulbs, strands of garland and tinsel, and hung the ornaments. When she finally finished, she could barely stand, yet she still wrapped the Christmas presents she hadn't gotten to before going into labor with Tommy. As Dad lay snoring, Ma collapsed into bed—only to be up around the clock with her hungry newborn.

On Christmas morning, functioning on barely two hours of sleep, Ma placed Tommy under the tree, presenting him as a gift to the younger kids who hadn't met him yet. Jimmy, almost four, was the first into the parlor. His eyes widened at the sight of the tiny baby swaddled in a blanket beneath the tree.

Ma brought him closer. "This is your new baby brother, Tommy." Years later, Jim said that as a little kid, he thought it was beautiful how Santa had brought him a baby brother.

Ma was worn out after Tommy's birth. The disconnect between her and Dad was so wide, they never even gave Thom a middle name, which used to make him feel left out as a kid. She didn't have the energy to deal with one more "minor" detail or any of the other many worries weighing on her. It said a lot about where she was mentally and emotionally—her life always teetered on the edge of unpredictability.

Chapter 22

Revolution

THE SUN DIPPED LOWER in the sky, and the chatter in my apartment wound down a bit. The streetlights outside flickered to life, casting a bluish glow over the wintry street. My siblings were launching into a debate over when the "baseball bat" incident happened—the time Jimmy snapped and nearly killed the old man. Everyone's voices spoke over each other as they debated the order of events.

Dan thought back. "...I don't know. I wasn't even there. I think I was in jail in Ohio then." That was the time he and his buddy stole a car in Boston, setting out on a grand cross-country escape from Dorchester to California. They didn't make it far before getting busted and locked up. "California or bust" didn't quite pan out.

Two culminating events, the baseball bat and the fire extinguisher incidents, had finally pushed Ma to file for divorce. As the years have passed, we've erroneously conflated the details and timelines like spliced film from two separate movies. But Jim, who took on Dad in one of them, was certain of the way the two events happened.

"No, they weren't the same incident!" Jim's voice cut through the room. "I'm the one who hit him with the bat. Don't you think I'd remember?"

Jimmy, the sibling we'd always thought of as the most nervous and least confrontational when we were kids, stood up to Dad in a way none of us had imagined possible. His breaking point came after Dad's fists landed on Ma one too many times.

ON A WINTER SUNDAY IN 1975, Dad was asleep on the couch—drunk, as usual. In the kitchen, Ma had dinner in the oven and was preparing to bake our favorite Sunday dessert: sweet cinnamon raisin rolls. She rolled out the pastry dough on a floured bath towel with her heavy wooden rolling pin and layered it with raisins, cinnamon, and sugar. Once rolled up, she sliced it up into pinwheel segments. We hung around Ma, drooling, watching her brush melted margarine all over the doughy goodness. The sound of Dad's stomping footsteps came down the long hallway, a sound which made us all freeze.

We exchanged nervous glances. *Oh no, what does he want now? Why can't he just stay asleep forever?* He stood in the doorway, arms crossed over his enormous beer gut, glaring at Ma. "Why the hell are you cooking dessert instead of supper?" he yelled, clueless about all she was pulling together simultaneously. One of Ma's many gifts Dad overlooked was her mastery of the kitchen. Watching her taught me how to juggle several side dishes and get everything to the table hot and on time.

Wiping her flour-coated hands on her apron, Ma adjusted her hair net, a cooking accessory Dad mandated. Visibly nervous, she explained that the pan of baked stuffed peppers was already half-done, and the rolls were about to be baked alongside them in the oven. Efficiency was her middle name, but as with everything, he couldn't, or wouldn't see it.

Spittle flew from his lips. "You can't even chew gum and walk," he sneered. Shows what he knew.

Dad grabbed the rolling pin—once a kitchen tool, now a weapon—and swung it at her again and again, like she was a piñata. We all scrambled out of the kitchen and into the long hallway. We watched as Dad shoved Ma against the refrigerator and kept striking her, ranting insults about her intelligence.

Ma cowered near the pantry, blood trickling from her nose. "Stop it, Dick! I am making supper! I told you, it's in the oven!"

Sixteen-year-old Jimmy was lingering near the kitchen doorway, his eyes darting nervously, as if contemplating what to do next. Tommy, Billy, Margie and I held our breaths in the hallway ten feet away, helpless to do anything. Then, something came over Jimmy. He shook his head, as if to say, *That's it, motherfucker, you're dead*, and fear hardened into resolve.

He bolted from the kitchen down the long hall, as if headed for the front door. The sudden motion caught Dad's attention and he staggered behind him, slurring, "Where the fuck you think you're going? Get back here." We all pressed ourselves into the boys' bedroom doorway, afraid we'd be next. Once Dad passed, Margie ran into the kitchen to tend to Ma, and we trailed him down the hall, keeping just far enough back to watch every move.

From the long hallway, we watched, frozen, as Jimmy stepped into the foyer. He moved with swift, unshakable purpose. His face tightened, eyes fixed on the baseball bat Dad kept propped behind the front door—the same one he attacked Johnny with a few years before. He seized it in one swift motion. Dad, drunk and stumbling in sock feet toward him, was still mid-rant, too wrapped up in his own psychosis to see what was coming. Jimmy followed him into the parlor, raised the bat high, and brought it down on the side of Dad's head three times. It was the only way to stop him, like dropping a charging rhino with a tranquilizer. I'll never forget his

300 pounds crashing down—The floor shook like a Big Dig dump truck hitting a crater on Mass Ave.

Still huddled together, we all looked on in horror. My mind screamed, *Holy crap! Jimmy's gone mad!* Of all the siblings, the last one you would expect—the nervous kid who'd stuttered through childhood on account of the old man—was the one who finally brought him down. *Go, Jimmy!*

Blood streamed from Dad's head, down his face and neck, staining his white undershirt before reaching parlor floor. He lay ranting, immobilized. While all this was going on, Margie was tending to Ma in the kitchen and had dialed 911. The waiting for help seemed to take forever. Police Station 11 wasn't far, so we were surprised it was taking so long. But the cops never came.

Jimmy, tired of waiting, ran three-quarters of a mile to Gibson Street with no jacket. When he arrived at Station 11, he was out of breath, covered in sweat, and so nervous he could barely speak. He stuttered his plea, "Y-You g-gotta go arrest my f-f-father, D-D-Dickie Dyer. He's beating up my mother again. I hit him. He's lying on the floor bleeding and my mother's bleeding. We need help." The police said they'd get there when they could. Jimmy ran back home in the bitter cold.

When Jimmy ran through the door, Dad was sitting on the couch, holding towels to his bloody head. The police never came. They didn't even do a drive-by. Maybe they were tired of being called to our house, fed up with dealing with Dad. By then, the neighborhood had seen a lot more crime, so maybe they were tied up elsewhere.

I can't recall much else about that awful day—either I blacked it out, or time has blurred the memory. He mostly left Jimmy alone after that, but his pattern of violence at home was far from over.

In my living room, retelling it to us, Jim said he always thought it was strange how Dad never even drove himself to the hospital for his head injuries. We all surmised it was because he knew he would have to explain how it happened, putting himself on notice as a domestic offender once again, and possibly going to jail.

Chapter 23

The End

By DAY's end of Dad's funeral luncheon, Jim shared a final thought about the baseball bat incident.

"Even though I'm not a religious person, I think some type of 'divine intervention'"—he made air quotes—"stopped me from hitting the old man a fourth time. I don't know why I didn't keep going. It was like an out-of-body experience."

"You mean about stopping?" I asked.

"Yeah. Something stopped me dead in my tracks, that's for damn sure, because I had no intention of stopping. Somehow the bat was out of my hand. It was just gone, as if someone took it from me—but no one remembers taking it."

I agreed with Jim. Whatever you wanted to call it, spiritual intervention or inner wisdom, something interrupted his fury so he wouldn't have to go to jail for murder. In that moment, protecting Ma and the rest of us from further attack mattered most, even if it meant killing him. That split second—when he didn't swing again —changed everything. It later allowed Jim to live a full, productive life as a beloved mail carrier on the same Comm. Ave. route for thirty years, not rotting in a jail cell. It had taken sixteen years of rage and all of his courage to stand up to our father.

When Jim finished, I was still unsure what event finally led our parents' divorce.

"So... the baseball bat—was that the last straw?"

"No!" Jim huffed. "The baseball bat was first. I said that already. It was after the fire extinguisher when we threw him out in the snow and Ma divorced him, not the other way around."

"Oh..." It came back to me in fragments, blurred by time. I shuddered, remembering mostly the fear and how everything escalated without warning.

As my siblings talked over one another, filling in details, the fire extinguisher incident came back clearer to me. Recounting parts of the story together, I could see it again, the chaos of the near-tragic winter afternoon.

AFTER THE NEW year in 1976, with me turning ten in two weeks, Christmas school vacation ended. The holiday had been peaceful so far. My father hadn't injured anyone—yet.

Jimmy was setting the kitchen table while Ma cooked a boiled ham and vegetable dinner in her five-gallon army pot.

My father usually operated in two modes: violent or asleep. We preferred asleep. On this winter afternoon, he was passed out drunk in the parlor. Johnny was mostly in the boys' back bedroom while Danny, exhausted from his 3:00 a.m. newspaper run for the *Dorchester News*, slept. I vaguely remember Johnny peeking into the kitchen once, hungry for supper.

I was elated because the week before, Santa Ma had brought me what I'd wanted most—a tall Howdy Doody puppet.

I remember Margie and me in the bedroom we shared, the two of us squeezed onto a twin bed with Billy and Tommy on the other, listening to some of Margie's records. Her *Carpenters Greatest Hits* album played in the background while we all quietly joked and talked, unaware of how everything was about to change. I was practicing my ventriloquism skills with Howdy.

Showing off, I turned the puppet toward Tommy and Billy. "Look! Watch how good I can make Howdy talk!"

I sat Howdy on my knee and pulled the string on his neck, making his plastic lips tap up and down, while I kept mine still.

In a pinched Howdy voice, I said, "Mary knows how to make me talk the best."

I made him nod for emphasis and had him add, "Karen Carpenter is my favorite singer."

We had so much fun taking turns with my puppet, especially when Billy took charge. He grabbed Howdy from me. "Lemme have a turn." He pitched his voice high and made Howdy say naughty stuff like, "Hey, who farted? Pee-yew! Oh, it was me. I crapped my pants!"

Billy was always a jokester when it was just us kids around each other. But if the old man was nearby, he immediately tensed up and the clowning would halt.

At one point, while we were passing Howdy around, we stopped, our noses wrinkling at the sharp smell of something burning. At first, we looked toward the kitchen, thinking perhaps Ma had burned something. Then came a crackle from the wall right beside us.

Tommy leaned forward, careful not to wake the old man. His whisper came out tight and panicked. "Whoa—sparks!"

Before the words even settled, the space heater cord spit more sparks from the wall socket. Small flames ignited along the edge of the wall. We bolted off the bed, eyes wide in panic, whisper-screaming, "We gotta get Ma!"

The run to the kitchen was a blur—arms flailing, feet tripping

—yet still no one dared make enough noise to wake the drunk, sleeping bear in the parlor. There were no smoke alarms back then to rattle him from his stupor.

Tommy grabbed Ma's arm and blurted, "Ma, the bed's on fire!"

Her eyes darted to the hallway in disbelief. "What?" They widened when she saw the glow of orange flames coming from the bedroom.

"Jimmy, help me!" she whispered urgently. They rushed toward the bedroom while the rest of us stumbled behind, tripping over each other in our panic.

In no time, Ma was back in the kitchen. "Margie, turn off the oven burners!" she snapped, her voice cutting through the chaos as we stared, frozen. Though she was accustomed to managing crises, she was clearly not prepared for this. She did her best to take charge. Fumbling, she grabbed the giant aluminum fire extinguisher out of the pantry—one of Dad's "free acquisitions" from either a hospital or a school, filled with water.

She ran into the bedroom with the fire extinguisher, but Jimmy pulled her arm to stop her.

"M-Ma, there's no f-foam in the fire extinguisher. You can't put an electrical f-fire out with w-water," he stammered, his hands shaking. He dragged the bed away from the wall and yanked the heater's electrical cord out of the melting wall socket.

Panic flickered across Ma's face as she hurled the useless extinguisher aside. She and Jimmy grabbed whatever was within reach —blankets, bathrobes, pillows. They moved fast, beating and smothering the flames as they crept across the bed, heat rising, smoke thickening. Margie jumped in with dirty bath towels, helping to suffocate the flames. In a matter of minutes, the fire was finally snuffed out under a heap of scorched linens. Ma grabbed the fire extinguisher and doused the smoldering bedspread with the water.

Peering through my siblings' bodies from the doorway, I saw

one of Howdy's red plaid arms sticking out from under a scorched blanket. I covered my mouth, silently crying his name. *Howdy!* Tears streamed down my face as I sobbed for my burning puppet and the entire situation. The soaked bed was smoking.

"I think it's all out." Ma sighed in exhausted relief.

She opened the bedroom windows to air out the room and she shut the door. We all followed her to the kitchen—Margie, Jimmy, and now Johnny leading. Johnny hoisted the massive fire extinguisher onto the kitchen table. Lingering smoke could be seen floating in the hallway off our bedroom.

Shock filled the room as we exchanged uneasy glances, looking at Ma for what might come next. A moment later, the floor began to shake underfoot. We knew what was coming. Dad was storming in, his heavy footsteps like the approach of a ravenous bear awakened from a deep winter sleep. He entered the kitchen without his glasses, squinting, disoriented, drunk, and groggy. He narrowed his eyes at Ma, sniffing the smoky air.

"What the hell's burning in here?"

Ma stammered. "Th-there was a small fire in the girls' bedroom. I put—"

Dad cut her off and headed to the hallway toward our bedroom. He threw open the bedroom door.

"What the fuck?" He charged back into the kitchen, eyes locked on Ma with rage, fists clenched.

Ma shrank back, her eyes wide with fear. She instinctively raised her hands to her face to block the blow she knew was coming.

"The space heater caught fire. I put it out, Dick! It's out!" Ma cried out, her voice shaking as she tried to head off the explosion of anger.

He shoved her against the fridge. "Get outta the way, you don't know what the fuck you're doing!"

Paralyzed by fear, we all retreated into the hallway again,

knowing one of us could be next. Dad picked up the fire extinguisher. But instead of heading to the bedroom with it, he swung it at Ma's head like a baseball bat. Her forehead split above her left eye and blood streamed down her face.

My mother endured many black eyes and bloody noses at my father's hands. I'd seen or heard him corner and strike her more times than I could remember, much of it a blur. But at almost ten, I'd never seen her bleed that much, and it made it all the more real.

Ma stretched out her arms, grasping at the air in front of her. "Someone help me! Get me a towel! I need a towel!"

Jimmy scanned the kitchen for the closest thing within reach and grabbed for the paper towels over the kitchen sink. He yanked the roll so hard the metal holder twisted on its bracket. He gathered a thick wad and, with shaking hands, pressed it to Ma's forehead to stem the bleeding, his eyes staying on Dad in case he made another move.

Ma sobbed in pain. "I need to get to the hospital. Dick, get me to the hospital," she begged.

Dad saw Jimmy helping Ma and lunged at him, pushing him aside. He refused to help her.

"I'm not taking you to no hospital. Go put a bandage on your head, for cripes' sake. You'll be fine."

Seventeen-year-old Danny was the only other family member with a car, but he was sound asleep.

"Danny! Danny!" Ma screamed from the kitchen. Her voice was raw with panic as she bled. "Someone wake up Danny!"

Johnny ran from the kitchen to get him, but Danny was already on his way when Ma screamed again.

"Danny!"

Danny entered the kitchen groggy, unaware of what was going on. Dad swayed, eyes fixed Danny, as if weighing whether he'd have to take him on next.

Ma crouched between the refrigerator and the pantry door to

shield herself from another attack. "Danny, get me to a hospital! I'm bleeding!"

Danny's eyes narrowed on Ma in the corner, clutching her bleeding head.

"What the hell!" he yelled. He jolted fully awake, the sleep gone from his eyes. Marj was already making her way to the wall phone when Johnny shouted, "Margie, call 911! Get an ambulance—now!"

Her fingers shook as she grabbed the receiver, but she managed to spin the rotary dial and call for help. I ran to Margie for protection, crying hysterically. She pulled me close. "It's okay, help is coming for Ma."

Dad started to close in on Ma again and Johnny stepped in to block him. Danny, shirtless and barefoot in the kitchen, started punching Dad in the head and the other boys ganged up on him like hyenas on an antelope. They knocked him to the kitchen floor. It shook under his fall as they kicked and punched him.

Danny yelled for the boys to back off and let him get up. Dad wobbled up to his feet. Once upright, Danny and Johnny pushed him out of the kitchen and down the long hallway, yelling, "Get the fuck out!"

Dad tried to force his way back to the kitchen, but the boys overpowered him and shoved him back down the hall. In the distance, sirens were approaching our house.

The boys pushed Dad into the foyer and out into the cold in nothing but his sock feet, pants and a white undershirt. Danny locked the deadbolt behind him and peeled back the curtain on the front door window to watch for the cops.

Dad pounded on the heavy wooden front door. Out on the porch, he pleaded, "Let me in! I surrender!" He held up two fingers in a shaky V sign, his voice growing fainter with each shout. "Peace! Peace!"

But Danny, furious, stood his ground, yelling through the glass, "You're going to jail, muthafuckah!"

Half a minute later, our house was bathed in the pulsating blue and red lights of ambulances, fire trucks, and police cars. The fire department inspected the bedroom and gave the all-clear, confirming the small fire was out. EMTs escorted Ma out to an ambulance with Johnny. Dad was handcuffed and taken out by the police. Another officer stayed to talk with Jimmy. He tried without stuttering to explain to the police what had happened. They didn't require lengthy statements. They were familiar with Dad's chronic history of domestic abuse. He was thrown in the back of a paddy wagon and promptly chauffeured to his home away from home—the Charles Street Jail. The EMTs took Ma, with Johnny riding along, to City Hospital, where she was treated for her forehead laceration.

Up until then, my father's brutality had been a chaotic blur I couldn't fully grasp or had failed to remember. When things turned loud and violent, Margie would crank up her record player and sleep with her big headphones on to drown it out, sometimes giving them to me. Oftentimes, I slept through the late-night beatings. I remember blocking out the noise, but I had never seen anything so violent up close before. Or if I had, time had erased the details.

For the older kids, this was very familiar, like a scene they'd already lived through many times. I'd always been too young to understand the depth of my father's mental illness. But now, I saw it clearly as our family's nightmare unfolded in the kitchen.

Overwhelmed, I sobbed while Margie held me. As I watched the ambulance pull away with Ma inside, I understood the full scope of how crazy my father was and the brutality he inflicted on Ma for so many years.

Once the house had quieted and we knew Ma was safe at the hospital with Johnny, my siblings and I stuck close together. The older kids cleaned up broken glass and smears of blood on the kitchen floor, while me, Tommy, and Billy lingered anxiously.

Margie did her best to assure us younger kids. "It's all right now. He's gone. Ma's gonna be okay."

Danny spoke with authority. "Mark my words, he's never stepping foot back in here again."

I listened to my siblings talk about next steps to ensure Ma would finally get rid of our father for good. I held Howdy close to me. His flimsy nylon belt and cheap plastic boots had melted in the fire, and his clothes were scorched. He reeked of acrid smoke and his neck bandana was gone. Even Howdy bore the scars of the hell he'd been brought into. But I was most upset about Ma.

I hadn't remembered my father's earlier incarcerations until this event. I vaguely remembered being sent to Grandma Dyer's for a weekend in preschool, without explanation. I later learned the reason: Dad had beaten Ma, landing her in the hospital, and he was in jail.

Now I understood fully—and I was in favor of him being locked up.

Jimmy mopped the kitchen floor, stuttering, "He's g-gotta go. We gotta m-m-make Ma get rid of him."

Margie swept up the last shards of broken glass and debris. Helping Danny get the kitchen furniture back in place, she sighed in relief. "Yeah, if it weren't for you boys, she'd be dead. She needs to divorce him A-S-A-P."

Danny added, "He's done. We'll figure out a way to help Ma pay the bills."

"I don't want him coming back ever," I sobbed, wanting to feel I was a part of the unanimous decision-making.

Later in the evening, Ma came home from the hospital with white bandages wrapped around her head. The only part of her I recognized was her right eye and the crown of her head. Her eyebrow and the left side of her head were shaved bald. The bandage covered a jagged, six-inch-long, stitched wound.

When I looked at her, overwhelming sadness came over me. My eyes welled up when I saw the severity of her injuries. It felt like I was looking at a beaten, broken, half-dead person I barely knew. Fear and insecurity overcame me as I thought I might lose my mother. I worried about our future. *Where do we go from here? Who's going to help us with whatever comes next? What if he comes back?* I followed her around for the rest of the evening, afraid to let her out of my sight. I feared she might die in her sleep if I wasn't right there next to her, keeping an eye on her.

Ma murmured, "I gotta go lie down. My head is pounding."

Downplaying my concern for her, I asked, "Ma, can I sleep with you tonight? I have no bed to sleep in."

"Sure, Mary. Just don't steal my covers or come too close to my head."

For the following week, Ma let me sleep with her. I even wore one of her nightgowns to bed every night so I could smell her scent as I slept beside her.

The day after the fire, the older kids gathered around Ma. Margie started the conversation. "Ma, you need to divorce him. He can't come back here, ever again. You don't need him for anything. We can help pay the bills. We're all working now."

Danny chimed in. "Yeah, Dorchester News said I can take more hours bundling papers. Like Margie said, he's not coming back. You don't need him."

Jimmy offered to take extra hours at the Swiss House, the bowling alley restaurant where he washed dishes after school.

"You need to file for divorce before he gets outta jail, or he'll try coming back," Johnny said. "Restraining orders won't stop him. He's a maniac."

Margie said she would pick up more weekend hours at Bradlees, the department store where she worked part time. "The court will help you file for the divorce. He can never step foot in here again. We'll help you take care of it all."

Ma sighed in exasperation. It would take tremendous courage, but she must have seen the truth in her older children's words. With an exhausted sigh, she surrendered. "Okay—if you kids help me."

And so they did.

Ma obtained legal representation through Dorchester District Court, which initiated divorce proceedings on her behalf. After twenty-four torturous years with Dickie Dyer, there was finally light at the end of the long, dark tunnel of abuse that had held all of us prisoners for so long—especially Ma.

A few days after the fire, when she could function better, Ma hand-washed Howdy's clothes and sewed his ripped trousers.

With a weak smile, Ma handed me Howdy. "Here, Mary, he's good as new. I put one of my hankies around his neck so he has a little bandana again."

Relief washed over me. Seeing her well enough to fix Howdy meant she was on the mend. I was grateful for my mother and relieved to know she'd be okay, with Dad locked up, and my older siblings now taking charge.

JIM CLOSED OUT THE STORY. "In court, I had to testify about what happened that day and in general, what was happening at home. I was so riddled with anxiety, I couldn't even state my name for the record. The old man, of all people, was in the courtroom trying to calm me down. 'Take it easy, Jimmy,' he kept saying. 'Take it easy.'

I found it odd, he was trying to be nice to me, since I was there to testify against him.”

He added, “I have a good memory for small details. I remember one of Margie’s album covers got ruined in the fire... It was completely soaked. It was George Harrison’s *Extra Texture*.”

“Oh wow, I don’t remember that at all,” I said. “Just the Carpenters album which was playing when the fire started. I guess the wet record got some extra texture that day, huh?”

Jim caught my attempt to end on a light note. “Yeah, no kidding. Margie and Johnny’s Beatles albums were always around. I never forgot it.”

It was after six o’clock when my siblings began gathering their things and we said our goodbyes. The day had been full of stories and shared memories, and it was good to be together after all we’d been through with our father. I wished Bobby had been there. As the oldest, he never talked much about what he’d endured growing up. I could only imagine it all through my siblings’ stories.

After everyone left, I was alone in my apartment. I tackled the leftover food containers and stray dishes. *Abbey Road* still played softly in the living room. “Golden Slumbers” came on, and I found myself doing what has grounded me for as long as I can remember —singing. As I scrubbed the soapy wine glasses, I sang along, thinking of my father in his own golden slumber, or at least hoping it was golden.

It was a day of finality, but also one of connection—a day when we came together, bound by the complicated legacy of the man who affected us, for better or worse, and by the triumphs we’d fought to claim for ourselves and for Ma.

At the office the next day, coworkers offered their condolences for my father’s death. Some insisted I should have taken more time off. It’s what most people do when a parent dies. But they didn’t know how estranged we were. Work was the distraction and focus I needed to slide back into my daily routine.

On the subway ride home to Quincy Center, my mind turned to the evening ahead. I felt relieved at the thought of playing some blues with Rob, my longtime drummer friend, and the rest of the band. With a gig coming up in a couple of weeks, band rehearsal was a welcome distraction. And after all the heavy Dad stories shared at my apartment, I needed to *get back* to my routine—back to where I once belonged.

Chapter 24

I'll Try Not to Sing Out of Key

Music has always been a big part of my family's life, woven into many of my earliest experiences. Years ago, when I ordered my birth record from Boston City Hospital, I noticed a nurse's note on my chart: "Baby has VERY healthy lungs!" It made me laugh, but it also made me wonder how much distress I might have been in, crying so much in the nursery. Either way, the comment has always felt fitting, given how much I've always loved to sing with full-breathed gusto.

With seven older siblings obsessed with rock and roll, early R&B, and Motown, I grew up on music recorded well before my time and developed a deep appreciation for so many styles. The older boys wore out records by Smokey Robinson, Stevie Wonder, the Beatles, the Rolling Stones, Jeff Beck, Led Zeppelin, just to name a few. Their 45s, LPs, and 8-track players ran a constant stream of hits. They wore out songs like "In the Summertime" by Mungo Jerry, "Get Ready" by Rare Earth, "Hocus Pocus" by Focus, "Na Na Hey Hey Kiss Him Goodbye" by Steam, and "Spill the Wine" by War, along with hundreds more. They spent every dime from their paper routes on records.

On the rare occasion when Dad's spirits were good, my parents danced in the parlor to his country and "Rat Pack" records —old 78s, especially Dean Martin's "Everybody Loves Somebody." Dad loved Dean's persona of drunkenness and flirtation— two of his favorite pastimes. He loved Louis Armstrong's "That Lucky Old Sun." A gem of a song—though as a kid I thought it sounded so old-fogey. A few times, he tried to teach me how to waltz, having me put my size-four feet on top of his while he led. But the smells of booze on his breath, sweat, and stale Hai Karate aftershave frightened me. I would recoil, thinking, *This doesn't feel normal.*

In those rare moments, Dad also liked to tinker with various musical instruments. His attempts at the bugle and harmonica were more comical than skillful, but I was struck by how music, accompanied by his booze, seemed to temper his volatile moods, offering him a few hours of peace.

In our shared bedrooms, at the beach, or just hanging out on our front stoop, our siblings always had an AM transistor radio tuned to WRKO, a local top 40 station. Once Margie had a part-time job, her record player was regularly stacked with at least five hit 45s, or three to five LPs playing back-to-back in our bedroom, many of them Beatles records. Music-themed TV shows like *The Monkees, The Partridge Family, Tony Orlando and Dawn*, and *Soul Train*, along with cartoons like *The Jackson 5, The Archies, The Banana Splits*, and *Josie and the Pussycats* kept us glued to the 19-inch black-and-white TV in the parlor. On Friday nights, I stayed up way past my bedtime to watch *The Midnight Special* with the older kids. Music was everywhere, surrounding us like a constant companion, softening the edges of a tense home life. When I was a teen, Ma shared a cute story I never forgot: "When you were a baby, you wouldn't go to sleep unless we played 'Pretty Woman' by Roy Orbison. The kids would have to play that song over and over until you fell asleep."

Looking back, my taste in music as a baby had already gained rock and roll credibility, thanks to my siblings. When I was nine, Margie told me the Fields Corner branch library had rock albums to lend. Instead of checking out books, I left with albums by Ringo, John Lennon, and other Beatles records, along with Bob Dylan and Simon and Garfunkel—anything I could get my grubby little hands on.

When my parents divorced, life at home became much more relaxed, and my family socialized more. Disco music was on fire, and on weekends, Margie and her girlfriends danced underage with fake IDs at discotheques like Boston-Boston. She taught my friend Joan and me all the dance moves she'd learned the night before, like the Hustle and the Bump. Joan and I were Dancing Queens at the Illusions teen discotheque and Spinoff, a roller disco rink. Our after-school dance practice paid off when we won a few dance contests at the Sunday afternoon teen disco dances at Dorchester's Kane Post. Joan and I obsessed on disco hits played on Boston's new Kiss 108 station, even stealing its advertisement signs off the Red Line trains.

I knew early on music was more than background for my life—it was calling to me. The catalyst was an unforgettable experience on October 30, 1978, when Margie took me to see Donna Summer in concert. I was already obsessed with her music and persona, and from the nose-bleed seats at the back of the Music Hall, I was starstruck and mesmerized. Donna was a Bostonian, so I felt a special kinship with her. After the concert, I started writing poetry and lyrics, thinking, *when I grow up I'll be a singer*, never imagining in my twenties I'd bring those words to the stage with Dan in our original rock band, Ns & Vs.

At home, I pretended to sing into a blue Soap-on-a-Rope microphone. Though it smelled repugnant, I treasured it. Every day after school, I finished my homework and put on Margie's Donna Summer records, trying to emulate her singing but probably sounding more like Peter Brady croaking, "when it's time to change."

At bedtime, Margie and I drifted off to her albums like *Jesus Christ Superstar*, solo Beatles' albums, the Beach Boys, Cat Stevens, Herb Alpert & Tijuana Brass, Heart, the Supremes, Peter Frampton, Carole King, and countless others. Those records, along with the ones Johnny and the older boys played by J. Geils Band, Blue Öyster Cult, Steve Miller Band, James Gang, Edgar Winter Group, and countless others, influenced my musical tastes. Dan and Bill's Who albums along with Jim's KISS and Aerosmith records filtered down to me. Tommy and I wore out Johnny and Dan's Queen albums. The songs I sang along with awakened my ears to a rich kind of self-expression, something we hadn't been allowed when our father was around. Music became our outlet—our creativity, our escape, our joy, and most of all, our bonding.

Although I was hooked on disco with Joan, Jimmy had other plans for my musical aspirations. Determined to steer me toward more complex, harder rock, he devised a plan, transforming my music taste from "Disco Duck" to "Disco Sucks" overnight.

When Margie lived away at Job Corps vocational school, I got our bedroom to myself. Jimmy, wearing his "Disco Eats Dogshit" T-shirt, secretly spliced his speaker wires into my stereo, hijacking it so his music played through my speakers. I couldn't escape it. Every night, I fell asleep to Frank Zappa, Genesis, and other eclectic bands. He flooded the rock station WBCN into my room, pulling me into Boston's local rock music scene and a wider world of international rock, punk, and new wave. When he wasn't blasting music, he played his raunchy George Carlin, Smothers Brothers, or Cheech and Chong albums, providing the comedic relief we all grew up appreciating.

When I was fourteen and Jimmy was twenty, he snuck me into The Rathskeller (The Rat), a gritty Boston nightclub, by lying about my age. He told Mitch, the doorman and a familiar face on the club scene, that I was eighteen. There, I saw my first live local band, a new wave group fronted by a girl singer with eyes rimmed in black eyeliner, a tight miniskirt, and ripped fishnets. She owned the stage, spitting out lyrics with a fury that felt relatable to me. The power she carried, the band, the crowd—the raw energy of it all—hooked me. I promptly traded in my dancing shoes, leaving disco far behind.

Around the same time, twenty-two-year-old Dan, with a bass guitar strapped over his shoulder, started pulling me into his rock and roll world as it took form. He let me tag along to his band rehearsals in a smoky, beer-soaked triple-decker in Dorchester, inhabited by a rowdy biker gang. Sometimes he let me sing a few songs with his bandmates. That's where my real singing took root. When Billy—also a bassist by then—formed a band, he let me join his practices too. With both brothers, I absorbed the collaboration, self-taught creativity, and the rock and roll camaraderie of their bands. Their rehearsals felt like sacred family gatherings to me. Dan and Billy taught me my first guitar chords on an old Sears guitar.

As my interest in singing grew, I started listening more closely to lead vocalists, mimicking a broad range of styles from my siblings' record collections and from the radio. I listened for harmony and phrasing, practicing vocal dynamics and control. Their records became my vocal teachers.

Our siblings who didn't play music were always part of the band fun. Whenever Dan, Bill or I had a band, they came to our rehearsals, and they all showed up at our gigs, cheering us on. We were a family who rose from the ashes of adversity, bound together by music.

In the days after my father's passing, my mind drifted back to the "hillbilly" country music he played. Drunk in the parlor most nights, Dad soothed himself with records—crooners singing about teardrops in beer and honky-tonk angels stealing husbands. At seven, I took Kitty Wells' "Only Me and My Hairdresser Know" literally, thinking women went to the beauty parlor to hide their sadness. He wore out records by Ray Charles, Johnny Cash, and Patsy Cline, along with the songs, "From a Jack to a King" by Ned Miller and "A Hole in the Ground" by Johnny Rivers.

As a kid, those old-timey records repelled me. Years later, playing in bands that weren't even country, I heard some of my bandmates leaning into that rootsy American style a bit and began to hear it differently. Their high, lonesome harmonies stirred something familiar—melancholy, disappointment, heartache, loss, and, at times, the sweetness of love.

Revisiting those songs now, I recognize some of the emotions my father might have felt when he played those records. I've come to understand him in small ways I never could as a child and, in a way, found an unexpected connection.

Chapter 25

All Those Years Ago

After Dad's funeral, Marj and I set out to find his long-lost big brother, our Uncle Bob. It felt like a mission of mercy to find him, and for me, a small way to connect with my late father and grandparents.

Marj reached a relative and confirmed Uncle Bob was living in a group home outside Boston. Fingers crossed, I called the facility and was relieved to learn he was still a resident. The house manager was thrilled to get the call. "Oh, I'm so happy to hear from Bob's family again. He hasn't had a visitor in quite a while. He'll be so happy to see you."

The following week, when Marj and I arrived for our visit, the years seemed to melt away from the moment we saw Uncle Bob. He smiled big, as if he'd unearthed a forgotten treasure. His physical resemblance to Dad struck me at once. He had the same brown eyes and prominent nose. Uncle Bob, now seventy-four, still had the same deliberate mannerisms and monotone voice I remembered, his deep voice landing in the slow, staccato rhythm I hadn't heard since I was about eight or nine. His toothless smile spread wide across his face, childlike and full of warmth.

Pointing to us, he said, "Yuh's Dickie's kids. I me-membah you when you w-was a b-b-baby. I-I changed your dia-puhs..." He smiled big in his made-up recollection. We went along with him, letting him take on the make-believe role of the wise elder. "That's right, Uncle Bob. You did change our diapers a long time ago."

"I g-got a guitar. I'll play it for yuh when I come to visit."

Marj and I exchanged a quiet nod. Another "musician" had joined the family.

We took Uncle Bob to his favorite diner for lunch. Sitting in a vintage booth with red vinyl seats, we reminisced with him over a burger, "Fwench fwies," and a Coke.

Marj started the conversation. "So, who do you remember from the old days, Uncle Bob?"

His face lit up. He pointed at us and repeated, "I memembah you."

We asked him if he remembered our mother, Doris.

"Y-y-yuhh!," he replied confidently. "She cooked suppah for me. She's my friend too. I g-gotta lotta friends."

"You sure do," we replied warmly. It was like no time had passed for him.

Marj asked the burning question. "Do you remember your brother Dickie?"

He thought for a second. "Y-yuh. He rode me on the back of his m-m-m-motorcycle."

Marj's face lit up with a big smile, remembering those times too, when Dad was good to his big brother. I vaguely remembered it. "That's right!" Marj said. "He used to take you for rides when you visited us for Sunday dinner."

Uncle Bob grew serious. "Dickie bwoke my m-muthah's parlor w-w-window."

We didn't know which memory he was recalling, but it was clear Dad's violent side had left an impression on him.

"Oh, he did, huh? That must've been scary," Marj said.

"Y-yuh. When I was a cop, I hit him with my billy club," Uncle Bob declared, swinging his hand with vigor, making us giggle.

I raised my eyebrows in mock approval. "Yup, you put him right in his place, didn't you?"

When we told him Dad had passed, he nodded as if he had some prior awareness, though of course, he didn't. He gestured towards his chest. "Y-yuh, it was his tick-ah."

"You're right, it was his heart. You're a pretty smart guy, Uncle Bob." We played along, exchanging a glance acknowledging the truth between us.

Uncle Bob grew serious and authoritative. "He's in the ground. If he g-g-gets outta that grave, I'll shoot him dead with my g-gun!" he exclaimed, sending us into fits of laughter.

After lunch, we dropped Uncle Bob back at his home, hugging him and promising to stay in touch. "I-I'll be coming to v-v-visit on Crissum. I'll dress up like Santa Claus for da kids."

"Oh, you'll be visiting us way before then," we assured him. "Easter and your birthday is coming next. But we'll see you way before then. We'll have you over with the family and all the kids."

Uncle Bob waved goodbye, his smile wide.

On the ride home, Marj and I basked in gratitude for seeing our long-lost uncle. "He looks so good," Marj said. "And he was so happy to see us. I can't wait to tell Dale about him. He's going to love him."

"Yeah, and he looks just like Dad. Or I should say, Dad looked like him."

Most of all, we were happy Bob knew he still had our family. "If Dad hadn't died," Marj said, "we probably wouldn't have thought of Uncle Bob for years. We definitely have to take him for an overnight stay and have a cookout with the family."

One door had closed, but another had opened, bringing family back into focus. For me, it felt like making up for lost time, bringing my father's big brother back into our lives. From then on, we included Uncle Bob in all our family gatherings. Marj and I took turns hosting him for overnight stays.

Some are Dead and Some are Living

Dickie (right) in the Army in Japan, 1947, sporting a racy new tattoo, age 18

Tommy & Ma 1973

Ma as a new mother at 19 with Bobby on Dorchester Ave., 1954

Dad working at a Dorchester gas station, late 1960s

*Me, Billy and Tommy, 1974. Boston Harbor family
boating day. Fonzie thumbs were cool*

*"Welly" meat in the can served over toast was a regular staple
in Ma's kitchen (drawing by author)*

*Practicing my Donna Summer chops with a Soap on a Rope
microphone, age 13. Behind me: Donna Summer concert
reviews from the show Marj and I attended.*

*Grover Pals in 1979: Joan, Me, Cheryl, Kristin (front). I'm
wearing a Beatles "Apple" T-shirt.*

Jim with Frank Zappa poster I gave him for his 20th birthday

Dan Danger, age 19

Me and Bill jamming, 1980, ages 14 & 18. I'm wearing Johnny's Boulder (jail) sweatshirt

Thanksgiving 1980 at biker house party. Back: John, Bill Front: Jim, Marj, Thom, Me, Dan

Dan, age 22 and Bill, age 18, 1980

Me & Marj, age 21 & 26

Johnny, Marj & Bill, 1988

Performing with Dan at Ns & Vs show at The Channel *club, Boston, 1990*

Me, "bossy," at Ns & Vs band rehearsal at the Studio in Ashmont, 1991.

Family photo, 1994 Bob, me, Bill, Dan, Charlie, Thom, Jim, John. Front: Marj, Ma

Bobby & Johnny, 1996

Marj, Uncle Bob and me on his 75th birthday, 2000

Me, Kristin and her sister leaving our mark on Siesta Key Beach, 2016

Bill a few years before he passed away

When there were two: Dorchester gas tanks as I remember them—a snowy scene I painted on wood during the 2020 COVID lockdown.

Ma in 2021, age 86

With Joan & Cheryl at a Dorchester restaurant, 2024

Me and Husband Bill, 2024

Everyone today: Dan, Jim, Thom, Marj's husband Dale, Marj, my husband Bill, Me

Chapter 26

I've Just Seen a Face

A FEW WEEKS after Dad died, I spent a weekend at Marj and Dale's, as I often did, for a belated birthday dinner. I loved the ninety-minute drive to see them in central Mass, surrounded by them, their two boys, Eric and Taylor, and the warmth of their home. With Dad's funeral behind us and the recent topic of Uncle Bob still fresh in our minds, there was plenty for us adults to talk about once the kids went to bed.

I brought up our grandparents' unmarked grave.

"Grandma couldn't afford a grave marker when Dad's father died but why do you think none of Dad's siblings ever put a headstone or even a simple, small marker on their grave?"

Marj shrugged. "It was probably a money thing. And Dad was never in his right mind to do it."

I let out a slow, disappointed sigh. "I guess."

"We should find out what a small headstone costs," Marj said. "Maybe we can all pitch in for one of those small, plain, flat ones and put their names on it."

"That's a great idea. They can't be that expensive."

"Yeah," Dale said. "That tiny, round stone under the snow was tough to find."

I changed the subject to the sibling who had concerned us all the most, especially for the past couple of years.

"Johnny didn't look too good the day of Dad's funeral. Every month when I give him his disability money, he's a little weaker. Social Security keeps sending me questionnaires, asking if he's in a detox or rehab program, and I always check the 'no' box, hoping they'll help, but they keep sending the checks. It's like they don't even read those things."

Dale leaned on the counter, his face showing concern. "Man, I heard Bill talking about that rooming house Johnny lives in. It sounds pretty rough over there."

"Yeah, it looks bad from the outside," I said. "That's why I wait in the car whenever I pick him up."

We'd all been at a loss as to how to help Johnny. We all saw the wear over the years. The decline was gradual but long, and it began with our father—the day Johnny was born.

John, my mother's second child, was born in 1955. Ma shared through the years how, from the time Johnny learned to walk, Dad hated him. His resemblance to her father, Ralph, whom dad didn't like, was the first thing which provoked Dad's mistreatment of him. The reasons only grew from there.

Early in their marriage, Ma thought Ralph could be a fatherly presence for Dad, filling the void left by the premature death of his own father. Conversely, she hoped Dad could be like the son Grandpa never had.

Perhaps seeking camaraderie with his father-in-law, Dad

would pressure Grandpa to go out drinking after work. Though Ralph hardly drank, he would agree to meet for a beer to appease him. I suspect Grandpa may have gone along with it to keep tabs on Dad, searching for signs of trouble at home. After one beer, Grandpa would glance at his watch, and announce, "Oh, Jeez, Louise. Look at the time. I gotta go, Dick. Kay's got supper waiting for me."

Dad grew to despise Ralph, seeing his mild-mannered nature and devotion to his family as weaknesses. Pushing him to stay out drinking, Dad took digs at Ralph's masculinity. "Come on, Ralph, have another beer with me. Who wears the pants in the family, anyway? For cripes' sake."

But Ralph didn't cave to Dad's insults. He wouldn't subject his wife to the endless waiting Ma endured, never knowing when her husband would arrive home.

As Johnny grew, relatives commented on his blond hair, blue eyes, and Danish-Germanic features, so unlike Ma and Dad's brown eyes and hair. Dad seized on it, mockingly calling Johnny "Ralph's Little Twin," a nickname steeped in bitterness. Through no fault of his own, Johnny became the target for Dad's resentment, as if resembling Ralph were a crime. In drunken rages toward Ma, he assaulted Ralph's character. "Your father makes me sick, I hate him! And now Johnny's starting to look just like him. He's not my son—he's your father's son!"

As time passed, Johnny could do no right in Dad's eyes. Every word, every action seemed to trigger Dad, as if Johnny's very presence reminded him of every disappointment and everything he despised.

Chapter 27

Live and Let Rest

It was a February work morning, about a month after we buried our father, when a call came through to my office cubicle at 11:30. It was Johnny on the line, calling from a pay phone. In the background, I could hear a Commuter Rail train clanging into the platform at South Station.

Once a month he came to my office to pick up his cashed Social Security disability check. As his state-appointed representative payee, I made sure his rent got paid, he had food, and suitable clothes to wear.

I picked up my desk phone. On the other end, Johnny spoke in a weak, faint voice. "Hey, Sis. I heard you finally got your birthday dinner at Margie's."

"Yeah, you know how it goes. Story of my life." I sighed. "I always got gypped on my birthday parties because of snow cancellations. Better late than never, though." I shifted the conversation to Johnny. "Everything okay? You sound... tired." I didn't want to say weak.

"Yeah, I'm good. I'm at South Station. Can I swing by for my money?"

"Sure. Come to my office now. I'll meet you out front."

I waited for Johnny in the icy air in front of my building on Summer Street, our usual meeting spot. I could tell from a distance something was off. He was moving more slowly than usual, wincing with each step. When he reached me, his breathing was labored. Johnny had been declining for years, but this day, he looked very tired and frail, and more disheveled than usual.

I handed him the cash. "Johnny, what's wrong? You look like you can't breathe."

He grimaced when he lifted his hand to put the money in his coat pocket. "I fell at Ma's. I'm fine."

"What do you mean, you fell? What happened?"

Looking back, I regret how judgmental I sounded, grilling him. In a tired voice, he recapped, "I was at Ma and Charlie's and I banged into the TV. I think I hit the corner of the VCR." He pointed to his rib cage.

Forcing a steadier tone, like he was trying to convince himself as well as me, he said, "I'll be all right. It's just a little bruise."

Ma still had her oak floor cabinet TV, the one Margie and Jimmy had bought for the family on Christmas 1977. It was the first "luxury" item we'd gotten after Ma's divorce, a symbol of our fresh start.

His breaths came in short, uneven pulls. "Johnny, I think you should get checked out. You're not breathing right."

He waved it off with a weak laugh. "It's copacetic. My side is sore but I'll be fine."

But I knew better. "You could have a broken rib, maybe even a punctured lung. You should go to City Hospital. Let me call you a cab."

Again, he brushed it off.

"Nah, I'll wrap some duct tape around my ribs. It'll heal," he joked. "I gotta go pay my rent. Talk to ya later, little sis."

I watched him walk toward South Station, his steps careful

and uneven, until he disappeared down the stairs to the Red Line, bound for Broadway, one stop away, where his rooming house was. With no cell phones back then, I had no way to check back in on him. I only hoped he was okay and tried to focus on my afternoon at work.

Wanting the full story, I called Ma after work to verify Johnny's account. She confirmed he'd visited, and added he'd shown up drunk and stumbled into the TV, backing up everything Johnny had told me.

Two days later at work, my desk phone rang from an outside line.

"Hello, Miss Dyer. This is Homicide Detective Gerald Mackey. I'm with the Boston Police Department at District C-6 in South Boston." He paused, his tone measured. "You're John Dyer's sister and legal guardian, correct?"

Oh, no. What's happened to Johnny? My gut wrenched.

"Yes. That's correct."

"I'm sorry to inform you... Your brother John was found deceased in his room last night."

My heart sank. I knew it. I let out the long breath I was holding.

"Ahmm... what were the circumstances?" I croaked, bracing myself for whatever horrid details were about to be shared.

"He was found lying prone on the floor," the detective said, choosing his words carefully. "There may have been injuries we couldn't see—possibly from a struggle, but we can't say for sure. He had some bruising on his torso. There was no visible blood, though that doesn't mean there wasn't significant loss internally."

He paused, then added, "Forty-three is young. Given his age, we've ordered an autopsy. We have to look at all possibilities. Someone that young doesn't usually die of natural causes."

My thoughts drifted back to my last interaction with Johnny

two days earlier. I insisted it had to be accident-related and shared everything I knew about Johnny's fall at Ma's. But given the seedy environment of the rooming house, filled mostly with homeless people and addicts, the detective pressed hard for other motives.

"Did he have any enemies you're aware of? Anyone in the rooming house who would want to hurt him? It's a pretty rough place."

"I don't think so. He kept mostly to himself."

"A drug dealer he may have owed money to?"

"I doubt it. He drank a lot. Too much. I know he smoked a little pot but I don't think he had any hard-core drug habits."

"A jilted lover?"

"None I'm aware of. He's been on his own for quite a number of years. As I said, he fell at my mother's. I told him I thought he might have a broken rib."

The detective said on the morning of Johnny's death, he'd tried to get himself to the hospital. The manager of his rooming house called a cab for him, but when it arrived, Johnny staggered out barefoot, underdressed, and disoriented. The driver took one look at him and drove off, probably assuming he was just drunk, leaving Johnny to limp back to his room. Unbeknownst to anyone, his "drunk" behavior was mostly due to internal blood loss. His autopsy would later confirm he'd hemorrhaged from a punctured lung caused by a broken rib, along with the expected advanced cirrhosis.

We never found out why the house manager didn't call an ambulance for Johnny after the taxi refused his fare. All we were told was that late in the evening, the house manager found Johnny dead on the floor. His attempt to save himself had come too late.

Johnny's life had never been easy. He bore the brunt of our father's cruelty, enduring physical and emotional brutality that left lifelong scars. As he got older, years of heavy drinking took their toll, resulting in cirrhosis, malnutrition, and mental decline. His body had been failing him for years, dragging him toward an end we all saw coming but couldn't stop. But knowing it was inevitable didn't make it any easier.

Despite our eleven-year age difference, Johnny had always been there through my younger years. Now he was the first of my siblings to die, just a month after our father. Sadness came, but more, I felt the pangs of guilty relief, knowing he was out of his misery.

Everyone grieves in their own way. For me, coping meant focusing on the logistics of Johnny's funeral arrangements—just as Margie and I had done the month before. It was easier to concentrate on the minutiae than to face the weight of it.

I couldn't bring myself to view my brother's remains. It had been hard enough seeing him in so worn down in his final days. The funeral director who had overseen Dad's burial allowed me to identify Johnny over the phone by describing his three amateur India ink tattoos: a heart on his upper arm; a simple two-line Dorchester cross with hash marks on either side above it on his forearm; and his initials, "JD," beneath it.

Over the few days before Johnny's burial, I stayed busy, although a quiet unease settled in—I knew I suffered an enormous loss but couldn't yet grasp its full weight.

Johnny said on a few occasions that he wanted to be cremated and have his ashes scattered in the Combat Zone, the place he felt at home. That may sound morbid and sacrilegious to some, but it made perfect sense to me. It was where he spent his longest and most-loved years working. Some of us were open to honoring his wish, but in the end, we decided as a family to bury his ashes in the Dyer grandparents' grave in Dorchester, where there was room for one more urn.

In those last few days, most of what I felt was sad relief for Johnny. Forty-three years of needless turmoil and suffering—first at my father's hands, then through his own struggles—had ended.

Chapter 28

This Song

THERE WE WERE AGAIN, gathered on a blustery winter day for another family funeral at Cedar Grove Cemetery. Bobby had work obligations with his Florida business partner, but this time, Ma and Charlie were at the cemetery with us. Together, we laid Johnny's ashes to rest under the great, bare weeping willow, the only landmark for a plot still with no headstone. It felt eerily similar to the month before. In the distance, I heard a southbound Mattapan trolley rattling over snowy tracks toward Milton.

A priest from St. Gregory's parish led us with a few prayers and blessed Johnny's urn before placing it on the frozen ground for internment. The day was both poignant and conflicted for me. I felt sad Johnny had never found his way through the darkness, yet relieved he wouldn't have to face another dismal day. And beneath it all was the uneasy sense we were leaving him behind, and none of it sat easily.

After the burial, we gathered at Jim's house for a luncheon he hosted. Somber as the day was, I sensed even Ma took some comfort knowing her son was no longer enduring the effects of his struggles which, many times, left him homeless and adrift. I was grateful she had Charlie for support, a kindness my father never provided her.

Jim brought generous platters of sandwich fixings and salads into the dining room, while most of us shook off the cold feeling inside with adult beverages—except Jim, who'd given up drinking in his early twenties, determined never to turn out like our father.

We settled in at the dining room table while Tony Bennett and Frank Sinatra crooned softly in the background. It was respectable American songbook music, but something felt slightly off.

Across the table, Dan and Bill whispered back and forth, their expressions pointed and animated. A few hushed words passed between them as they shot looks at the stereo. I could tell they were gearing up to object to the music choice.

Dan used his standing as the oldest sibling in the room to bring the music back on track.

"Jim, why are we listening to this elevator music? We should be playing Johnny's kind of music. Why don't you put on some classic rock or something? It doesn't have to be loud, just put it on low volume while we eat."

"We like the music," Ma protested from across the dining room table. Charlie backed her with an affirming nod.

Dan pressed on, undeterred. "I know you like it, but Johnny wouldn't want us listening to this. If he were here now, he'd say, 'Put on some Grand Funk! Or at least some instrumental Jeff Beck, or even jazz.'"

"Or Santana," Thom suggested. "Nothing too heavy."

I winked at Marj with a smile. "Or some Beatles." She knew.

"Just throw on the entire *In-A-Gadda-Da-Vida* album and call it a day," Bill added, deadpan. Jim switched the FM dial to classic rock on WZLX. The familiar sounds of Jimi Hendrix, the Stones, Creedence Clearwater Revival, and other bands Johnny loved filled the room. Dan leaned back with a satisfied look. "This is better, much more Johnny's style."

A self-taught bass player since age sixteen, Dan reflected on how much Johnny had loved rock music, particularly the rarer, eclectic deep cuts. "One thing's for sure. Johnny knew good music. He influenced most of what I listened to growing up. I learned to play bass to all his albums. Same with Bobby's music. Mary, remember the Australian band, the Skyhooks? Johnny got me into them."

"Yeah, I still have that album. And *The Point.* Johnny knew so many great, obscure bands."

The Point album by Harry Nilsson tells the whimsical story of a boy, Oblio, and his dog, Arrow, set to a delightful soundtrack. Under my breath, I sang a line from the chorus, "Me and My Arrow."

Jim concurred. "Yeah, Johnny and Bobby definitely influenced my music taste. Dan, I listened to all your music, but I mostly remember Johnny's albums. When I was ten, I was still into the bubblegum crap like the Partridge Family and the Archies, but he was listening to Steppenwolf, Led Zeppelin, Deep Purple... the real heavy stuff you, Johnny, and Bobby liked, which I wasn't ready for yet. A few years later, though, I started to get into it. Johnny had the drum set, and he was always playing along to those heavy songs."

A flicker of the drum set from my preschool days hit my brain, with Johnny playing along to the Surfaris' "Wipeout."

"Oh, yeah, I remember his drum set. It was red with sparkles."

Dan and Bill lived and breathed cars and musical gear. They knew guitars and amps inside and out, and Dan knew a bit about drum sets.

"Yeah, he stole that drum kit from some kid's basement on Bowdoin Street. It was just a small Gretsch trap set. He only played it when the old man wasn't around."

Ma sighed softly. "Those drums were so loud. I was glad when he got rid of them."

While Johnny never pursued drumming further, it was clear as a teenager, he had a natural love for anything rock and roll related.

Musicality seeped into all of us as kids. We quoted lyrics to express how we felt, or made up our own to fit the moment. I still do. When I'm walking my dog on a beautiful day, I'll sing to her "Good Day, Sunshine" by The Beatles or "Hey there, Chaqui girl," to the tune of "Georgy Girl" by The Seekers.

In crowded Dorchester in the '6os and '7os, kids everywhere had their transistor radios tuned to the latest AM hits. WRKO spun tracks by Tony Orlando and Dawn, the Beatles, Neil Diamond, Tommy Roe, the Grass Roots, Neil Sedaka, and hundreds of other great artists. Musically, childhood was such a fun time for us.

Talking about music eased our conversations into stories—both the funny ones and the hard ones—about the person who was obviously missing: Johnny. Our table of siblings, spouses, and again, Dan's friend Ted, shared our memories of Johnny, many marked by the weight of what Dad had put him through or the messes he'd gotten himself into.

Marj brought up our other sibling who wasn't with us. "Too bad Bob couldn't make it up. But I get it. He hates winter. Florida would be pretty good right about now, huh, Ma?"

Ma wasn't one to show much emotion. She ate quietly, offering a few words here and there. "I guess. It's a long way for him to fly up just to turn right back around again. Airfare's so expensive."

"Yeah, he'll come up in July like he does every year. I'm sure he'll stay with us for a while to get out of the heat."

Charlie grinned. "He's no dummy. He's staying where it's warm. Spring training's right around the corner. He's probably already schmoozing with the Orioles, selling his pitching machine. He could sell ice to an Eskimo."

He was referring to Bob's baseball pitching machine partnership.

"If he were here, I'm sure he'd have some crazy stories to tell about Johnny," Thom said, setting his sandwich down.

With Bob in Florida and Johnny gone, Dan carried a wealth of early family memories. "I remember a lot of stuff from when Johnny and Bobby were young. Don't forget, Johnny and I were close in age, and we hung out a lot at Ronan Park, the First Parish Church area, and all around Uphams Corner through the '60s and early '70s."

Dan tipped his beer bottle, letting the beer fill into his glass. His voice carried a wry edge. "One thing I'm sure you know... Johnny was a firebug. The old man was always kicking his ass for playing with matches and lighting things on fire."

As he spoke, a heavy quietness settled over me. I knew Johnny's history, how my father's abuse and scapegoating early on had set him on a long slide into rebellion, poor judgment, and recklessness.

Chapter 29

Boy, You're Gonna Carry That Weight

Dan set down his sandwich reflecting back on Johnny's fire obsession. "So, Ma..." "When did we live in Quincy? I vaguely remember it when I was a preschooler, so it must've been, what... the early '60s?"

"Yes, that sounds about right, 'cause Jimmy and Margie were born there, in Houghs Neck. Your father was still working at Boston Gear Works then. He didn't like being away from Dorchester for very long, so Quincy only lasted maybe two years."

Ma and Dan always said the apartment in Houghs Neck was a dilapidated one-bedroom, in-law apartment which sounded like it had all the charm of a shack.

Dan continued. "I remember Bobby and Johnny shared a twin-size mattress on the floor, and I slept on the couch. It was a tiny place. It was where the old man burned Johnny's hands for starting the bedroom fire. I was little, but I remember it."

Ma wasn't one to dredge up the past when it involved Crazy Dickie Dyer. Plus, for years, Charlie had heard enough drama about him to fill one of his episodic novels, with Dickie as the antagonist.

But a few conversations about Johnny that day seemed to loosen her up a bit.

"Yeah, I guess," she murmured sadly, her voice trailing off. Then, deciding she'd shared enough, she gave her usual response when she wanted to get off a subject. "I don't know, Dan. I don't remember that far back."

It had been a hard day for everyone, especially Ma. She'd tried to protect Johnny from Dad all his life, but she wasn't spared back then, either.

Since her divorce, Ma rarely spoke about our father except to make a few well-deserved cracks about him. But, now in her sixties, those memories were further away—and so was her desire to revisit those dark times.

Dan picked up the fire story, recalling it as best he could—how Dad had tormented Johnny the day he started a fire in the Quincy apartment.

He paused to think back. "Johnny loved playing with matches as a kid. He'd steal them from the old man's Bugler tobacco can. Back then, the old man hand-rolled his cigarettes."

In a surprise turn, Ma added a detail. "He'd even sneak your father's snuffed-out cigarette butts when he was about ten."

Bill chimed in. "I blame the candy companies... starting with the candy cigarettes with the bubble gum filters." He held an imaginary cigarette to his lips. "Hey, watch me, kids, smoking's cool!" He shook his head. "What a scam—no scruples."

Johnny's childhood fascination with lighting fires grew as he did. After stealing a pack of matches from Dad's tobacco can, he'd set fires in a vacant lot or alley, with whatever he could find—gum wrappers, a toilet-paper core, a twig. But it went too far at age seven, when he started a fire in our parents' bedroom while baby Margie was in the crib.

On this particular day in 1962, Ma was multi-tasking in the kitchen. Dinner potatoes boiled on the stove while she scrubbed soiled diapers in the sink and kept an eye on two-year-old Jimmy in the high chair. Johnny crept into our parents' bedroom. On Dad's nightstand, he found what he'd been looking for—the dazzling, bright yellow-and-red matchbook advertising Paragon Park, Johnny and Bobby's favorite amusement park.

Johnny sat down on the bed, studying the matchbook's back cover: "World's Largest Roller Coaster. Paragon Park, Nantasket Beach, Rte. 128 and 3A."

With each match he lit on the striker, he stared, mesmerized, as the flame slowly burned down to his fingertips before blowing it out like a birthday candle. He struck the last match in the pack. When it got too close to his fingers, he reflexively flicked it onto the bed. The threadbare blanket immediately caught fire. Johnny panicked. He hadn't meant to start a fire. He knew the old man would kick his ass if he found out he'd done it, so he bolted. He ran out the front door, not thinking about baby Margie, asleep in the bedroom.

The smell of smoke wafted into the kitchen. When Ma saw flames in the bedroom, she leapt into action. She scooped Margie from the bureau drawer crib and ran back into the kitchen to turn off the pot of potatoes. Juggling Margie in one arm, she frantically dialed the operator for police help, gave the house address and hung up. With her free arm, she pulled Jimmy out of the high chair.

A neighbor woman downstairs heard the commotion and ran up to help. She grabbed Jimmy and Margie while Ma ushered Bobby and Danny, fleeing from the house. Johnny was nowhere to be found.

The fire department extinguished the blaze, keeping it contained to one corner of the bedroom. When it was safe, Ma and the kids were allowed back into the apartment. The fire chief approached her.

"Mrs. Dyer, we found burned matches in the bedroom." He

held out an empty matchbook. "This was near the front door. It may have something to do with how the fire started."

Ma tucked the matchbook into her apron pocket, dread settling in. She knew: Johnny was playing with matches again. Dick would be home from work in half an hour.

When the fire department left and the commotion subsided, Ma sent nine-year-old Bobby out to look for Johnny. "Check the backyard, the cellar. Walk the neighborhood. He can't be far."

Fifteen minutes later, Bobby came back alone. "Ma, I can't find him anywhere."

When Dad returned home and saw the damage, he went ballistic. "Johnny did this! I know he did!" he screamed, his face reddening. "That little punk. I'll teach him not to play with goddamned matches. He could have killed Margie! He did it on purpose! Where the hell is the little bastard?"

Ma stammered, fearful of Dad's wrath on herself and Johnny. "I-I don't know, Dick. He was here when I was cooking supper. We can't find him. Bobby looked everywhere."

About a half hour later, Johnny ascended the apartment stairs to the second-floor, shoulders hunched, bracing for a beating if the old man had put two and two together. Dad yanked him into the apartment by the collar and slammed the door, hollering about him being a "no-good, firebug punk." Four-year-old Danny ran crying to Bobby on the couch, scrambling into his lap. Bobby held him close but didn't move. He knew Johnny was about to get it. He froze, his eyes fixed on the scene, his whole body rigid with fear. Dad dragged Johnny into the parlor by the arm and slammed his small hands onto the red-hot grates of the whole-house metal gas heater. Johnny screamed, jerking and twisting as the heat bit into his hands, but Dad's grip didn't loosen. Ma rushed in, her face stricken with fear, clawing at Dad's arms to pry him off.

"Stop, Dick!" she screamed hysterically. "You'll kill him!"

"No—he needs to learn a goddamned lesson, once and for all!"

He swung around and punched her, sending her staggering back. Rage twisted his features as he pressed Johnny's hands harder onto the blazing metal. Sweat ran off his nose and hissed as it hit the hot grates, Johnny's screams filling the tiny apartment.

Bobby and Danny sat huddled in horror, crying.

"Have you had enough yet? Huh, you little punk? You tried killing your baby sister. How do you like it?"

When Dad finally released Johnny, Ma rushed him into the bathroom to run cool water over his blistered, raw hands. Sirens in the distance indicated the lady downstairs had called for help.

Ma and Johnny were taken to the hospital. Johnny's burns were severe, requiring extensive treatment and a hospital stay for the deep, charred wounds across the tops and bottoms of his little hands. Ma had to have two teeth extracted where Dad's fist had landed again.

Ma pressed charges against Dad from the hospital. Since she feared for her and the kids' lives, it must have taken all of her courage and strength to do it. Perhaps she had no choice, with the police involved, or maybe she saw a rare chance to protect her children—if only for a while. She never shared her feelings about these things with us.

Dad was sent to Boston State Hospital in Mattapan for a month-long, court-ordered psychiatric evaluation. I wonder if there was ever a diagnosis or a treatment plan, or if it was just another wasted holding period. Once he was out, his drinking resumed, his manic swings grew sharper, and his grip on reality slipped further. The rages returned with a vengeance, with Johnny as Enemy #1.

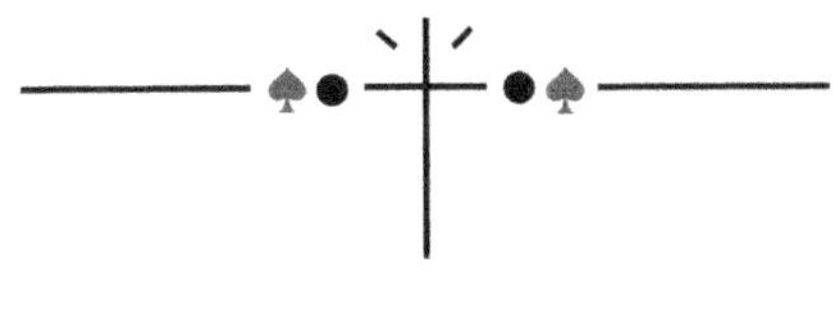

I've tried to stand in Johnny's seven-year-old shoes, walking through the door to face our father after the fire, unaware of what was about to happen. Of course, I couldn't. What he endured would have been unbearable for any adult, never mind a child.

Most of what I know about Johnny and Bobby comes in pieces, fragments passed down over the years. But one thing feels certain: that day, and so many others like it, stripped Johnny of whatever innocence he had left. For the rest of his life, Johnny carried the marks of the faint scars on his hands and the deeper ones in his psyche. By age three, he'd already learned who he was supposed to be: a troublemaker. By seven, the lesson had hardened into something final—you'll never be anything but a loser, punk, piece of shit all your life.

I remember Ma once said, "If Johnny so much as had dirty hands at the supper table or forgot to close a door, your father beat him and sent him to bed without any supper."

Each time Dad beat him, Ma tried to protect Johnny.

"Enough, Dick!" she would cry, attempting to pull him off him. "You've made your point. Leave him alone!"

But Dad was a raging bull, impossible to hold back. He would fling Ma across the room like a rag doll, beating on Johnny, Bobby, or all of them at the same time. Bloody noses and black eyes had become a common occurrence with Ma and the boys. If Bobby or Danny was within eyeshot during one of Johnny's or Ma's beatings, they got a beating as well, just because. Dad's paranoia rendered everyone suspect.

With the continual beatings, Johnny grew into a rebellious, delinquent juvenile. He started pinching from Dad's narcotics and alcohol bottles whenever he had the chance. He got into trouble for stealing merchandise from stores and often skipped school. He sniffed glue, paint, and other toxic fumes to get high. Johnny would have large bruises on his body, which people assumed to be from roughhousing with his brothers or neighborhood boys. Neighbors who lived above or below our family knew better. They heard the beatings firsthand and saw the unmistakable marks. But no one dared get involved. They were afraid of becoming the target of Dickie's retribution.

By age eight, to escape the beatings and emotional torture, Johnny started running away from home. He bounced between juvenile detention centers for stealing and chronic truancy, disappearing from school completely by tenth grade.

Ma always told a story about Johnny running away from home at eight to escape a beating for shoplifting a yo-yo. When he realized he had nowhere to go, he concocted a scheme which seemed ironclad to him at his young age. He stole a bottle of black shoe polish from the corner store and dyed his blond hair black. He hoped the old man wouldn't recognize him sitting on the front steps, and Ma could sneak him back into the house. Of course, Dad recognized Johnny right away, but he was in a happy drinking mood, so he let Johnny back in with berating insults instead of a beating.

Around those same years, Dad's violence escalated and he subjected Ma to a brutal beating. The severity of his assault rivaled the kind he would unleash on a man in a barroom brawl. The attack landed her at the hospital with extensive injuries and she'd lost additional teeth.

Massachusetts Child and Family Protective Services placed the five kids in a family shelter while Ma recovered in the hospital for two grueling weeks. Dad served another jail sentence for domestic violence at Deer Island Prison.

After another violent incident that year, one of Ma's sister's took her and her five young children to a battered women's shelter in Boston.

"Doris, you and the kids are safe. He can't find you here. These people will help you with whatever you need."

Fearful of Dad's retaliation, Ma called Dad the same night and he convinced her to tell him where she was. He promptly drove there and removed the family from the shelter.

The next day, Dad stormed over to our grandparents' apartment in the projects, furious Ralph was behind getting Ma into the shelter, and looking for a fight. But Ralph, Kay, and a couple of their older teen daughters fought back, kicking and punching until he tumbled down the hallway stairs.

Ma's family, worn down by Dad's wrath and retaliation, were at a loss for how to help. One afternoon over tea, Ma sat across from Grandma Dyer with a black eye, bruised limbs, a swollen cheek, and a few less teeth. Alma urged her to file for divorce.

"Doris, I don't even know my own son anymore. When he was a kid, he had his bad moods, but nothing like this. You can't keep living like this. For the kids, for yourself—you've got to get out. Call the Dorchester courthouse. They should be able to get you a social worker who can help."

But Ma was rightfully paranoid Dad would follow through on his threats to kill someone—probably her or Johnny. She couldn't bring herself to act. Family social services at the time were limited, and she dreaded the thought of her kids being placed in foster care. This led her and, by default, us kids, to endure ongoing struggles with our father for many more years.

As Johnny grew up, his mischievous nature led to riskier behavior. It was a vicious cycle: the more Dad beat Johnny, the more ways he found to get into trouble. Having no outlet to vent his frustrations and pain, and no match for the old man in a fight, he asserted control by acting out—more glue sniffing, stealing cars, skipping school, and setting larger fires. Ma wore herself out trying to keep him from sinking deeper into trouble, to no avail.

Even after Dad burned his hands, Johnny kept playing with

fire—both literally and figuratively. At age eleven, he started a trash fire in the boys' bathroom at Benjamin Cushing Elementary School. The damage was minimal, but when Johnny was found to be the culprit, Dad dealt him a severe beating.

Later that year, Johnny set another fire in the bathroom at Lucky Strike. After he was identified as the arsonist, Child Protective Services intervened, and Ma had to accompany him to juvenile court once again. The judge ordered him into a youth facility, which led to more beatings when he was released. When Johnny was sent away, Bobby and Danny started calling it "going to Juvie."

Chapter 30

So, I Lit a Fire

WHEN WE FINISHED lunch at Jim's, my siblings talked in the kitchen and dining room, while Dan and I sat with Ma in the living room. Charlie and Thom crossed the room, zipping up their jackets to step outside for a smoke, Charlie with an unlit Benson & Hedges dangling from his mouth.

"Sheesh. Smoking again? I wish you'd all quit," Ma muttered, her voice dripping with disgust. "I never smoked a day in my life."

"I quit smoking once. Worst fifteen minutes of my life," Charlie joked.

Ma shook her head, knowing it was a battle she'd never win.

Overhearing Ma's comments about smoking, Bill strolled in with his usual sarcasm. "Not me. I've never smoked a cancer stick. Maybe they all want lung cancer."

He smirked and took a long swig from a bottle of pink alcohol. Normally, he drank exotic Bavarian bock beers, dismissing American beer as "saltwater swill."

In the foyer, Charlie pulled open the heavy front door, settled his felt fedora on his head, and lit his cigarette with a flick of his butane lighter. He passed the lighter to Thom as they raised their coat collars and stepped out through the storm door.

"What's this you're drinking?" Dan asked, eyeing the bottle as Bill handed it to him. "Cisco?" He squinted at the label. "What is it, a wine cooler?"

"No. It's kinda like a carbonated, sweet wine. This one's strawberry flavor. But yeah, I guess it sort of looks like a wine cooler."

"Never heard of it." Dan examined the label. "Fortified wine...." Then reading further down, he exclaimed, "18% alcohol!"

Bill let out a laugh. "Yeah! I get it at the packie up on Stoughton Street. It's the only place I can find it. The brothers in the 'hood call it liquid crack because of the high alcohol content." Bill smiled, proud of the hidden gem he'd discovered.

Dan sniffed the bottle opening. "Smells like friggin' cough syrup."

"It's cheap, high-octane stuff. Try it, it's not bad."

Dan took a tiny sip and gagged. "That's gross, man. Why are you drinking this crap?"

"It packs a good buzz! One of these and I'm good for the night." Bill let out his sinister laugh—the one hinting he'd found a "loophole," which for him meant a bargain, a workaround or a way to stick it to the man.

Dan was about to hand the Cisco back to Bill but then offered it to me to try.

"Oh, no..." I waved it off with my hand. "I don't want that rotgut... I've tried it before. It's putrid."

Charlie and Thom smoked on the blustery front porch. Through the front window, I could see Charlie's cigarette tip glowing, bringing me back to stories of Johnny setting fires as a kid.

"Dan, didn't you once say Johnny burned down a church or something?"

"According to what he told me and Bobby, anyway. It was

when we lived on Hancock Street. Johnny came in, all out of breath, claiming he set the fire to that old brick church."

Dan began to piece the story together.

It was an October evening in 1970 when a massive fire nearly destroyed a church in Uphams Corner. Out of breath, Johnny ran into the boys' bedroom and quietly shut the door behind him. Dan was tinkering with an old flashlight on the floor. On the bottom bunk, Bobby flipped through a *MAD Magazine* he'd swiped from Jimmy, its cover parodying *Easy Rider* as "Sleazy Riders."

Danny looked up. "Did you get me that blue rabbit foot keychain from Mighty Midget?"

"Shhhh. Forget about the stupid rabbit's foot! Get over here, Danny!" Johnny pulled him off the floor and led him to Bobby's bed.

Huddling around the boys, Johnny whispered, "Don't tell anyone... I set fire to that old church down the street."

Danny leaned closer and whispered. "The one where you smashed out the window?"

Johnny nodded, his face pale.

"Horse shit!" Bobby wasn't buying it. "Stop lying, Worm." He went back to flipping through his magazine.

"No, I really did," he said, his face flat.

Bobby got up, about to laugh off another of Johnny's tall tales. But Johnny's face was different this time, caught somewhere between worry and excitement, though Bobby couldn't tell which was which.

"Turn on the TV. All the news stations are down there." Johnny's voice was edged with urgency.

Danny flipped the switch on the tiny black-and-white TV and adjusted the knob on the tin foil-covered rabbit ears antenna. Channel 7 news showed the church's roof engulfed in flames, with firefighters above the roof spraying water down into the sanctuary.

"Don't fink on me!" Johnny's voice cracked, panic creeping in.

"The old man will kick my ass and send me away again. I didn't mean for it to get outta hand. I was smoking in the upper pew, and, I don't know... those dried out palm things just started burning."

"Johnny, you're a fuckin' firebug!" Bobby snapped. "Why the hell were you smoking in there, anyway? You better quit burnin' shit down. You wanna get caught? What's wrong with you?" He punched Johnny's arm hard.

"I dunno. It was an accident."

"Accident, my foot! The old man's gonna fuck you up if he finds out. You wanna get sent away again? You better cut the shit!"

"Come on, man, don't fink on me, please?" Johnny pleaded.

Danny and Bobby exchanged concerned looks. They couldn't understand why Johnny kept lighting fires. But out of protective brother loyalty, they kept quiet, not wanting the old man to beat Johnny up again—or worse, send him away to Juvie.

The boys kept the fire a secret for years. Our parents never learned of Johnny's supposed role in it back then. Somehow, he avoided suspicion entirely, slipping past what could have been a severe beating for him, and probably everyone else—guilt by association. Ma only heard about the incident secondhand long after Johnny had grown up.

"I vaguely remember you kids mentioning some church fire, and Johnny claiming he had something to do with it." Ma gave a faint shake of her head. "I can't keep up. He was always getting into some kind of trouble."

Even now, when I'm in the area and I pass that church, I wonder if Johnny really set the fire—or if it was one of his tall tales.

Chapter 31

He Would Steal, But He Did Not Rob

WHEN MY FATHER was sober or not suffering the effects of a severe hangover—which was rare—Dad seemed to find genuine moments of joy in fatherhood. He could be generous and cheerful with us when his spirits were high, passing as a "normal" dad.

Dan talked about when he, Bobby, and Johnny were little, and Dad had more good moments in him, before the drinking got worse.

"When we lived on Adams Street in the mid-'60s, the Park Theatre was a five-minute walk up on Dot Ave. Every Saturday, Dad would give me, Johnny, and Bobby a dollar and some pocket change so we could go to the Saturday matinee. He'd say, 'Here's an extra quarter each so you can all get an ice cream at Charlie's after.'"

I smiled for Johnny, thinking, *Well, at least he got some joy*. It sounded like such a nice, fatherly gesture.

I could picture the area Dan was referring to. "Oh wow, I remember Charlie's! The frappe place in Fields Corner, right?"

"Yeah, across from Adams Appliance. He'd give us money and let us go on our way. No adults, just us little kids crossing busy

Adams Street and Dot Ave. alone. Back then, kids went everywhere alone. The older kids watched the younger ones. That's how we all learned street-smarts so young."

Ma added, "Well, by fifth grade, Bobby was already taller than most adults. We always let him take care of you younger kids."

Marj, Dale, and Jim joined us in the living room. Dale took a seat and joined in the conversation. "More Johnny shenanigans?"

"Who else?" Dan said.

Not all of our reminiscing was sad. Much of it was comical.

Dan was eager to get to the good parts, including his earliest memories of Johnny stealing.

"So anyway, when we went to the movies on Saturdays, every kid got a ticket stub when they paid admission. During intermission, they'd play a movie clip of a car race. If our ticket stub matched the number of the winning car, the kid won a prize. It was awesome."

On one of their Saturday movie outings, during the intermission between *Tom and Jerry* cartoons and *Munster Go Home*, Johnny yelped with excitement when his ticket matched the winning race car. He exchanged his winning ticket for a toy motorboat and ran to the boys in their seats, smiling big, rocking the boat over imaginary waves. "I won! I won! Look what I got!"

Dan's smile deepened as he recalled the day. "Johnny ran through the front door all happy. 'Ma, look! Look! My ticket matched the car race. I won this cool boat!'"

My chest warmed as Dan recounted Johnny's good fortune as a boy. Back then, it wasn't very often he had a reason to be so excited about something.

"After the movies, we'd sometimes stop at Woolworth's and browse around the toy department, and sometimes Johnny would steal a small toy. One time he stole a Slinky, but it was usually something smaller, like a Matchbox car or marbles. Whatever he could fit in his pants pockets. Anyway, when we got home, Johnny would show his new toy to Ma and Dad, saying, 'Look, I won the car race again!'"

"So, after the third time Johnny 'won,' Dad got suspicious," Dan laughed under his breath. "He goes, 'Johnny, something's not right here. You keep winning the race every week. How's this possible?'"

"Dad's rule had always been clear: 'If anyone asks you anything about me or about what goes on in this house, you tell them you don't know anything.'"

"Because I was the youngest then, the old man would grill me every time, figuring I'd fink on Johnny for stealing. He'd asked me, 'Did Johnny steal that toy?' I always stuck with the only safe answer I was taught—'I don't know.'"

Every once in a while, if Johnny kept his mouth shut, he escaped punishment for stealing. It often depended on Dad's mood. Sometimes he would let Johnny's winning claims slide. Other times, he would impose his own brand of justice with a severe beating, whether he thought Johnny was guilty of stealing or not.

Thom and Charlie came back in from their smoking break and Thom re-joined the conversation.

"At least Johnny never robbed a bank or anything."

"None we know of, anyway," Dan tossed back, jokingly. "He knew how to steal, but a robbery would've gone sideways."

"True," Thom said. "He never took it that far. Remember how he used to say 'dieve'—for when he stole something or snuck in somewhere for free?"

"Oh, yeah, his made-up word for devious." Dan smiled as

memories of teen Johnny flooded back. He added, "Johnny mostly stole things from stores, occasionally a B&E if a door was unlocked. So many kids we knew took whatever wasn't nailed down."

"Whatever he wanted, he just took it," Thom said smiling, amused by Johnny's gumption.

Like many kids from Dot, Johnny's education came from the streets, the school of hard knocks. His work life never rose above low-wage, menial jobs. So he stole to get by.

"He stole a lot of cars," Dan said. "If there was an unlocked car, especially a Mustang—he loved Mustang convertibles—Johnny just took it. He didn't care. Back then, cars were so easy to hot-wire."

"He didn't need to own a car," Bill added. "He'd steal a car, use it for a week, then ditch it in some alley in town."

"Then do a 'chew 'n screw' in Chinatown." Thom lifted his beer can. "With a few cold teas, of course, to wash it down."

"That was nothing," Dan's friend Ted said. "The biggest classic Johnny theft I remember was the three-way dieve, right, Hook?"

"Yeah, he'd start out in town at Filene's or Jordan Marsh, try on a leather jacket, and walk around like it was his. Then he'd hit the record department and fill a paper shopping bag full of albums. From there, he'd hit the shoe department, putting on a pair of expensive sneakers."

"And he walked out the door with it all," Ted laughed.

"I remember the 'Gary Dieve.'" Jim said.

"Yup, the good old Gary Theatre," Dan chuckled.

I hadn't heard this expression before. "What's the Gary Dieve?"

Dan explained. "So—one day Johnny says, 'Hey, let's go in town and do the Gary Dieve.' I asked the same thing you just did, Mary. 'What the hell's that?' Turns out it was Johnny's code phrase for sneaking into the Gary Theatre near the Boston Common. He showed a bunch of us how to get onto the roof of a building next door to the movie theatre. The two roofs were practically connected. We'd jump onto the Gary Theatre roof and then sneak in through an unlocked door, right into the theater. We caught all the latest movies for free. We saw *Taxi Driver* there."

I remembered bits of what they were talking about, but most of it was vague since I was still playing with Shrinky Dinks and doing latch hook rugs when the boys were teens. Still, it was easy to imagine.

I said, "It's too bad Bob's not here. He'd have a ton of Johnny stories."

"Yeah, for sure," Marj said. "But I think when he moved to Florida, he pretty much washed his hands of all the Dorchester stuff. The good and the bad."

At twenty-three, Johnny's dieving caught up with him when he stole an Impala in Boston, planning to head west. I don't know if he had a destination in mind. I think he just wanted distance from the life he hoped could be better with a fresh start. His joyride ended in Colorado, where he spent a year in a Boulder jail.

While incarcerated, he enrolled in culinary classes and trained as a sous chef. In letters he sent me—ones I still have, thoughtful and well-written, from a time before drinking and cirrhosis clouded his mind—he described the life skills he was learning and his plans to return to Boston to work as a chef in a posh hotel or restaurant.

I could see Johnny was dreaming of a better life for himself. But when he returned from jail, he slipped back into the familiar rhythm of his old Dorchester life and heavy drinking. He had a brief stint test-flicking Bic lighters at a local factory. For extra "easy" money, he and Billy volunteered for paid drug studies, becoming human pincushions with round-the-clock blood draws and weekend stays at university research facilities. When they cut him off because they'd stuck him too many times, Johnny became a salesclerk at an adult bookstore in the Combat Zone.

Amid the rough streets and colorful characters, Johnny felt a deep connection. Under the neon glow of X-rated theater marquees like the Naked i Theatre and the Pilgrim Theatre, and among the workers he befriended in the peep-show joints, he felt welcome. Johnny was a storyteller by nature, and in the Zone, he had a captive audience. In the chaotic energy of the Combat Zone and in Chinatown's gritty alleyways, Johnny found camaraderie among the strippers and outcasts who, like him, were just searching for a place to belong.

Chapter 32

Oh What Joy, for Every Girl and Boy

THE LONG DAY of Johnny's funeral was winding down. The winter sky darkened and a quiet reality settled over me—Johnny really was gone. With all the reminiscing to distract me from my own quiet feelings, I'd momentarily forgotten them. My family started gathering their belongings to leave, some still lingering to talk.

Marj lightened the mood for us, and especially Ma, with a fun memory.

"Ma, remember when you took us to *The Bozo Show*?"

Ma smiled a little. "Oh, sure. Johnny won a huge box of toys..."

"Right, it was called the Treasure Chest." Marj's smile broadened. "He won it in the dance contest."

Murmurs of "Oh, yeah," and "That was cool," came from my siblings who were old enough to remember. I'd heard the story countless times before, but today it was a welcome distraction—a lighter memory of Johnny, and a reprieve from the thought of returning to my empty apartment alone. Moments like these made me wish I had someone to share life's ups and downs with.

"I took you kids to Bozo a few times," Ma added. "We'd take the bus to the television studio where they taped it, remember?"

"Channel Five," Jim said. "When it used to be on Morrissey Boulevard. Waaaay back when."

"It got you kids away from your crazy father for a few hours, anyway."

Marj recalled how all the kids were dancing, and one by one, they were tapped on the shoulder to sit down. Johnny was the last one standing, winning the Treasure Chest.

"Johnny could dance. We all could," Dan said. With a touch of pride, he added, "Me, Bobby, and Johnny went to all the school dances at St. Ambrose. We learned how to do the Watusi and the Twist there. Johnny knew all those dances."

This brought a smile to Ma's face. "And some other crazy dance he used to do—I think it was called the Monkey or something. When the huge box of toys came to the house from the Bozo show, it was like you kids got Christmas all over again."

Marj smiled. "Yeah, I got a huge plastic tea party set. Dolls, games..."

Dan added, "Yeah, we got the Gunfight at O.K. Corral game, a bunch of Army guys... Oh, and those slot car sets... We loved those."

He smiled as the memory carried everyone back to a simpler, innocent time with Johnny—treasured youthful moments which happened well before my time.

Bill shot Dan a flip look. "Ha! Then I got those hand-me-down slot cars for Christmas one year, right, Ma?"

"We were too broke to get new toys for all of you. I did what I could for you."

"Yeah, but I didn't care. I liked snapping the tracks together and setting up the houses and trees."

These were the memories which made us smile for Johnny's good fortune. Despite the abuse shadowing him, Johnny experienced true childhood joy the day he won on The Bozo Show. He became the center of attention for something positive. He was the hero, with all of his siblings sharing the windfall of the many toys he won.

Marj zipped her coat and paused.

"When Johnny slept over our house a couple of weekends ago, he said something weird. We were up until four in the morning, just the two of us, talking about anything and everything. He said he thought Dad was still out to get him. Like, from the grave."

Those words gave me goosebumps. Dad had died only a month before Johnny. It didn't feel like a coincidence.

Marj looked off, thinking. "Or maybe," she said, "maybe Dad was finally helping Johnny out. Like telling him it was time to rest. I like to think of it that way."

I liked how she put it. I held onto that, too.

Chapter 33

It Don't Come Easy

Bill zipped up his coat to leave, sharing his matter-of-fact synopsis of Johnny's life.

"Johnny lived how he wanted to. His Combat Zone days... the peep shows, the strip clubs, all the shady poseurs he hung with... Hey, it's what he liked."

Thom hung out with Johnny the most during that time. "Yeah, those were some strange people, but Johnny definitely felt right at home there. I saw some crazy stuff—one guy who always dressed like a woman in see-through dresses. Girls turning tricks for five bucks."

"No doubt, the Zone was his happy place." Jim added. "As Bill said, he lived how he wanted. That takes something, considering the way the old man treated him all his life."

"I wonder whatever happened to that woman he married?" Thom pondered aloud.

Johnny met her at a bar in the Combat Zone. Their whirlwind romance led to a quick wedding, but it unraveled within a few years. Johnny's drinking had cost him his health, his job, and eventually, his marriage. At thirty-five, he was scraping by on Social Security disability checks, his heart as broken as his dreams.

Dan shrugged on his coat and pulled his keys out of his pocket. "Bill, you need a ride?"

"Yeah, I'll take the ride to Quinky," Bill quipped, mispronouncing Quincy for whatever zany reason he thought up. "Just drop me off at my kid's house. I have to watch him tonight."

Dan nodded ok and finished the final sip of his warm beer. He handed the empty glass to Jim, eyeing the last trace of foam at the bottom—a quiet reminder of Johnny's struggles.

"Johnny was always getting his ass kicked by the old man. It's probably why he drank so friggin' much. But even as a little kid, he just loved booze, man." He lingered to add more context. "He was stealing the old man's booze when he was eight. I remember him sneaking it when we lived on Bowdoin Street. Even earlier..."

"Wow... so young..." The weight of it hit me. But I knew alcohol was Johnny's ally, his coping mechanism. My mind flashed to when I was fourteen, drinking Lowenbrau and Riunite like every teen I knew—Dorchester kids, school friends. I was no angel. None of us were. Taking a sip of Merlot, I thought, *Was it my coping mechanism too? Is it now?*

Dan glanced around the room as he spoke to all of us. "Let's be real. In Dorchester, everybody I knew was partying, drinking Dorchester Martinis."

I blinked. "Wait—what? What the heck's a Dorchester Martini?"

"Kool-Aid and vodka." Dan said proudly. "All of us poor Dorchester kids drank them."

We all shared a quiet, much-needed moment of humor. It felt good to laugh with my siblings. I liked to think Johnny was right there with us.

Dan paused. "It's too bad. Johnny was a good kid. He just never got things figured out."

"He had a heart of gold," Marj said softly, looking down. Dale reached for her hand.

Talk of early drinking brought me back to when I had my first unplanned encounter with alcohol. I couldn't resist stalling everyone for a few more moments to share my own comical memory.

"I drank booze once when I was four."

"Huh?..." Their faces showed a mix of disbelief and curiosity, waiting for the punchline.

"Yeah, one summer day, I was on the back porch on Hancock Street. I was thirsty, and I saw a short glass of clear liquid on the railing. I thought it was water."

They weren't shocked. Between my father's heavy drinking and all the chaos in our home, encountering alcohol young was inevitable.

"I saw the glass and thought, *Oh, goody, a glass of water!* I took a big gulp, and in no time, I was gagging and my mouth was on fire. I was like, *That was no water!* I lay down on the porch twin bed, thinking I'd drunk some kind of poison. It scared the crap outta me. I didn't tell anyone 'cause I was afraid I'd get beat for touching something I wasn't supposed to. Dad probably left it out there in one of his drunken stupors."

But Dan had another theory. "I bet it was Johnny's. He was always sneaking the old man's booze. It was probably vodka he put out there to hide from the old man and he probably forgot all about it."

"Oh, wow. Maybe." The possibility hadn't occurred to me.

Dan moved toward the front door. "All right, I gotta be up early for work. Bill, you ready?"

Bill gave his best sarcastic reply. "Whaddya mean, ready? I've been standing here with my coat on for fifteen minutes. You're all still yappin' like the *Golden Girls*."

He was right. I guess we were lingering to keep Johnny's

memory with us a few minutes longer. With final hugs goodbye, everyone departed Jim's and headed home.

After my brother was laid to rest, I found comfort in being surrounded by my family. But once alone in my car, a bleak quietness settled in—the kind which comes when the world feels a bit off balance. On the drive home, I cranked the heater to full blast, but it couldn't cut through the cold clinging to me. Heading south on I-93, the massive rainbow-painted liquid natural gas tank loomed large on my left—a familiar Dorchester landmark, and a comforting marker of home, carrying both the weight and the joys of our shared past.

"Highway Star" came on the car radio, a song by one of Johnny's favorite bands, Deep Purple. I thought about how he would sit and strum made-up, dissonant chords on an out-of-tune acoustic guitar, pretending, yet honestly believing he could play. He idolized rock stars. Seeing Dan, Bill, and me playing in bands for years made him proud, like he had rock stars in his own family. He introduced us all to so many good bands, always holding a soft spot for the Beatles, like Bobby had. For my musical education, I felt grateful.

I thought about Johnny's generosity, and how proud he was when I started college. Even with so little to his name, he would hand me fifty dollars on my birthday or Christmas. "Here, Mary, buy yourself a school book. I know how expensive they are."

The small gesture, coming from Johnny's meager income, spoke volumes about his heart. Johnny was one of the good ones. And despite life dealing him a harsh hand, he always gave his time and money to help someone out.

A couple of weeks after Johnny died, our family gathered at Ma and Charlie's to celebrate Dan, Jim, and Eric's February birthdays. Bill did a very sweet thing, passing around a Valentine's Day card for Johnny, and we all signed it with our own personal messages to him—a metaphorical love note. Bill always kept that card in a suitcase of sentimental items, holding onto it as a way to honor Johnny's memory.

I reflected on how Johnny's life had unfolded, how his innocence was ripped away so young, something none of us could have prevented. There was no silver lining to soften the truth. But in his love of music, his fake-it-till-you-make-it optimism, and the way he lived by his own rules, he remains with us through the wild stories we still keep alive.

To our family, Johnny will always be a true Dot Rat.

Chapter 34

It Can't Get No Worse

THE YEARS after Johnny's death passed mostly uneventfully for me. My life revolved around family, work, singing, friendships, and dating. Dan and I played in our own bands, gigging off and on, while Marj and Dale hosted most of our family celebrations. Work and music were the steady areas of focus for me. By November 2005, I'd just been promoted to office manager and was living with my two cats in a condo I'd purchased. Life was pretty good.

A week into the new job, my world was shaken. I had just gotten home from work, a plate of pasta in hand, with the 6 PM news next on my agenda.

Our top story... An armed robbery occurred today at the Ace Pawn Shop in Worcester. Police report a suspect shot a store owner and a clerk. Both were taken to a local hospital with serious injuries...

I dropped my fork. *What? That's Bill's store!* I felt the blood leave my face. *The owner and a clerk? That's Bill and Don. Holy crap.*

With shaky hands, I grabbed the phone and called Marj.

"Are you watching channel five news?"

"No, we just sat down for supper, why?"

"Bill and Don were shot at the pawn shop!"

"What?" She yelled for Dale to put on the news and put me on speaker phone. I told them what I'd just heard, and that Bill was at a local hospital. Marj sprang into action. "We'll find out what's going on. I'll call you right back."

Ten minutes later, my phone rang. She and Dale had reached the ER staff. Bill was in surgery with multiple bullet wounds to his arm and back, in critical condition.

"I'm on my way. I'll meet you and Dale at the hospital."

I hung up, fed my cats, and headed out the door. We divided up the phone calls. Marj would let Ma and Dan know, and call Bob in Florida, and I would call Jim and Thom.

Once in my car, my first call was to my new manager. Being in my position for just a week, I worried about the optics of it—admitting I had a brother who'd just been shot, as if it placed him on skid row, which wasn't the case at all. In the end, I told the truth. "I'm sorry, I won't be in tomorrow. My brother was just shot. I just found out about it on the six o'clock news."

He didn't hesitate. "Take whatever time you need. I hope he pulls through. Family first, Mary."

Relief washed over me.

During the hour-long drive to the hospital, I called Thom and Jim with the news. Everyone was concerned for Bill and asked to stay updated.

For the rest of the drive on the Mass Pike West, my worried thoughts went straight to Bill. I thought about how much he loved working at the pawn shop, how he'd said it was the best job he'd ever had, because he got to repair and restore musical instruments —straightening warped guitar necks, filing frets, installing pickups, strings, and tuning heads, as well as rewiring electronics—taking pride in making each used instrument play like new. He even gained a working knowledge of instruments not typically found in rock and roll—banjos, mandolins, and violins. It wasn't long before all of our musician friends went to Bill for their guitar repairs. The owner trusted him and left him in charge when he needed to step away.

When Bill was moved to a patient room, he was groggy but talking with Marj, Dale, and me. He recounted what had happened.

"I was behind the counter when this guy—a regular customer —walked in. I stood up to shake his hand hello like I always do, and he pulled out a gun, shot us, and grabbed a load of jewelry and cash."

The gunman was apprehended and sentenced to prison. Bill underwent surgery for a gunshot wound to his back, a collapsed lung, and shattered bones in his wrist, forearm, and elbow. He would need many months of rehab and physical therapy. His boss had serious injuries as well.

Bill's life wasn't in danger, and the lung would eventually heal, but the question hung over everyone—would he ever regain full use of his arm enough to play and repair guitars again?

Bill endured months of painful recovery. Even with a fundraiser the family held to help with his bills, he spiraled into a financial crisis. To make rent, he was forced to sell twenty rare and custom guitars. He was devastated. I could see the physical and financial toll it took on him. He eventually found work again, but in my opinion, he was never the same. It seemed to me the trauma and losses had left their mark.

Chapter 35

This Bird Has Flown

IN THE SPRING after Bill's shooting, our family came together to celebrate both Easter and Uncle Bob's birthday. He had become a permanent fixture at every gathering, fitting right into our noise, laughter, and more often than not, our friendly heated debates about everything from rock bands to who remembered a family story the right way. Dale, with his smart aleck humor, had Uncle Bob cracking up, teasing him as a "crazy old coot." For his birthday, Bill and Marj pitched in and gave Uncle Bob a banjo. He lit up, cradled it in his lap, and plucked the same string over and over, smiling like he'd nailed it.

Bill was healing slowly from his injuries, but I could see the mental weight of selling his guitars and dealing with so much physical pain still hung over him. He was tired and seemed down.

Around this time, Charlie's health took a turn. As his needs increased, he was transferred to a nursing facility. Jim and I lived closest to Ma, so we took her to visit him a few times a week.

As usual, talk at Margie's drifted to the old days, with Bobby's name surfacing more than usual. My family's walks down memory lane, like so many before then, gave me more glimpses into where Bob's life started.

BOB, my mother's first child, was born in 1953. When I came along in 1966, he was already a grown-up in my eyes. He left home before I entered kindergarten, trading whatever was left of his innocence for an escape from Dad's violence. Thirteen years and countless miles separated us, so in many ways, he was more like an uncle to me than a sibling. The six boys shared three bunk bed sets crammed into one bedroom, so they weathered Dad's outbursts with Bobby. John, Dan, Jim and Marj, closer to his age, had grown up alongside him. Their history with him was richer, more adventurous, and undeniably closer.

Through the years, Dan liked to talk about the older boys' "camping" nights on our third-floor back porch on Hancock Street. As we sat around chatting, we listened as he described how he, Bobby, and Johnny would drag out pillows and old army blankets and camp there during the summer, trying to escape Dad's chaos. It wasn't exactly camping in the Blue Hills, but it was good enough. One night on that porch stood out.

What follows is just another cog in the Dickie Dyer wheel of craziness, but there's something darkly comical about imagining Bobby and the older boys' teenage antics and their attempts to fend off our father.

On a September night in 1970, the back porch buzzed with the three older boys' voices as they gathered for one of their usual camping pow-wows. The porch light cast long shadows over a twin bed Ma kept there, and their circle of plastic milk crate seats. The large gauze bandage on sixteen-year-old Bobby's hand was hard to ignore. Fifteen-year-old Johnny and twelve-year-old Danny demanded all the details.

"I got jumped at work today," Bobby said angrily. He held out his bandaged hand to the streetlight's glow so they could see it better. He was working part time in the stockroom at the Jordan Marsh department store in Boston.

"I was on my lunch break—just cashed my check at the bank, and three Black guys followed me back to work in the freight elevator. Two tackled me while the other guy tried to grab the cash out of my pocket. I says, 'No way, man!' I wasn't giving up my money. I had to fight them off."

Bobby's expression hardened. "It ain't gonna be me getting robbed... Fuck that! I pulled out my box cutter and just started slicing, man. When the elevator opened, they ran off. They didn't get any of my money."

Half listening and lost in his Slush Puppie, Danny wiped his sticky hand on his dungarees. He was adding up in his head how many more Paw Points stood between him and a tiny harmonica. "Wait—so you got beat up?"

"No! Stop cutting in," Johnny snapped. "He's tryin'a tell us."

Johnny leaned closer, impressed as always by Bobby's toughness. "Oh, shit, Bobby—did'ja mess 'em up?"

"I think so. I dunno how bad. I sprained my thumb, though. Ma wrapped my hand up. There's blood all over my new suede jacket." He paused. "But it ain't my blood, that's for damn sure." His voice dipped, more annoyed than proud. "I just bought the fuckin' thing."

Johnny picked at a scab on his knee—road rash from wiping out after jumping a plywood bike ramp. "Aw, what the hell? That jacket's hip, man! I was hoping to get it next."

"Yeah, then me!" Danny added.

Johnny assured the boys. "Ma'll fix it, though. She's good with sewing clothes."

"Yeah," Bobby said. "She says she has some leather cleaner to get the stains out. But some of the fringes got torn off. You know what...I don't care, I wasn't backing down. That's my hard-earned money."

"Ma can sew new fringes on," Johnny said. "When I cut over the fence at Fields Corner station, my jeans got shredded and she fixed them."

Bobby's good hand tightened on a Kool cigarette, the menthol tip glowing red. He stared out at darkened Glendale Street. "Everywhere I go, someone's getting jumped or hassled by n——s. Can't even walk down the fuckin' street anymore without wondering if it's gonna be you next. I'm sicka this shit."

Johnny sang just loud enough to tease him: "You never give me your money..."

When Bobby didn't laugh, Johnny dropped it. "Least you fought 'em off. Sounds like you did some collateral damage." He fished out a bobby pin, pinched a tiny pot roach into it, and took a puff. The pungent pot smell drifted into the crisp night air. He shifted the conversation to cars and the pretty girls who hung up at Ronan Park. Bobby, feeling grown up with his job and bored by the juvenile chatter, rested his cigarette on the railing.

"Gimme that thing." He snatched Johnny's roach and sucked it down to nothing, blowing the smoke out slowly.

"Shit's getting worse around here." Bobby's voice dropped. "The old man's beating on Ma again. Two months in lockup did nothing. He'll never change. She should've divorced him when she had the chance. What the fuck..."

Jail never made a difference. Dad always came out just as unhinged as before.

Danny frowned. "How come she took him back?"

Johnny rolled his eyes. "Duh! Because she's scared he'll kill her. Why ya think?"

Bobby handed the empty bobby pin back to Johnny and took a long hit off his cigarette, exhaling the plume of smoke from his nose. He nodded, his gaze distant as he let Johnny's response settle.

"And he will too. He'll put her in the hospital again, and next time she won't come back alive." Danny glanced between his older brothers, unsure if they really meant it.

Johnny lit a hand-rolled cigarette and swigged from a Fanta root beer bottle filled with whiskey—both pilfered from the old man when he was drunk. He shook his head. "He's gotta go, man. His craziness and paranoia keep getting worse the more he drinks. Ma needs to divorce his ass already."

Bobby exhaled another plume of smoke, deep in thought. "I'm outta here soon. A guy I work with's got a room I can rent on Tremont Street, right across from the Common. I'm sicka fuckin' Dorchester, sicka the old man beating on everyone. I'm sicka looking over my shoulder all the time when I walk down the street. I'm sicka these shithole winters too." He paused, picturing a better future. "I'm thinkin' I'll prolly end up in Florida or Texas someday —someplace warm."

Bobby, a solid six-four, was the only one who might have been able to stand up to the old man, who was pushing a bloated three hundred pounds. Johnny, dreading the thought of Bobby leaving, changed the subject. The boys settled into their usual routine— smoking and hoping to drift off to sleep as they did on their Blue Hills camping trips. But the streetlights on Glendale dimmed the stars. Instead of crickets, Dorchester's cacophony filled the air: speeding cars barreling down Hancock Street, barking dogs, drunk couples fighting, and distant sirens wailing from Columbia Road, where Glendale Street ended.

The boys settled in for the night, spreading their Army blankets across the porch floor. Danny got the twin bed since he was the youngest.

A sudden commotion rose from inside. Johnny turned toward the back door, straining to hear. The old man was home drunk from Mallow's Bar, his voice slurring as he ranted about a skipping record.

From the parlor, Dad's 78 RPM country record droned on, skipping on the same line:

"I've got a tiger by the tail, it's plain to see. I won't be mu—I won't be mu—I won't be mu—"

"Who the fuck's been playing my Buck Owens record?" he hollered. He staggered up and dragged the needle across the vinyl, gouging it as he lurched it toward the next song.

He lumbered into the kitchen in his sock feet, where Ma was baking his favorite midnight snack—stuffed quahogs—jumbo clam shells packed with breadcrumbs and bits of clam, smothered in Tabasco sauce. A "delicacy" he swore by, though it always set off the gout in his foot the next day and sent him into one of his full-blown fits.

The yelling got louder. "I know Johnny scratched my record! I'll kill that punk! Where the fuck is he?"

Bobby whispered, "He's coming for you, Worm. Hide the shit."

Johnny turned down the static transistor radio playing "Girl Watcher." The boys heard the sickening thuds of Dad hitting Ma.

Bobby turned to Johnny, his face set with resolve. "We gotta do something, man."

"Yeah, let's take him down," Johnny said, brimming with confidence—the kind he only ever mustered when Bobby was around.

Bobby got up and, with his good hand, grabbed the old, rusty axe from the corner of the porch and handed it to Johnny. "I'll knock him down with a kitchen chair. Then Johnny, you hit him in the head with the axe. And make it count. I can't do it with my bad hand."

Johnny ordered Danny, "You stay in the hall as backup. We got this."

Bobby and Johnny eased their way through the back door, nudging it enough to slip inside unnoticed. Dad had Ma pinned against the refrigerator. Her nose was bleeding.

"Get your hands off my mother, you muthafuckah!" Bobby yelled.

Drunk and unable to focus without his glasses on, Dad slurred, "You swearing at me?"

Bobby swung a metal folding chair at Dad's shoulder, knocking him off balance to the floor. Johnny followed with the axe, his hands shaking as he aimed for his head. Dad dodged in time, sending the axe blade slicing into the linoleum floor. He got up, roaring like a cornered silverback. The boys bolted out the back door. Back then, Ma had milk delivered in glass bottles. Dad ran after them, hurling empty milk bottles at their heads, his curses mixing with the crash of glass echoing down the three flights of stairs.

"Don't you ever come back, you cocksuckahs! I'll kill you all!"

Two weeks later, just shy of his seventeenth birthday, Bobby quit school, stuffed what he could into a duffel bag, and left home for good. He was determined never to live under our father's roof again.

I remember when I was in preschool, one day, he was just— gone. But after hearing Dan's story, I grasped the depth of Bobby's determination. I remembered how years later, Bobby said he had to escape the chaos of home before it turned him bitter enough to kill the old man. I thought it took guts for Bobby to leave home so young and find his own way in the world.

Chapter 36

He Took a Sad Song and Made it Better

After he left home, Bobby bounced around a few apartments before settling in Malden, north of Boston. Now and then he would come by for Sunday dinner on Bloomfield Street, but those visits tapered off since Dad was still around, wreaking havoc. He made his feelings about Dorchester and Fields Corner clear in passing remarks like, "I'd never live here again," or "Ma, why are you still living in this dump?"

As a young man, he did time in a Louisiana jail, which he chronicled in a long block of writing tattooed along his inner forearm. It read something like: "When I die, I won't go to hell, because I did my time there already in a Louisiana jail cell."

He never let us read it, always pulling his arm away if we tried. I never knew the reason for his incarceration. None of us had much insight into the life he lived after he left home.

Bobby took trips to far-off places and came back with souvenirs for me from San Francisco, Texas, and New Orleans—pieces of a new life he was building bit by bit, somewhere else. For me, those trinkets sparked curiosity about the bigger adult world he was stepping into.

In the early '80s, fed up with Boston's long winters and restless for something else, Bobby moved, trading the cold, gray strife of Massachusetts winters for the bright, sunny shores of Florida. Over time, when he occasionally came back to visit, his thick Boston accent had softened. The dropped endings gave way to a slower drawl, and his "aah" endings on words were traded for hard Rs.

Bob became a key player in a business venture with a guy who had invented a baseball pitching machine used by major league players. He loved meeting team owners, coaches, and pro players. I got the sense he felt like a rock star around them. He worked hard and played harder, building a life far removed from our troubled upbringing. From what he shared about his Florida life, it seemed like he was doing well, albeit partying a lot. But who wasn't?

Every July, he came back to Boston for a quick break from Florida's oppressive heat. For me, those visits were brief—quick hellos, a few laughs about the old days, and comments about how much he loved his life in Florida. Seeing him just once a year in the nineties, I started noticing changes in him. He'd put on a lot of weight from drinking and seemed less pulled together than I remembered.

By the early 2000s, Bob's health was slipping. He was thinner and weaker, with low stamina. His girlfriend finally convinced him to see a doctor, and the diagnosis came back: advanced cirrhosis. He had several hospitalizations and his condition worsened. It felt like a familiar pattern—first our father and Johnny, and now our oldest brother fading due to hard living.

Marj and I flew down to Florida to help Bob and to assess what his health situation was. Walking into his trailer home, I saw how small his life had become. Bobby, the tough, towering six-foot-four brother who once seemed invincible, seemed frail and vulnerable. We spent a few days sorting medical paperwork, cleaning up his place, and bringing him groceries, trying to bring some order to the disorder. On our last day, as I shut the door behind us, I thought, *How does someone who once seemed to have it together end up at rock bottom?* But I knew.

In 2006, Bob flew up to Massachusetts to visit. He looked even more worn down. Marj and Dale didn't hesitate; they told him he was staying with them, no arguments. They moved Eric and Taylor into a shared bedroom and gave Bobby a room. They took him to medical appointments, administered his meds, and made sure he was eating well. But the cirrhosis was advancing and it was clear he was not going to get better. When summer ended, he stubbornly refused any more help from them and flew back to Florida for what turned out to be the last time.

A couple of weeks later, Marj learned that Bob didn't have much time left. She packed a bag and flew Ma down to see him briefly one last time.

A week later, on a Saturday evening, my flip phone lit up with Marj's name.

"Hey, what's up? I'm in the car, heading to a gig in Raynham."

She sounded subdued. "Oh, okay. I'll make it quick, I don't want to mess up your night, but I thought you should know. Bob passed away at the hospital about a half hour ago."

As I steered my car down Rte. 24 South, her words hung in the air, heavy and surreal. "Geez, okay. Thanks for letting me know," was all I could manage. After a pause, I said, "Well, I'm glad he's not struggling anymore."

We knew it was coming, but hearing it still hit hard. We hung up, and I kept driving, letting it settle. *Another brother gone too young at only fifty-three.*

WHEN I GOT to the club, I told my bandmates about Bob's passing. They huddled around me, concerned.

"Are you okay to play?"

My drummer friend Rob added, "We can pack it in and leave. Just say the word."

"I'll be fine," I said, though I wasn't sure. "I'll dedicate a song to him tonight."

Scanning the evening's set list, nothing felt quite right. I thought back and one came to me.

"I know we haven't played it in a while, but let's open the first set with 'Paranoid.'"

"Good choice," they said. "Yeah, we can pull that one off the back burner for your big brother."

When we took the stage, I leaned into the mic and said, "This one's for my brother Bob. He's no longer with us, but I think he's here in spirit tonight."

Then we launched into the Black Sabbath song—loud and heavy.

The night of my gig, the music wasn't just a tribute. It was a connection. For a few minutes, the years between us disappeared, and Bobby was right there, rocking out with me, just like he used to do with my older brothers.

Bob was cremated and a few weeks later, his ashes were shipped to our family. Ma kept a small tin of them on her mantle with his picture on it, about the size of a cocoa can. She told Marj, "When I die, I want the tin of Bobby's ashes buried with me. He was my first baby."

In the months that followed, Charlie's health deteriorated quickly. In early December, after a rapid decline, he passed away peacefully in his sleep at the nursing facility.

His death felt different somehow, not as sad and heavy. Maybe it was the Christmas season, or maybe because he hadn't suffered the way my father and my brothers had. For Ma, life was taking some adjustment, but she had us kids, which seemed to help a lot. For us, Charlie had given her the life she deserved, and for that, we were very thankful.

Chapter 37

He Had Blisters on His Fingers!

We came together at Marj and Dale's the Christmas after Bobby and Charlie died. Ma felt lonely living on her own for the first time. Marj and Dale had already set plans in motion and were now moving forward with placing her in elderly housing closer to their home. Everyone, including Ma, breathed a little easier.

In the living room, Dan and Bill were showing our nephews Eric, Taylor and Dayne some guitar and bass parts from an old Ozzy Osbourne song. The aroma of Italian shells and meatballs wafted through the house—Ma's Italian Christmas tradition we've kept through the years.

As usual, when reminisced about the old days. Dad's presence loomed over many stories, either with him stirring up chaos or stepping in as an unlikely protector. He would provoke fights over real or imagined slights, and when it came to defending his family, he did so with the same intensity. Physical punishment was his sole domain—no one else was allowed to lay a hand on his kids.

With Johnny and Bobby gone, Dan was a key link to their early years. At the dinner table, he passed around a plate of Scali bread and buttered a slice.

"I remember when Bobby got hit by the car. He was crossing Adams Street—right in front of our own house, right, Ma?"

"Right, it was in the fall when we lived above Sand's Café—where Mary was born—across from Lucky Strike. The car came out of nowhere. It hit him so hard, his face shattered the headlight and his sneakers flew right off his feet. It was terrible. It's a wonder he wasn't killed."

Dan added more details. "He had to have massive reconstructive surgery—metal rods and screws in his knee, and it took 244 stitches to repair his leg."

"Yeah, he was still in a cast when he went back to school," Ma said. "He got kept back that year, though, from missing so much school. Cripes, he was so tall, he looked like an adult in sixth grade. I remember the time of year because Mary was born shortly after his stitches came out."

Dan glanced from Jim to Marj. "And that principal, McAdams. He hit Bobby with the ruler when he was in the leg cast. Remember that?"

"I don't recall that at all," Jim said. "I was probably too young. But, yeah, I remember the principal, for sure. He always had that thick wooden ruler in his hand, walking the corridors. And the assistant principal, Mr. Burns."

Marj added, "Yeah, back then, public school teachers could still hit kids like the Catholic schools used to."

I sipped my Merlot, thinking back to my brief time teaching, when I couldn't live on the salary and moved into the corporate world. Back then, Charlie, a former teacher, joked, "Denial is a river in Egypt, Mary. You never wanted to hear it."

Dan returned to the wooden ruler story, repeating what Bobby had told him as a kid.

. . .

At the local middle school, Principal McAdams used to make students walk the corridor stairs in pairs in straight military formation. Any kid caught using the handrail got the "rat hand," as we called it. Bobby was in a leg cast, so he had to hold onto the handrail to climb the stairs. One day, McAdams caught him. He halted the line and pulled Bobby out to make an example of him.

"Young man, you're not allowed to use the handrail."

He then whacked the ruler down on Bobby's knuckles in front of the whole class. Bobby hobbled back into line, embarrassed, fighting back tears from the sharp wallop.

He came home from school with his knuckles swollen and bruised. At supper, Dad noticed his hand.

"Who'ja get in a fight with?"

"No one." Bobby said, nervously, and he told him what the principal did.

Dad saw red—and not just the red welts on Bobby's knuckles. He slammed his Schlitz down on the card table they ate their meals on. Foam spilled over the rim, and Ma and the kids flinched.

"Are you telling me the principal hit you for using the goddamned banister with your leg in a cast? You better be tellin' me the truth, son."

Dan said our father always told the boys, "If you're in the right, I'll back you a hundred percent. If you're wrong, or you lie and make a fool of me, your ass is grass."

Bobby was shaking. "That's really how it happened, Dad." Dad took a sip of his foamy beer. "Okay. I'll be taking care of this tomorrow." Bobby knew what that meant. Someone was about to get their butt kicked.

The next morning, hungover and smelling like stale beer and cigarettes after a long night at Gallagher's bar, Dad was on a mission. He put Bobby in the car and drove directly to the school.

He stormed into the school office with Bobby at his side on

crutches, demanding to see the principal. After getting his name, the secretary asked, "Mr. Dyer, do you have an appointment?"

"No, I wanna see the principal. Now. Hurry it up, miss. I'm already late for work."

As Dan told the story, I pictured the 1960s secretary in a plaid mini skirt, peering over crystal-rimmed cat-eye glasses, while Dad sized up her bosom, his gas station uniform greasy and rumpled, the name patch over the pocket reading "Dick."

When the secretary led them to the principal's office, he was sitting behind his stately oak desk. The boys always said he looked like he was dressed for Sunday Mass—Saville Row pinstripe suit, starched white shirt, and mirror wingtip shoes.

Dad barged in with Bobby. "You the principal?"

McAdams rose and extended a hand to shake, but before he could answer, the old man started blasting him with questions.

"You gave my son the rat hand yesterday for holding onto the goddamned banister? Are you a fuckin' imbecile? He was hit by a car!" He pointed to Bobby's leg. "Can't you see he's got a goddamned cast from his hip down to his ankle? How do you expect him to get up and down the stairs without holding onto the banister, huh, asshole?"

I could picture Dad's red face and spittle flying from his mouth onto McAdam's wingtips.

"Errr, well, Mr. Dyer. The rules—"

Dad cut him off, demanding, "Show me the ruler you used on my son." When McAdams pulled the hefty wooden ruler out of his desk with a shaking hand, Dad snatched it from him. He sized up McAdam's smooth, pale hand and said, "Looks like you've never seen a day of hard work in your life." Then he gave McAdams a hard whack on the knuckles with the ruler and flung it on the desk.

McAdams recoiled in pain, rubbing his hands together to lessen the burn.

"You ever touch one of my kids again, I'll kick your ass right in this office. Don't make me come back here a second time and be late for work again like today, you fuckin' moron."

Dad stormed out, Bobby hobbling behind him toward the schoolyard. He turned to Bobby. "That prick ever touches you again, you tell me. I gotta get to work—so long."

Bobby watched him light a cigarette, get into the car, and peel out, nearly careening into a school bus full of kids. He never heard another word from McAdams or Burns, and his cast came off in time for Christmas vacation.

Ma snapped at the memory. "I don't know if that's exactly how it went. Bobby always told it that way. It was so long ago... But no one at the school laid a hand on any of you kids again." Then she threw in a deserved jab. "But it was okay for your father to hit ya's." She shook her head in disgust.

We all shared the moment of comic relief, though a trace of sadness lingered with Bobby now gone. His story had become family lore, a reminder of Dad's fury and twisted, albeit well-intentioned, sense of justice.

I was born a few weeks later in January. Our apartment sat above the rowdy Sand's Café, a convenient spot for Dad to slip downstairs for a couple drinks (or six). I was my mother's tenth pregnancy, but only the eighth living Dyer child.

By the time I came along, my thirty-two-year-old mother had endured more than most women her age. She now wore partial dentures, a lasting mark of the toll from multiple pregnancies and my father's abuse. At eight pounds twelve ounces, I was her heaviest baby. I arrived with enough force to leave her with an umbilical hernia, keeping her in the hospital for two extra weeks, the longest rest she'd had from motherhood in thirteen years of marriage that wasn't abuse-related. Margie joked that when Ma brought me home from the hospital, she had to cut Margie's long ponytail into a short "pixie" haircut, after Dad let her unbrushed hair turn into a "rat's nest" for the two weeks she was gone. I entered the world with six older brothers and one sister, each shaping me through example and hands-on lessons. In my mind, I grew up with seven fathers and two mothers—a pretty lucky last born.

With the age gap between me and Bobby and him leaving home so young, we had always lived in different worlds. The stories my siblings shared offered rare glimpses into his early life, snippets which helped me feel closer to him. My own memories of Bobby are few, but they still make me laugh, and they give me something to offer when the family starts reminiscing about him.

Like when he was a teen, he was the brother who teased and terrified me, probably thinking it was just harmless fun. When my parents were out, he was in charge of watching us younger kids. He would leave the phone off the hook, and perfectly time when the piercing warning pulse tone would start up. Once it did, he would whisper and make a scared, wide-eyed face. "Mary, listen. There's a monster in the phone!" It sent me running in panicked tears to Margie or whichever sibling was nearby. He and Johnny liked to pull down the shades to darken the boys' bedroom and play a macabre, psychedelic song called "D.O.A." by a band called Bloodrock. The song is about a guy dying after a plane crash, with eerie sirens wailing in the background. Time after time, I heard the funeral-like organ chords and the singer asking God to teach him how to die, and I was sure the people in the song were coming to get me next. Even now, the song makes the hair on my neck stand up.

Bobby hadn't set out to introduce me to Black Sabbath when I was four, but he blasted the *Paranoid* album whenever Dad wasn't around. I can still picture him grinning mischievously. "Listen to the monster, Mary," he would say right before Ozzy's robotic voice growled, "I am—Iron Man," and the spooky guitar riff droned. I thought a big, robot-monster was coming after me.

But Bobby wasn't all mischief and pranks. He taught me card tricks and the tongue-twister song, "The Name Game" by Shirley Ellis. He cracked me up playing the hand-slap game, Red Hands with me. Even back then, though, I didn't spend enough time around him to really know him. From the stories I heard later, it was clear he'd always been dreaming of something beyond Dorchester. His restlessness—planted in moments like the Sally Camp trip, being jumped in the elevator at work, and my father's violence—became the push he needed. It took real determination to choose a different life for himself, far, far away from Dickie Dyer.

As we sat in her living room, the Christmas tree lights twinkling softly, Marj told us about visiting Bob in Florida with Ma shortly before he died. Knowing the end was near, he told her, "I have no regrets about how I lived my life. I had a lot of fun."

Chapter 38

If We Ever Get Out of Here

THROUGH THE YEARS, we slowly got used to holidays and cookouts without Johnny and Bobby, and now Charlie. Ma missed him, but time seemed to soften the sadness. Each family gathering seemed to get smaller, but we still found ourselves laughing and revisiting the fun, wild, and often chaotic experiences of our Dorchester childhood. Gatherings still brought out the best—and sometimes the worst—of our collective memory.

One Easter, we gathered to celebrate Uncle Bob's birthday, as we did every year. We traded stories about our childhoods, the soundtrack of classic rock and the back-and-forth of Bill and one of our nephews on guitar drifting through the house. Our stories lingered alongside accounts of growing concerns about our safety in our Fields Corner neighborhood and some of the challenges we faced at school. Thom and Bill recalled their experiences at the Grover—the after-school shakedowns when they were outnumbered, harassed, and jumped.

Dan had attended the school eight years before me and had a better experience.

"When me, Bobby, and Johnny went there, it wasn't like that. We had fun there in the '70s."

"Same for me and Marj," Jim said.

But by the time Billy, then Tommy, and eventually I attended the school, it was a different place, its halls teeming with a diverse mix of students from every corner of Dorchester. It wasn't the Grover my older brothers knew, before forced busing began and before Fields Corner and Uphams Corner were more fully integrated.

I recalled my freshman trepidation.

"I was so nervous about going to the Grover. After hearing Tommy, Billy, and other neighborhood kids talking about getting jumped, Cheryl and I were terrified to go. The John Marshall was like Miss Jean's *Romper Room* compared to there."

Dorchester was a tough place to grow up, no matter what section you were from or your background. A lot of kids carried the weight of troubled homes or neighborhoods, which pushed us into survival mode far too early. Being "offered out"—getting dared to fight after school—was one of the ways territorial lines got drawn. So we blended in, kept our heads low, and chose alliances wisely.

Conversations about school got me thinking about how I met my friend Joan at the Grover, how we clicked right away. We were two of the five White kids in Miss Morrison's homeroom, and we stuck together, much like the bond Cheryl and I had forged in third grade. Cheryl was assigned to a homeroom on the opposite end of the sprawling school. After dismissal, she met me at the side door, and we bolted toward the Geneva Ave. area where we lived, while Joan took the Red Line home to her safer Savin Hill neighborhood.

I joked with my brothers that in my first week at the school, teachers teased me about my last name at attendance because of their shenanigans.

"Mr. Stephens said, 'Another Dyer. I hope you're more like your sister, Marjorie—your brothers were another story.'"

Bill whipped his head around in indignation. "I was a good student," he said, pouring pineapple Cisco into a tall glass.

Dan waved it off. "We weren't that bad."
"Then Mr. King in math: 'Another Dyer? I had your brother Bob, John, then Dan... Are you the last one? I hope so.'"

In Spanish class, my teacher assigned a boy to sit beside me, an angry kid who looked disheveled and had body odor. I felt bad for him and wondered if he was homeless. If I glanced his way, he curled his fist at me, grumbling, "What-choo lookin' at, White cracker bitch?"

I kept my eyes in my book or straight ahead, not wanting any trouble. I suspect the teacher had paired us because I was too scared and obedient to provoke him.

The conversation shifted from school trouble to the neighborhood incidents that led us to leave Fields Corner. Deep in birthday cake dessert, Jim and Bill debated which event finally pushed Ma to move.

Jim set down his fork, thinking. "Marj, didn't you and Ma get jumped or something?"

"We almost did. But luckily the guy ran off."
Jim was referring to the time when Margie and Ma were coming home from the Park Theatre one night. Walking up Bloomfield Street, a man tried to snatch Margie's cross-body purse. He kept pulling, but she wouldn't let go. He finally gave up and ran off.

Another time, in the 5:00 a.m. darkness, biking to her paperstand job at Brian's Donuts, Margie saw two men blocking her path ahead. Panicked, she pedaled harder, barreling straight through them down the steep hill. Her bike wobbled uncontrollably, but she made it away, shaken but unharmed.

These and other frightening encounters deepened our sense of being vulnerable outsiders in a racially changing neighborhood, as most White families had already left. Ma's divorce was well underway. But living on welfare, she couldn't afford higher rent, so we stayed where we were. She also had no experience looking for an apartment. By then, our older siblings were all working and helping with the bills. With Dad gone, Margie and the older boys once again took charge. Together, they sat Ma down.

"We gotta move. It's gettin' too crazy around here…"

"Yeah, we can't keep looking over our shoulder every time we walk down the street… We gotta leave.

Ma shrank back. "I don't know how to find an apartment. Your father always did everything."

She looked around the kitchen, her gaze moving from one appliance to the next.

"And what about getting all these heavy appliances and the furniture moved?"

Moving without a man felt unfathomable to her.

Margie put it plainly. "I'll find us a nice place. You have us now to help you."

"Yeah," the boys added. "We'll take care of it. Just start packing."

On Sunday, sixteen-year-old Margie sat at the kitchen table with the classifieds from the five-inch-thick Sunday *Boston Globe* and *Herald* newspapers, determined to find us an apartment.

A week later, she announced the good news: she'd found a beautiful, clean apartment in Savin Hill and Ma signed the lease. We felt relieved to be leaving our apartment and the painful memories that came with it. I was sad to be moving away from Cheryl, but I consoled myself with the thought we would still see each other at school, and on weekends by train.

Monday morning in the school yard, I told Joan my great news. "I'm moving to Savin Hill in November!"

Her face widened with delight. "No way! Where?"

"Sydney Street, near Savin Hill Ave. Do you know where it is?"

"Do I know where it is? It's right around the corner from me—like, a minute's walk. You're gonna love it there. Savin Hill train station's right there. We can take the train to school together!"

Woo-hoo! It was the happiest I'd been yet, aside from my father's eviction to prison over the fire extinguisher ordeal.

My last memory of Bloomfield Street is from moving day. Billy, Tommy, and I took turns, rebelliously scrawling the names of every rock band we could think of with a permanent black marker, covering almost every inch of the inside walls of the boys' closet. We wanted the next occupants to know we'd been there, what we stood for, and to get a surprise when they went to hang up their clothes. It was the last happy memory I had of that apartment, and it came from knowing we were finally leaving it.

Life was looking up for us, and we felt *free as a bird*. Especially Ma.

Chapter 39

Starting Over

Easter dinner was winding down. Marj's boys were outside throwing a football around, the dishes were drying on the counter, and the stories kept circling back to Dorchester and our old apartment. Thom poured the last of his Natty beer, shaking his head. "Well, at least we finally moved out."

Ma agreed. "And life was so much better without your crazy father around. Cripes, Savin Hill was like living in the suburbs."

In the winter of 1977, with Ma's divorce in progress, our family was settled into our clean, peaceful triple-decker apartment. Free from the old man's grip and the chaos of our old neighborhood, we barely thought of him or Bloomfield Street anymore. Savin Hill was a five-minute train ride from Fields Corner, yet it felt worlds away. For the first time since busing started, I felt safe walking around my neighborhood.

I remember on one of Bobby's visits, he was glad to see we'd left the old apartment and neighborhood. "About time you got out of there."

Ma began to heal, both emotionally and physically, from years of fear and strain. At forty-two, she began to reclaim a normal life.

Her contact with family grew steadier, something she valued. She also built a social life, joining other divorced women her age for evenings out.

To improve our finances, Ma returned to the workforce, something she hadn't done since her days living with her parents in the projects. At the Women's Industrial Union in Boston, she enrolled in a homemaker-health aide course. Before long, she had a full-time job helping elderly and disabled clients.

The role suited her domestic skills perfectly. She cooked meals, shopped for groceries, gave baths, and provided companionship to housebound clients, treating each one as if they were family. One client, Herman, awaited her visits every Monday with cookies and tea ready. He shared stories of his harrowing escape from an Auschwitz concentration camp in Nazi-occupied Poland, a part of his past he rarely spoke about with others. Her clients adored her. "Send Doris," they would insist to the agency. "No one else will do."

Since becoming a mother at nineteen, Ma felt a renewed sense of purpose. Her steady paycheck, along with the older kids' incomes, brought small improvements in our lives. Real eggs and milk replaced powdered versions. Butter replaced margarine, which Johnny loved to drizzle over popcorn, shaking the kernels in a brown paper bag as Ma had taught us. Jimmy reminded me of JJ from *Good Times* with his bucket hat when he joked, "Who would've thought we'd be eating cube steak? The old man was the only one who ever got steak around here!"

In time, Ma transitioned us from welfare to fair and well—something my father had never achieved. Groceries were now bought with real currency instead of plastic food stamp coins and Monopoly-looking bills from a coupon book. Medicaid health and dental coverage was the only federal help we still received. Life was *getting better all the time.*

She also indulged in small luxuries my father had long denied her. Margie brought her to the "Dot House" Health Center and got her ears pierced and showed her how to apply makeup. Ma got her hair colored and permed regularly, now free to express herself in fashionable outfits in ways she never could before.

Her growing transformation and confidence drew admiration. Her new friend Judy knew Ma's history and joked, "You're like a real-life Cinderella, Doris."

With time, Ma started dating, leaving behind the shadows of her past. In 1980, at the lounge of the upscale Lenox Hotel in Boston, she met Charlie.

To some, they seemed like a mismatch, but after bad first marriages for them both, their relationship worked. After all Ma had been through, she deserved a man like Charlie, who treated her well and helped around the house. And in Ma, Charlie found a grateful woman who didn't "hen-peck" him the way he said his first wife did. They offered each other stable companionship. That steadiness meant more to Ma than it might have to someone else.

Nearly a decade after they met, they married. Doris Dyer shed a last name burdened with pain and embraced a new one, along with a future filled with companionship, stability, and humor with Charlie.

Chapter 40

I'll Never Lose Affection

Talk of our move to Savin Hill reminded me of my blooming friendship with Joan. Once I moved around the corner from her, we were always together: Lenny and Squiggy, Fonzie and Richie, Mork and Mindy, Laverne and Shirley.

Even though Ma was a little more financially stable, every penny still counted. Trendy designer jeans and Nike sneakers—the staples of Dot and Southie kids—were out of reach. Ma couldn't afford to buy me a Baracuta jacket, a short jacket with a plaid lining kids wore flipped inside out to show the tag's authenticity. Nor could she buy me an "alla-gatah" (alligator/Izod) shirt like the cool kids wore with their collars turned stiffly up. Still, we were doing all right. Margie's hand-me-down corduroys and dungaree jackets were stylish enough for me.

Though Joan and I stayed clear of serious trouble, like many Dot Rat kids, we flirted with mischief. Designer clothes were so important, even poor kids like me found ways to keep up trendy appearances—even stealing to avoid peer rejection. Stealing makeup from department stores like Bradlees or Woolworth's wasn't beneath me.

At twelve, older kids bought us Newport cigarettes, the brand Joan insisted on us smoking because it had a Nike-looking "swoosh" logo on the box—our low-budget attempt at being trendy. On Monday nights, we attended Catholic catechism classes at St. William's Parish, where we made our Confirmation together.

Since we had a few years before we could legally work, Joan suggested we become candy stripers at St. Margaret's, Dorchester's Catholic maternity hospital. I thought it was a job putting frosting stripes on candy.

Joan pinched my chubby cheeks. "No, silly. We'd deliver flowers, magazines, and snacks to the new mothers. We'll get to see all the newborns in the nursery. It's a volunteer job, for fun."

It sounded like a good way to stay out of trouble. A few days a week after school, we donned red-and-white-striped smocks and matching caps. Looking like pilgrims, we pushed sundry-filled carts to patients. We also helped ourselves to plenty of candy swiped off the cart. In our minds, it was fair compensation for unpaid child labor. Imagine—stealing from a Catholic hospital!

Later, I got an after-school job at Arnie's, a shabby five-and-dime on Savin Hill Avenue. Like every kid I knew who worked there, I pocketed fistfuls of Swedish Fish, Fortune bubble gum, Mary Janes, Squirrel Nuts, and bricks of Bubblicious gum. My preschool gum obsession hadn't waned. At least now, I wasn't eating it off the streets. By twelve, I needed a root canal.

At thirteen, Joan and I lied about our age to get jobs at a mail plant near South Station. We said we were sixteen and hand-sorted endless buckets of mail after school while supervisors timed our pace. It paid for Jordache jeans, Members Only jackets, and Newport cigarettes.

Back on Leroy Street where Cheryl lived, things were heating up. More families were moving to the South Shore, and those who stayed were dealing with rising crime. Break-ins, muggings, and vandalism became more common, and houses grew harder to sell, some sitting empty for months on end. A few desperate owners turned to arson, torching their own homes for the insurance payout to make their escape.

One night in 1979, Cheryl's father spotted an orange glow outside her bedroom window. The house behind them was engulfed in flames, burning so intensely, it melted the vinyl siding on Cheryl's family's house. Her father learned the owner, unable to sell the property, had set the blaze for insurance money. Furious, he confronted the guy, shouting that his children could have died in their room. He hit his breaking point, sold the triple-decker, and moved the family south to Braintree. He took a significant loss on the home sale, but chose his family's safety over equity.

When Cheryl first moved to Braintree, it felt like the country to me—far from Dot, though only nine miles away. I was glad she was safe. We stayed in touch, bonding over *Tiger Beat* magazine and our growing Scott Baio obsession. Her mother even took us to meet him at the Hynes Auditorium car show, where we got to kiss him. We visited each other by subway once a month for sleepovers, and once we got our driver's licenses, we saw each other more often.

Cheryl, Joan, and I made countless memories in Dorchester, greater Boston, and beyond. I cherish those bonds, rooted in our formative years—not just in the search for safety and belonging, but in shared experiences, small rebellions, and the many lessons that stayed with us. We were girls figuring things out together, growing into ourselves. Our friendship has stood the test of time, and we still get together a few times a year, reminiscing. The memories we made in Dot will always hold a special place for me.

Chapter 41

Two Of Us

From my earliest memories, Margie has been my guardian, friend, teacher, advocate, and second mother. Long before I started kindergarten, she'd already taught me counting and the alphabet. She had an eager student in me; I wanted to be smart like her. In elementary school, I found myself bored and unchallenged, so I took it upon myself to tutor the other kids. Teachers would call Ma because after finishing my classwork, I'd leave my seat and begin helping classmates as if it were my job. I was simply copying my big sister and best friend, teaching and helping, just like she'd done for me. At the end of each school year, like a nerd, I asked all my teachers for their leftover worksheets to re-do over the summer. While other kids played house or went to summer camp, my favorite activity was playing school.

At a family gathering one Fourth of July, Marj reflected on those times, saying, "It gave me a sense of fulfillment to see what I could teach you. Plus, it kept you occupied so I could give Ma a break. I loved to learn, and teaching you gave me something to do, an escape."

Margie loved me, but I was a pest when I was little. I stuck to her like glue, constantly getting in her way and demanding to go wherever she went. I wanted to be with her all the time. At ten, she preferred being outside with her friends on Glendale Street, playing Old Lady Witch and Red Rover. If she was inside, she liked being with Ma, watching soaps and game shows—not hanging out with her five-year-old sister. I would cry until she gave in.

Dale's burgers sizzled on the grill while Bill rationed the sparklers and firecrackers, just enough to keep things lively. Marj and I sat with our wine as Eric and Taylor argued over who got what fireworks. She began reminiscing about the old days.

"When you were like four or five, you used to beg me to take you on walks. So, I'd take you out and force you to walk and walk," Marj recalled. "You'd cry, 'I wanna go home now.' I'd say, 'No, you wanted to walk. Now, keep walking.' Then, late at night, I'd lie in bed thinking about it, and I felt bad for what I did."

But Margie was my savior, my safe haven. Whenever there was chaos at home, I found solace by her side. Ma couldn't comfort me when Dad was beating one of my siblings, or her, when she tried to intervene. I would shrink in fear, hiding near Margie in our shared bedroom until the noise of the beatings passed.

Plenty of kids I knew in Dorchester came from tough homes, some with no positive role models. But I was one of the lucky ones. I had Margie, who taught me academic appreciation, social graces, and etiquette.

Margie didn't get into as much mischief as the other Dyer kids, but she had her moments. At fifteen, she briefly smoked cigarettes with her friends to fit in.

She worked at Bradlees Department Store after school, and earned a healthy paycheck for a teenager. She always had money to buy herself clothes and to go out with her friends. On Saturdays, she went into downtown Boston with her friend Nicole, who regularly stole things. One time, the girls went shopping at Jordan

Marsh and Margie, taking her cue from Nicole, stole a blouse, slipping it into her Woolworth's bag. As she stepped outside, two security guards pulled her aside. Ma had to take the train into downtown to pick her up. When she got home, Dad punished her with a beating.

Between the police interrogation and our father's wrath, Margie never stole again. She avoided the trouble that landed our brothers on his bad side on a regular basis.

From a young age, Margie often took me downtown in nicer weather to people-watch and window-shop. When we moved to Savin Hill, Joan was always included in the outings. Margie's plans with Joan and me, and sometimes just me alone, were simple, yet fulfilling and enriching:

"We'll take the train to Park Street and walk through the Common to Copley Square. We can end at the Prudential Center and then walk back again."

Each time, I made sure to ask if we could visit our distant Quaker ancestor's bronze statue on the State House lawn. "Can we go see the Mary Dyer statue?"

We would wing it, meandering through downtown all day, but spending time with my sister was enough for me. For Joan and me, it was the perfect day, a two-mile round-trip walk lasting us hours, filled with cheap, endless fun. The three of us would sometimes take in the Swan Boat rides in the Public Garden. There were free-spirited people to see on the Boston Common. Hari Krishnas chanted and banged on tambourines, while a short walk found folk musicians playing guitar and singing. Margie would give me a quarter to throw in their empty guitar case. A guy we looked for each time on the Common played nothing but Beatles songs, and with Margie's help, I wrote him a poem called "The Music Man" and presented it to him one day. A twelve-year-old kid's gesture acknowledging his talent and appreciating the Beatles humbled him.

I'll never forget Captain Don, the tattooed sword swallower, and some church hippies offering free personality tests to lure young recruits. Joan and I loved doing the quiz while Margie shopped at a used record store on Newbury Street. At the church, we would listen to their pitch long enough to get our personality results. When they asked us to sign up for their church, I used Jimmy's phone-prank tricks, writing down a fake number—(617) 637-1234, the time-of-day service.

Taking in the scenes downtown exposed me to all kinds of cultures and personalities. A tourist city and diverse in its own right, Boston brought us shoulder to shoulder with people from all over the world, widening my growing sense of it.

There were always perverts trying to flirt with young girls on the Red Line, so we learned to stay on guard.

I benefited not only from Margie's financial generosity, but also from her academic and social guidance. Thanks to her, I was never interested in getting into serious trouble. While I dabbled in mischief during high school and college, I stayed on the right path when Margie was around.

On many Sundays, Margie took me to the "Beatles Festival" movie day at the Harvard Square Theatre in Cambridge, and we spent the afternoon watching back-to-back Beatles movies for one admission. They showed three of the Beatles' five films: *Yellow Submarine, Let It Be, Magical Mystery Tour, Help!, A Hard Day's Night*, and George Harrison's *Concert for Bangladesh*. Watching the Beatles on the big screen, I felt like I was getting to know them personally. It made me wish I could meet them. Spending a Beatles-filled Sunday afternoon with my big sister felt so special.

Before Margie, I'd never eaten at a restaurant. When I was eleven, she took me to a lunch spot on Tremont Street. Watching people eat and the employees work in the busy restaurant fascinated me. I didn't know it was customary to leave a tip on the table for the waitstaff. When I saw Margie do it, I snatched the bills off the table.

"What are you doing? Don't leave the tip money out in the open! Someone's gonna steal it and the waitress'll think we cheaped-out on her!"

"No, goofball. That's how it's done. No one's gonna steal it."

To be sure, I moved the dollar bills under my water glass as we left. Coming from where we did, I couldn't quite trust the idea.

In 1979, Margie graduated from Boston High School and she enrolled in Job Corps, a vocational school in western Massachusetts. There, she met Dale, her future husband, who was from central Massachusetts.

One weekend, Marj brought Dale home to meet the family. She'd warned him ahead of time he'd be meeting a bunch of "characters" and might see a few odd things. Sure enough, when he walked into the kitchen, Ma had clothes draped across the curtain rods and shirts on hangers over the door frames to dry.

Marj covered her eyes for a second. "I told you it would be weird."

But Dale thought everyone was very cool and down-to-earth, and ended up having a blast all weekend.

In 1981, Marj and Dale got engaged. The family was thrilled. I was so happy when she asked me to be her maid of honor. Dale fit right in with our crazy family, keeping us all laughing with his quick-witted humor. Shortly after their engagement, they got an apartment with Jim in Quincy, which was always buzzing with lively parties and late-night card games.

Marj and Dale married in 1983 and together, they've raised two wonderful sons. Their loving, enduring marriage has long been an example that others look up to.

I don't know how Marj developed such social, emotional, and intellectual astuteness, given our early home life. I suspect she tapped into her *inner light* and innate wisdom early on. She looked to role models at school, observed healthier families, and quietly passed what she learned on to me. Despite our upbringing, she cultivated a sharp curiosity, sound judgment, and a diplomacy beyond her years. She has always indulged and nurtured my insatiable curiosity, encouraging me to stretch further and reach higher. *If I needed someone,* she's always been there, and is still my biggest influence (the Beatles aside).

Chapter 42

Magical Misery Tour

IN 1980, I graduated from the Grover Cleveland with respectable grades; Cheryl was already in suburban Braintree, getting ready to start high school there. Joan's father, a postal employee, worked double shifts to send her to St. Gregory High School in Dorchester, rather than enroll her in Boston Public Schools for four more years. I, however, wasn't so lucky. I was bused forty-five minutes away to Mission Hill in Roxbury to attend Boston English High School. I was nervous. My brothers' troubled busing experiences and dropouts loomed large in my mind.

On my first day at school, I saw I was in the White minority, like in my previous schools. At fourteen, worry about my safety came back. I leaned on a familiar strategy and made a point of getting to know the other White freshman girls. Eight of us—from Roslindale, Hyde Park, Southie, and Dorchester—were scattered across different homerooms, but we found ways to stay close.

In the bathrooms, girls would ask to try on our jewelry or accessories and sometimes take them anyway—slipping a bracelet off a wrist, pocketing our cigarettes or lipstick. They had small ways of intimidating us, like flicking the back of our hair as we passed into the stalls. Before long, we never went to the bathroom alone. We made safety pacts with each other:

"Carol, go to the bathroom with me after period six art class."

"Okay, but then you have to come with me after science class tomorrow."

One afternoon in the bathroom, a group of girls moved in around us. One stepped closer. "You got some pretty hair, honkey-bitch." I kept quiet, too scared to respond. Another blew cigarette smoke into Carol's face and asked to try on her earrings. She shook her head. "My godmother gave me these. I don't take them off. Sorry"

"I'll give them back. What—you don't trust me?"

Carol said no again. The girl brought her cigarette close and singed a few ends of Carol's permed hair. When another student opened the door, the girls shifted just enough for us to squeeze past and get out—never even using the bathroom. After that, all eight of us stuck together more.

English High was massive, with ten floors of escalators carrying hundreds of students to classes. It felt more like a Macy's department store than a school—Language Arts on eight, Science on three, History on nine. Between periods, the escalators bottle-necked. It was like the Running of the Brides sale at Filene's Base-ment—hordes of women shoving for a cheap wedding gown. We were packed in tight, and things could happen fast. One morning, in the mob of students, I was on the down escalator when a kid on the up escalator reached over and ripped the thin gold chain from my friend Joanne's neck. I kept my eyes and ears more open after that.

With so many new kids around me, I started finding ways to go along with the crowd and took more risks. I tried getting high before school once. Being so crammed in with the crowds made me more paranoid than I already was. Jammed hallways and escalators were no place to be high and off guard. I never did it again. I saved my partying for weekends.

As the school year went on, I drifted more towards drugs and alcohol. I obtained a fake ID so I could make all the "packie" runs to the liquor store for my friends. Smoking pot and drinking led to more risk-taking, and I started stealing more. I gave myself a five-finger discount on bottles of Riunite wine and clothes from department stores. With Margie not around as much and Ma working full time, I fell in with an unspoken rule: *If it ain't nailed down, take it.*

A night after a concert with Cheryl was a perfect example of my teenage freebie philosophy. Leaving the Orpheum Theatre, we saw a few older teens getting high, too caught up in their reefer rally to notice us. I noticed a cool-looking leather biker jacket draped over a fire hydrant. I whispered to Cheryl, "I want that jacket. It looks like it would fit me."

She wanted nothing to do with it but she knew she couldn't stop me. I slipped it on under my dungaree jacket and we quickly tore out of Hamilton Place. The guys saw the jacket was gone—and so were we. They chased us toward Tremont Street, yelling obscenities. We sprinted through oncoming traffic to Park Street Station, through the turnstiles and down the stairs, catching an Ashmont train just before the doors closed.

I'm not proud of the theft, nor any of the others I committed when I was young. It was the Dot Rat life I started falling into. Despite its shady origins, the jacket symbolized the rock and roll lifestyle I yearned for. I never wore it to school, afraid someone would steal it.

Before high school, I'd been a strong student. Now, with no interest in staying in a school that felt unsafe, I cut classes most days after lunch and somehow got away with it. Except for my favorite classes—Art and English, where I liked writing poetry and essays—my grades fell fast, and by the time my final report card came back, I could see where things were headed. I barely passed half my classes.

At the end of my freshman year, I knew those grades—and the poor choices I was making—would carry into the fall if something didn't change.

Margie had attended Jeremiah Burke High School, then Madison Park High School, taking the train to school each day. Feeling unsafe in the neighborhood, she later enrolled at Boston High. There, students split their day between academics and work, and she graduated with honors. Watching her succeed, I wanted to follow suit and get my own academics back on track. Boston High felt like my only hope. I begged Ma to apply for a transfer. When the application went through, I needed to meet with a faculty member for a prescreening interview.

When Ma and I arrived, the guidance counselor asked me to read a paragraph from an open page of *Treasure Island*, which I did easily. He pushed his glasses to the tip of his nose, eyeing me with a look that said, "You're kidding, right?"

He peered over his frames, his expression softening. "You're an excellent reader, Mary. But I'm afraid... you don't belong here. This is a school for kids who struggle academically." My stomach dropped. *Oh, crud. I should have downplayed it.* I knew I had to advocate for myself.

"Margie was an honor student, and you let her come here. If you don't take me, I'll quit school. I won't graduate or do anything with my life. Three of my brothers dropped out of Dot High, the Burke, and Madison Park because of the trouble there. Most days, unless I have Art or English, I cut out after lunch so I don't have to stay or take the bus home. It's too dangerous. I can't go back. I need to be transferred here."

Ma gave him a small shrug, as if to say, "She's said it all."

Pleading my case seemed to make him realize he'd be denying a promising student a chance at a better future. It helped that I was the sister of an alumna. Thankfully, he enrolled me for the 1981-1982 school year. I was flooded with relief, knowing I wouldn't become another dropout statistic.

At Boston High, my days were filled with early-morning work commutes and afternoon classes. The school didn't bus students, so I took the Red Line, then the Green Line train, to get to my 6:00 a.m. job at a gourmet coffee shop on Boylston Street. Serving lattes and croissants to mobs of people in the sophisticated Back Bay neighborhood exposed me to an eclectic mix of people. I waited on corporate executives, Emerson and Berklee College students, employees from posh retail stores and hotels, and art gallery cura-tors from upscale Newbury Street.

At noon, I clocked out, scarfed down a croissant, and walked the half mile to school for four hours of classes, getting home in time for supper and homework. It made for a long day, with little room for trouble. I was grateful to be in a school where I could focus on my school work, not on watching my back.

There was a waiting list to get into Boston High, so we all knew how fortunate we were to attend. Students wanted to be there, the administration kept order, and kids from all backgrounds got along well—*ebony and ivory*—creating an atmosphere that felt more harmonious than divided, like school had been before busing started in third grade.

The work-study model set Boston High apart. Students not headed to college were steered toward corporate jobs, while college-bound students like me followed a more academic track. Many students arrived in the afternoon in suits after working morning shifts at banks and large Boston companies. Some went on to become bank managers and executives.

In my forties, I reconnected with Kristin, an old pal from the Grover middle school. Turned out, her high school freshman year experience mirrored mine. After a year of commuting by MBTA bus to a neighborhood where she didn't feel safe, her mother withdrew her. Like me, Kristin pleaded with Boston High to let her transfer in so she could focus and graduate. Because she attended morning classes and I was in the PM session, we never crossed paths at the school, unaware we were both there. We've stayed in touch, often trading memories of the old days in Dot, including some from our time at the Grover. Those memories remind us how precarious things had become and make us grateful for the steadier ground we later found at Boston High.

I'm grateful to Marj for her encouragement, and to the faculty at Boston High School—they got me to college and saved me from becoming another dropout. Looking back, I wish my brothers had pursued that option before giving up on their troubled schools. I listened to Marj and my teachers about staying focused on my studies and living up to my potential. I knew they believed in me, so I believed in myself.

Chapter 43

Not a Second Time

WHEN I WAS YOUNG, I threw tantrums over the tiniest things. My mother would say, "You're just like your father." I hated the comparison. I never wanted to be like him, yet I may have been copying him subconsciously. Still, I know his tenacity runs through my blood. That determination has served me well in many life situations, especially when I needed to escape a toxic, abusive relationship.

In my junior year of college, I started dating someone I really liked. After four months of dating, we rented a studio apartment together. At first, everything was great. I was on cloud nine, juggling college and playing house while he worked full time. He paid all the household bills and showered me with affection and surprise gifts. As fall turned to early winter, his flowers and gifts thinned, and he turned a cold shoulder. Then he gave silence and small slights. Being young and immature, I demanded, not asked, for answers. He got colder, and our arguments sharpened.

On New Year's Eve at our apartment, after the party hats came off and the keg ran dry, I nagged at him, insisting he help me clean up the butt-filled ashtrays, empty bottles, and Doritos crushed into the rug. He slapped me across the face in front of our guests. I was stunned. Not just by the slap, but by how the few men lingering quietly went back to their beers. My college friend was the only one who spoke up. "You friggin' coward—Mary, are you okay?"

I'd seen my mother endure years of abuse, and I swore I would never be in the same situation. Yet, as the months followed, we fell into a destructive cycle, with that first physical altercation setting the tone for our future conflicts. He should have known physical force was the wrong way to engage with me. I was still an ornery Dot Rat, and after years of being bullied at home and at school, I didn't take well to being pushed around. My mindset was to meet aggression with aggression. *If he hits me, I'll hit 'im back harder* At the same time, I realized I was becoming someone I didn't want to be. I heard the chorus of George's "Isn't It a Pity" in my head.

The turning point came one night before my overnight shift where I worked part time. We were already fighting when he told me to get out, and never come back. When I didn't move fast enough, he grabbed my cat by the scruff of the neck and held it up, threatening to kill it. I put my Himalayan, Dusty, into his carrier and put him in my car. The boyfriend followed me outside to take my house key away. As he leaned into the open passenger door to grab it from me, I heard Paul in my head singing, "Step on the gas and wipe that tear away." This person had grown up in a quiet suburb and his street smarts were no match for mine. I fought dirty. I hit the gas and sent him tumbling to the curb, the passenger door slamming shut as I cut the wheel hard.

I worked my night shift, leaving Dusty in my manager's office all night. I wasn't going to go back to Ma and Charlie's. I'd gotten a taste of independence and felt I'd come too far to go backward. I was determined to go to the "home" where I belonged and sort out my relationship, so I came back to the apartment the next day. When I walked in with Dusty, no questions were asked—we just made up. Still, in the back of my mind I didn't hold out much hope; deep down I knew I needed a Plan B—and the time to piece it together. We held on for another two months, but after a few more explosive fights, I knew the relationship had to end. I didn't know where I would go next, but nothing was going to stop me from finishing college.

I quietly plotted my exit. During this turbulent time, Marj was my main confidant and support. "You gotta get out of there, Mary. You can stay with us as long as you need to."

I landed a live-in nanny job, which gave me a safe place to stay. When the day came to leave, a friend of mine adopted Dusty, with the promise that I could visit him anytime. Billy and three of his friends packed up their vehicles and moved me out. Marj and Dale let me store all my belongings in their basement. The now ex-boyfriend came home that day to a stripped apartment, devoid of everything except what he'd come in with—his clothes and some music gear. I owned the rest.

It was the first and last time a man ever put his hands on me. Unlike my mother's generation, I had choices. I also had a fiery stubbornness in my veins. I graduated college the following year and never looked back. Never again would I sacrifice my independence in exchange for a man supporting me financially. It came at too high a price.

As a battered wife, my mother had a completely different experience. Her life was rooted in an era when women relied on men for financial support, and people rarely intervened in couples' domestic struggles. Wives seldom fought back or voiced their opinions against their husbands.

I love watching '70s sitcom reruns, especially *Good Times*. In one episode, Florida sits in on a "Women's Awareness" meeting where one of the women casually mentions being hit by her husband, as if it were just part of married life. Other women in the meeting chime in, complaining that their husbands believe a woman's best work is in the kitchen or the bedroom.

Watching the episode five decades later reminds me that women of my mother's generation didn't have a fraction of the rights I have. Back then, there was no easy way out, and women could risk losing their children if they were seen as breaking up the family.

Until 1974, women couldn't open a bank account, rent an apartment, or take out a credit card or car loan in their own name. They needed a male relative to co-sign. They were limited in where they could go, what they could say, and how much control they had over their own bodies—even within marriage, without consent.

When I came of age, enough had changed for me to imagine a different path. At twenty-two, I understood the challenges my mother had faced and was determined never to experience the same hardships. I knew hard work and focus, along with support from my closest allies, would get me places.

Chapter 44

It's Getting Hard to Be Someone

When I chose elementary education as my college major, Charlie tried to dissuade me from it. He was a former Boston public school shop teacher who left the profession after a traumatic experience.

In the late '70s, Boston was still raw from the unrest surrounding school desegregation. Charlie taught vocational classes at a middle school in Dorchester, so his homeroom was the woodworking shop. One afternoon, after he kept three students for detention, they overpowered him and injured his hand on a table saw. He left teaching for a security guard job which paid even less than his menial teacher's salary. He didn't want me to face similar hardships.

"Mary, teaching is hard. The pay is abysmal, parents don't always support teachers, and some days, it's like glorified babysitting."

"I'm not expecting to get rich, Charlie." I said. "As long as I can pay my bills."

"Do what you will. It's a noble undertaking, but don't say I didn't warn you."

At eighteen, I believed I'd have a better outcome. I ignored Charlie's advice and pursued my degree.

My first teaching job at an elementary school was, as Charlie had predicted, hard work for very low pay. On weekends, I drove import cars coming off ships at the Black Falcon Terminal to make ends meet. After three exhausting years, I switched to teaching special needs students. The salary was still low, but I finally had health insurance.

Growing up poor, it was hard to imagine doing anything other than low-paying, general labor jobs. That was what pushed me to go to college. But after four years of being worn down and broke, I found myself thinking: *general labor would be a picnic compared to this.*

I struggled to pay my living expenses, buying groceries on credit cards. Student loans were deferred multiple times, adding to the debt. Still, graduating college gave me the confidence to do things on my own terms, starting with leaving a profession where I was barely getting by. There had to be a way to earn what I was worth. Without a plan in place, I surrendered. One Friday, I walked into an employment agency in downtown Boston.

"I can type ninety words per minute, answer phones, and I'm ready to work today." By Monday, I was a receptionist at a company where I was treated well and paid enough to support myself and even afford a new car.

My "dream small" mentality stretched beyond its comfort zone when I entered the competitive corporate world. It's where I began to thrive. I learned to move at a breakneck pace, handling back-to-back deadlines, navigating office politics, and reading people in boardrooms and break rooms alike. The experience sharpened my skills and showed me what it meant to work with integrity in a professional setting. In my younger days, I lacked the skill and patience it required, but over time I came to rely on a gentler kind of persuasion built on teamwork, trust, and camaraderie.

Within a few years, I paid off my mountain of student loans and moved from managing debt to building a future I assumed I'd be navigating alone. Managing a team later on taught me how to interact more effectively with others in every arena of life. I had grown up, and my teaching days were a distant speck in the rearview mirror.

Meanwhile, my love life still lagged. By my late thirties, I finally admitted I'd been following a questionable dating strategy—choosing party boys, or men who looked out for #1, and it wasn't me. Too often, I gave away my worth to men who liked what I had to offer, but they just weren't buying. They were window-shopping. I was told I was too much of this, not enough of that—never enough. And, if I'm honest, I was guilty of the same churn, mistaking wit for character and swagger for substance. One after another, I dated guys who made promises they couldn't—or wouldn't—keep. My radar was tuned to the ones who needed saving, fixing, or mothering. I thought I was choosing love, but really I picked smooth talkers posing as Mr. Right. It was my own doing.

By my forties, I took an honest look at my choices and got clear about what I deserved. But by then, most available men were divorced with young kids and carried complicated baggage. My carry-on baggage fit neatly under the seat in front of me, while theirs had to be checked. Some of the higher-caliber men who showed interest in me were married. I knew I deserved to be someone's priority, not leftovers they could just reheat when it was convenient. I focused on my career, singing, and an active lifestyle, surrounded by a loving family, great friends, and a circle of talented musicians to inspire me. If love came, great. If not, I was content being single and independent. What mattered most wasn't whether I found love but the bonds I already had.

Chapter 45

A Day in the Life

One Memorial Day, we celebrated Marj and Dale's birthdays, along with their son Taylor's, as we always did. Cold beers were passed around on the big back deck while Dale's steak tips and hot dogs sizzled on the grill. The weather was perfect. Marj and Dale always made sure the elders were included—Ma, Uncle Bob, Dale's two elderly uncles, and Hattie, their ninety-year-old widow neighbor. Over the years, those gatherings became an important source of connection for all of them as they aged.

Across the street, two young boys were tossing a ball. The older boy kicked it into the road, and the younger one sprinted after it. His mother lunged, catching his shirttail just before he reached the curb.

As if on instinct, Marj rose from her seat, then lowered herself again with a long exhale once his mother secured him. "Cars fly down here doing seventy," she said, relieved he wasn't hurt.

The moment sparked a round of stories about Thom at the same age. He was the most active and sports-oriented sibling. His constant motion as a kid made him the most accident-prone of us, and Ma made more than a few trips to the Carney Hospital emergency room with him.

Bill leaned out of the breezeway slider. "Ma, remember when Tommy fell out of the apricot tree on Hancock Street?"

"How could I forget? I've lost count of how many times he got banged up, but that one was the worst."

Thom defended the scrapes he got into when he was young. "Well, it's not like any adults were around when we were outside playing. And most of the time, the older kids were off doing their own thing. Someone kicked a ball into the tree, so I went and got it."

Tommy, AKA "Monk," could climb just about anything—trees, fences, poles, like a monkey hunting for coconuts. Whenever one of us needed a daredevil, whether it was to scale a fence or rescue a ball, he scrambled after it for us.

When he was seven, he got about twelve feet up into an apricot tree and a limb snapped. He crashed into a wooden fence on the way down before hitting the ground. The fall left him with a broken arm, a fractured collarbone, and a concussion. In agony, he crawled into the house and went straight to bed, terrified of what the old man might do if he found out. In our house, getting hurt didn't always mean seeking help—it meant risking a beating.

Ma found him injured and crying in bed. Miraculously, Dad didn't hit the roof—he must've been in a good mood that day. She got him to rush her and Tommy to Carney Hospital, where they patched him up. Tommy spent the summer healing and was ready to start second grade on time in the fall.

Bill brought up another Thom debacle. "And what about the time you split your head open diving into the shallow end at the Marshall pool?"

Thom sipped his Natty, searching for a comeback. "Well, yeah, that was just a dumb kid move."

Talking about Thom's childhood scrapes pulled me back. I

glanced across at the young boy from moments before, and suddenly I was four again, remembering an accident with a neighbor girl.

It was an early, quiet Sunday morning. I stood alone in front of our house on Hancock Street, bored, looking around for someone to play with. I'm not sure why no one was watching me.

Eileen, a little girl from across the street, saw me and called out for me to come and play on her back porch. I yelled back, "No, I'm not supposed to cross the street. Come over to my house."

"Oooh-kay..." Eileen hesitated, knowing her parents didn't let her cross the street alone either. She called over, "You look for cars! Say go, and I'll run over to your side."

Where were our parents or older siblings? Why were two preschool girls out playing alone on a busy city street?

I glanced up and down Hancock Street, confident in my four-year-old logic: if I didn't see anything big and loud, it must be safe. "Okay, go!"

The memory of the car hitting her is gone from my mind.

The next thing I remember, I was playing in our yard with Tommy and Billy. I don't even remember how I got there. Out of nowhere, Dad appeared, barking, "Stay in the yard!" as he slammed the tall wooden gate shut.

It didn't feel like he was angry with us. It felt more like he was protecting us from something, but what?

We did as we were told. We played on the swing set, the striped legs lifting and pounding back down, the rhythm carrying on as if nothing had happened.

It was like being in a waking dream, trying to understand... Did I cause something? Why was there commotion out front? I heard adults yelling and a siren blaring. Why did Dad look worried? Something was going on, but I couldn't make sense of it.

Chaos and commotion were a daily part of life at our house, so it didn't feel out of the ordinary. I was too young to comprehend what had just happened.

The next day, I learned Eileen had been hit by a car and had broken her leg. Some of the kids in the neighborhood told me it was my fault, and I carried some burden and guilt about the confusing event. Afterward, I never played with Eileen again. Maybe our parents decided it was best we avoid each other. Whatever the reason, two little girls had been outside alone, and one paid a dear price for it.

Chapter 46

They Took Me Where I Should Not Go

With my siblings and I on the topic of childhood, another memory of mine surfaced. It was a sight burned into my young brain, and I shared it with my family.

"Back when I was about four or five, two older kids on Glendale Street took me to see a dead guy!"

"What?"

"Who?"

The questions rang around the lunch table, none of them having heard about this before.

"Well, he wasn't really dead." I gave a chuckle and told my siblings about how at that young age, some boys on Glendale approached me, saying, "Hey, there's a dead guy in the alley up at the yellow house!" One boy urged me on. "Don't believe me? I'll walk you up there now."

We headed up Glendale Street, past about fifteen houses and the boys stopped. "Go ahead, chicken, walk down the alley. You'll see him lying there dead at the end."

Frightened but young and dumb enough to be curious, I made my way down the long, narrow alley, past the garbage cans leaning against the house. At the end, a young man with a goatee lay sprawled on the concrete, unmoving. The smell emanating from him reminded me of my father—familiar but indescribable to me as a preschooler, as I hadn't yet learned the concept of alcohol. His mouth hung partially open and his eyes were half closed, unmoving. He looked dead. A thin stream of pink-tinged liquid trickled from the corner of his mouth into an expanding puddle of vomit. Frightened with goosebumps, I bolted from the scene, back down the alley to the safety of Glendale Street. Years later, when I understood what alcohol was, I realized it was a drunk teenager who had passed out in his vomit—something most kids don't understand, which is why we all assumed he was dead.

Fear and confusion were things I was no stranger to, whether it was from the so-called dead guy or the constant violence at home. Another time, I found myself caught up in a far more unsettling experience. This time, it happened with a movie I had no business watching.

I remembered back to 1973 when I was seven. One of our older brothers took me, Tommy, and Billy to watch the PG movie *The Sting* at the Puritan Mall Cinema. When our movie let out, the boys spotted an unattended door to the second theater showing the new R-rated film, *The Exorcist*.

"We can sneak in," I heard them whispering. "*The Exorcist* just started ten minutes ago." Since the boys were responsible for me, I had no choice but to go with them.

Unaware of the horror awaiting me in the theater, I took my seat. For the first half hour of the movie, I was unfazed. Then it turned. The demonic voice of Regan was the first jolt, followed by her gory, disfigured appearance, and terror took hold.

Billy was cracking up laughing through it, because he knew it was fake, but fear paralyzed me, watching her grotesque face contort into gruesome expressions. Two swollen, white eye sockets rolled up into her head and her neck swelled up while she floated off the bed in her nightgown. The movie's most damaging impact on me was seeing a little girl my same age, ravaged by demonic possession, her eerie devil voice tearing through my psyche. Coupled with the violence I experienced at home, it was over-whelming. But I was stuck with the boys until the movie ended.

For a couple years afterward, whenever I saw my shadow on my bedroom wall at night, I thought it was the devil coming to possess me. Watching the movie so young disturbed me for many years, shaking what little sense of safety I'd known. Some things aren't meant for young children. But boys will be boys. *Jaws* kept me out of Savin Hill Beach the summer of '75 but I was older and came to realize it was all special effects.

Chapter 47

If You Don't Know Where You're Headed, Any Street Will Get You There

On July 4th, my family gathered for Ma's upcoming 74th birthday. We were listening to music and enjoying a great cookout. In the kitchen, some of my siblings were reminiscing about the July 4th celebrations at Ronan Park growing up. They swapped stories about walking the "100 Steps" on Hancock Street, a steep path of stairs that led to a narrow side street of triple-decker houses.

Thom brought up his legendary "Thomas Spit-bomb Diarrhea" story.

"What about the time I got lost in Mattapan on July 4th?"

He was referring to an incident we'd heard many times over, with Ma and our older siblings' details as the backdrop.

Ma often took us to hilly Ronan Park when we were young, and the 4th of July was a huge deal there. We would join hundreds of other families for relay races, tug-of-war games, and treasure hunts, followed by fireworks at night. The crowds were massive, so parents had to keep a tight grip on their kids.

On July 4, 1969, Ma took all eight of us up to Ronan Park. If she had to tend to a scraped knee or a fussing kid, she'd put Bobby,

Johnny, or Danny in charge of us until they ditched us to flirt with teenage girls.

Ma could delegate like George Washington holding down Valley Forge. "Bobby, take Margie to the porta-potty. Johnny, take Tommy and Billy to the clown show. Danny, get Jimmy out of that mud hole."

We were always pestering and interrupting Ma—soiled underpants, loose shoelaces, hungry bellies. Whines followed her all day at Ronan Park.

"Maah, I'm staah-vin'. Can I have a Fluff-a-nut-ah sandwich?"

From her side, someone pleading: "Ma, can I get a Hoodsie?" —a small cup of vanilla and chocolate ice cream. She needed five pairs of eyes to keep track of us. Somehow, she always managed. Except on this day.

One of the older boys took their eyes off five-year-old Tommy for a moment and he wandered off. Ma and the kids looked all over for him—searching the swings, the benches, the perimeter of the park—shouting, "Tommy! Tommy!" By then, Ma's panic and dread had set in. They couldn't find him. Other parents and kids joined the search. She had no idea he was already long gone.

Ma flagged down a horse-mounted cop to help.

"We'll find him, Mrs. Dyer," Officer Kenneally assured her.

An hour later, an officer drove Ma and us younger kids home, with still no sign of Tommy, while the older boys continued searching the park.

"We'll call you as soon as we hear something, Mrs. Dyer. Kids get lost from time to time on July 4th, but we always find them. We'll find your boy."

Ma was a nervous wreck, pacing and praying Tommy would be home before Dad woke up to start his evening job pumping gas. Three hours had passed with no update. Finally, the phone rang.

"Mrs. Dyer, we found your son, Thomas Spit-Bomb Diarrhea," the officer chuckled. "We'll drop him home in ten minutes."

Ma nearly dropped the phone in relief. As she hung up, she muttered, "Why the hell would he give a crazy name like that?"

Reminiscing that July 4th, Dan reminded us of the reason.

"The old man always told us, 'If you ever get in trouble with the cops, give 'em a fake name—"

"I gave the best fake name I could think of," Thom shrugged. He'd walked close to five miles from Ronan Park to Mattapan, where he showed up in the yard of a family of Black kids playing outside. Their grandmother, concerned for a "lost little White boy," called the police.

When the cruiser pulled up to the house with Tommy, Ma was grateful Dad was still asleep, none the wiser. Thomas Spit-Bomb Diarrhea's tour ended without consequence, and Ma had dodged another bullet.

Chapter 48

Our Mother Should Know

As Ma aged, Dickie Dyer was a name she rarely spoke, usually brushing past it if it came up. But for us kids, the shadow of him lingered, and we sometimes pressed her for glimpses into what life had really been like for her, beyond what we heard or witnessed.

On Thanksgiving 2009, our conversations over pumpkin pie turned to the usual topic of the old days and, of course, the Dickie Dyer stories surfaced. Usually tight-lipped, Ma openly shared some incidents which were new and surprising to us. Perhaps she felt less guarded now that Charlie was gone, or maybe age had softened her reserve—or maybe both.

Dan, delving deeper into the past, brought up a provocative question. "So, Ma, throughout all those years, didn't anyone ever step up to defend you from the old man?"

Ma waved him off. "I don't know, Dan. It was so long ago."

He probed a bit further. "What about all your sisters' husbands? Did any of them help you?"

"No. I'm sure they were all afraid of him."

Then, in an unexpected turn, Ma paused, reflecting for a moment. "Well, actually, my father beat him up once."

We exchanged curious glances. This was new to us.

"Your father beat me up so bad, I was in the hospital for a week. Back when we were living on Freeport Street."

"So, around 1955?" I asked.

She sighed heavily. "I guess. I don't know."

This new revelation caught us off guard. Grandpa had always seemed so mild-mannered. I never knew he had it in him.

Dan nodded, urging her on to share more. "So, what happened?"

"When your father got out of jail, he headed right for Foley's Tavern like he always did. My father dragged him off the barstool and kicked the shit out of him outside."

We were intrigued. Dan urged her on for more. "Good for Grandpa. He kicked his ass good then, huh?"

Ma, who rarely swore, answered like it was nothing. "Yeah. Your father was shitfaced drunk, so it wasn't too hard to do. It didn't change anything. You know that asshole never changed."

She paused, as another memory surfaced. All eyes went to Ma. This was getting good.

"Then there was a time in the pantry on Bloomfield Street... I hit him pretty good."

It was hard to know which time she meant—we'd lost count of all the times he had her cornered and she tried to fight him off.

I jumped in, leveraging my youngest birth order to get her to open up. "Which time? I was too little to remember. Did you kick his ass?"

Ma's expression shifted, a flicker of pride in her eyes. "He had me cornered, so I grabbed a glass ketchup bottle. It was one of those big, heavy bottles. And I smashed it over his head. That got him off me for a little while."

We smiled, feeling a rush of pride. *Good for Ma. She fought back.*

When it seemed she was finished, she leaned back, as though

turning something over in her mind. "Well, there was another time…"

Dan's face lit up. "What? Tell us!"

She stopped. "Oh, it doesn't matter, it's ancient history."

"You can't leave us hanging!" Marj chided.

Ma sighed and gave in. "I did try to kill him once."

A sudden silence swept the room. We listened in, like Gordie's Lard Ass story in the movie *Stand by Me*, waiting for the big reveal. Ma went on.

"Do you remember your father used to keep a glass mayonnaise jar full of ice water on his nightstand, so he wouldn't get dehydrated from drinking?"

Dan moved her along, grinning. "Yeah, yeah. I remember the jar. What about it?"

"Well, one night, I emptied all his sleeping pills into the jar. He drank it all but nothing happened." She paused. "Nothing could kill him!"

Bill was eager for more. "So, what happened? Did he have to get his stomach pumped?"

Ma shook her head, frustration crossing her face. "No. The bastard just slept for three days. He wouldn't die!"

Thom chuckled. "So… Did he ever find out it was you?"

"No, he just thought he had the flu with a bad hangover and stayed in bed."

It was a rare conversation with Ma, one which gave more insights into what she lived through with Dad.

Old age sure brought Ma's memories into clearer focus.

Chapter 49

Cry Baby, Cry

A FEW MINUTES LATER, the topic of the first baby named Billy came up—the one who had died in early 1957, presumably from SIDS. His death had always seemed straightforward, rarely mentioned. But this time it was told differently. Since Billy was given the same name, he asked, "Ma, why did you name me after a dead baby?"

"I don't remember," she said. "I think your father named the first Billy after his uncle. He liked him a lot. So, we named you Billy, too."

I had to know more, so I dummied up to keep her talking. "So... How did the first Billy die again?"

I didn't expect her to share anything new, but the story she proceeded to tell was something none of us had heard before.

IN DECEMBER 1956, Ma welcomed baby Billy #1 to the Dyer family. His early days were difficult because of colic. She said he cried nonstop at night. Despite Ma's best efforts to soothe him, sleep eluded him, Ma, Dad, and his two big brothers, Bobby and Johnny.

Dr. Linden, the family doctor, reassured Ma, "Mrs. Dyer, your baby is healthy. Colicky babies usually cry because of stomach indigestion. Most pass this stage by three months. Be patient, dear —it's exhausting, but it won't last forever."

Night after night, Ma followed the doctor's advice—rocking, burping, holding him upright—but Billy never slept. In January, when he was six weeks old, Ma had another tough night with him. After a half hour of sleep, he'd wake up crying again, and the pattern continued.

At 11:30 p.m., Dad came home from his part-time evening job at a gas station. It was a bone-chilling two-degree night of pumping gas, checking tire pressures and oil dipsticks, and washing frozen windshields. His nagging shoulder bursitis ached like hell, and his back was acting up again. He desperately needed sleep and was glad to be home.

Nestled under the covers in the drafty, sixty-degree bedroom, the piercing wails of baby Billy sliced through Dad's throbbing spine like a burning dagger. Ma was up and down, out of bed, back in bed, tending to Billy. She tried to comfort him, but he only settled momentarily before erupting into frantic cries once more. This pushed Dad's patience and nerves over the edge.

Ma threw the bed covers off to tend to Billy again.

"You stay here, Dot," Dad ordered. "I'll check on him this time." This was noble for him to offer since he was never any help to her around the house, let alone with "baby duty."

Exhausted and grateful for a break, Ma said she closed her eyes and instantly dozed off. Billy never cried again. When she finally awoke at 3:00 a.m. to feed him, she found him cold to the touch and unresponsive, his pillow turned toward his face instead of tucked on the side of him. Panic set in. She wrapped him in his blanket and ran to the kitchen, dialing the operator for emergency help.

Dad followed, wincing, one hand at his lower back. He lifted the limp baby from her arms. "He's gone," he murmured.

Emergency responders arrived seven minutes later, but it was too late. Based on his core body temperature, the coroner estimated Billy had died a few hours earlier. Ma was devastated, questioning how her baby could have died so suddenly.

"Dr. Linden said he was healthy," she cried, looking to Dad for comfort. But he offered only a practical response. "He's had a rough time. We'll bury him in Blue Hills Cemetery with my uncle."

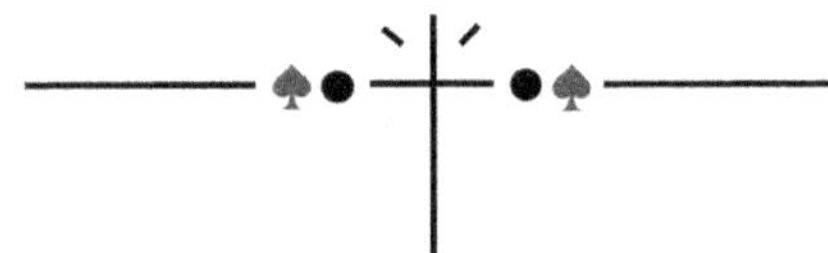

Ma's added details that Thanksgiving offered new glimpses into the tragic loss of our brother, Billy #1.

On a call with Marj the next day, I shared my thoughts about what we'd learned. Had Dad played a role in baby Billy's death? What about the oddly placed pillow? A newborn can't move a pillow. I wondered what really happened to baby Billy. I quietly imagined the big brother I never knew—what he might have been like, who he might have looked like, where he might have fit into our family as the third oldest before Dan, and where his life might have taken him.

Over the years, Ma shared a few pregnancy struggles—two at my father's hands, as far as we know.

During one pregnancy, we were told that on the Tobin Bridge in Boston, he either tried, or at least threatened, to throw her over. We don't know any other details.

In January 1958, at eight months pregnant with Dan, he kicked Ma in the stomach, sending her down a flight of stairs. She carried Dan to term, and he was born healthy.

In 1959, Ma lost a full-term baby girl due to a nuchal cord, where the umbilical cord wraps around the baby's neck. She never said anything more about it. It always seemed straightforward.

In 2024, I ordered Billy #1's death record. The cause of death shows: "suffocation, probable accident."

Given what we know, it's reasonable to wonder if we were all in fetal distress long before any of us were born.

<h1 style="text-align:center">Chapter 50</h1>

<h2 style="text-align:center">Love Comes to Everyone</h2>

BY EARLY 2014, Uncle Bob didn't move around the way he used to. His age had been showing more. He'd relied on a cane for years, but now he could barely take a few steps, even with two people helping. We knew our time with him was limited. During an overnight visit at my house, I brought up the delicate subject of his end-of-life wishes. I wanted to understand what he might want—if he even understood death. Knowing there was space in Dad's plot, I gently broached the subject.

"Uncle Bob, when you go to heaven, do you want to be buried in Dorchester, with your brother Dickie?"

His expression sharpened, and his voice rose with defiance. "N-No! I wanna be buried with my m-muth-uh and f-fath-uh. If Dickie gets outta dat grave, I'll shoot him with my gun so he goes back down in there!"

His adamant stance and animated gestures made me laugh, the humor cutting through the seriousness of the moment. The conversation about Dickie getting out of the grave had become a long running family joke when we first reunited with Uncle Bob, one he relished as much as we did. But beneath the banter this time, his wishes couldn't have been clearer. Like all of us, he wanted to stay as far away from his brother as possible—even in death.

Nine months later, Uncle Bob was admitted to the hospital with severe pneumonia. Marj called to say he was in critical condition and I should come right away if I wanted to say goodbye. I dropped everything and drove straight there, hoping to reach him in time. When I arrived, he wasn't lucid, but I like to think he knew I was there, reminding him of the good times we'd shared during sleepovers at my house and at Marj and Dale's, and all the cookouts we had. I told him how much the family loved having him around, and how Marj and Dan's boys adored him playing Santa Claus every "Chrissum" at their house. I knew how much that meant to him. I didn't say the word goodbye. Instead, I told him I would see him again someday.

Later in the day, Uncle Bob passed away at age eighty-nine. He'd outlived all of his siblings—remarkable given the challenges he was born with and the many years he spent in state care and group homes since age fifteen.

Though his parents' grave was full, the Dorchester cemetery with the trolley running through it made a rare exception, allowing one more smaller urn to be interred. Surrounded by family and a few extended relatives, we laid Uncle Bob to rest with his parents, in a grave marked by a headstone we placed years earlier, already bearing his parents' and Johnny's name.

His farewell service was filled with warmth and dignity. He was surrounded by people who loved him and wanted to honor him with the care and respect he deserved.

I'm deeply grateful that even though Dad wasn't part of our lives for many years, Uncle Bob was. Reconnecting with him late in his life but in time to share fifteen years of memories was a gift for us all. Dad's passing closed one chapter, but it opened another for Uncle Bob and us. For me, he was always a small, living link to my father and his parents. Who knows, maybe a higher power or Grandma Dyer had a hand in sending Uncle Bob to us after Dad and died. I hope our Dyer grandparents know what a happy ending their special son got.

Chapter 51

I Think I'm Gonna Be Sad

BILL HAD FULLY RECOVERED from the injuries he sustained in the pawn shop shooting. In time, he was playing music again and living what looked like a productive life. He landed a job as a clerk at a liquor store in central Mass—one that happened to carry his favorite, hard-to-find beverage, Cisco. Soon enough, he was drinking them nightly.

Somewhere along the way, he and his son had a falling-out, and they stopped speaking. Over time, his heavy drinking caught up with him, and he began to acknowledge it. He'd put on weight and felt run down and sluggish, and he made up his mind to quit drinking *cold turkey*. A couple months later, unexpectedly, he was diagnosed with cirrhosis and Hepatitis C.

"What the hell? I did a good thing by quitting drinking on my own, and now I find out my liver's going?" It felt like a cosmic joke. Usually, it goes the other way around.

Bill followed every directive from his medical team, determined to save his liver and his life. He stuck to a strict, nearly salt-less diet, making most food bland and unenjoyable. Fruit was the only thing he could eat freely, and the sugar sent his weight higher.

Sobriety, the unenjoyable diet, and experimental liver drugs kept him alive, as his world dimmed again.

Bill, once "hyper," as we used to say, and quick-witted, had slowed way down. He'd once fired off sharp, off-color comebacks without apology. Now, he had little to look forward to. He told me every day felt the same—depressing. Each time I saw him, he seemed increasingly defeated and hopeless.

I'd say, "Bill, try to find something small to be grateful for each day. The sun shining, a hot cup of coffee..." But he saw no way forward, only the distant sliver of hope of getting a new liver someday, if he was extremely lucky.

In the spring of 2016, severe stomach issues caused him to be admitted to the hospital for two weeks. When he didn't improve, doctors attempted an emergency liver transplant, thinking it was the root of his issues. When they opened him up, they found far worse complications than expected—a large section of his intestines had turned necrotic due to *C. difficile* ("C. diff") bacteria, leading to widespread organ failure. No one knew where he contracted the infection. After removing several feet of intestine, the surgeon kept him sedated on life support through the weekend. By Sunday, he wasn't improving. The doctor explained that even if he survived, he would face lifelong dialysis, a colostomy bag, oxygen support, and a liver transplant he was too weak to undergo. Bill wouldn't have wanted that. Guided by his doctor, our family chose not to prolong his suffering.

Over Sunday and Monday, my family and some of Bill's close friends visited him. He remained heavily sedated and unresponsive but surrounded by love. At his bedside, we played Bill's favorite songs through earbuds, mostly Who songs. During my alone time with him, I told him it was okay for him to leave and asked him to send me a sign when he reached the other side.

Even though Bill wasn't conscious, Dan explained to him what had happened. He believed Bill deserved to know why he was dying, even if he couldn't respond. The last thing Bill knew before surgery was that he was getting a liver transplant—a new lease on life.

Late Monday afternoon, we removed Bill from life support. Surrounded by his family and closest friends, Marj and I each held one of his hands.

"Bill, we're all here with you. Ma came earlier to see you." We listed the names of everyone who had visited over the weekend and those standing with him now. Though Bill was unresponsive, Marj and I noticed a tiny tear forming at the corner of his left eye. He heard.

To watch someone I loved die in front of me was beyond diffi-cult, but we were all grateful to be there for him when he passed. Johnny had died alone in a rooming house, and Bob had died in Florida with just his significant other at his side. We were grateful to have a couple of days to do it differently for Bill.

After Bill's cremation, Dan and I scattered some of his ashes in Dorchester Bay, just as he'd told Marj years earlier: "feed me to the fish." We released them off the Malibu drawbridge, with the massive rainbow painted Boston gas tank on the left, a fitting trib-ute. The following month, a friend and her husband took our family out on their boat to scatter the rest of his remains far out in Boston Harbor.

In large families, some siblings grow closer than others, whether by age or shared interests. Bill and I shared both. Over the years, we grew close through music, a similar sense of humor, and a love of words—always looking for new ones to add to our vocabu-lary—which made his passing especially hard on me. He was a rebel and a comedian, someone who could get under people's skin, but he never put up a front. That honesty mattered to me, even when it annoyed me.

Shortly after he died, I got the sign I'd asked him for when I said goodbye. As I poured his ashes into a glass jar, a titanium screw from his reconstructed arm clinked loudly. Staring at it, I thought how indestructible it was, like the cars he always picked out for me.

In my dreams of Bill, we're usually driving around in an old GM car, like the "tank" he told me to buy when I got my license. It was the same advice Dan had given him—get something big, something safe, in case I ever crashed. Billiam, as Thom called him, rides with me in memory, in dreams, and when a song by The Who comes on my car radio—which it does a lot more now.

Chapter 52

All I've Got Is a Photograph

In August, we chose not to hold a wake or funeral—exactly what Bill wouldn't have wanted as an unwavering atheist and nonconformist. Instead we honored him with a huge music jam at a function hall. Nothing fancy, just a party for anyone who wanted to "join together with the band," as Bill's favorite group, The Who, sang.

Marj came up with a great idea. With a few helpers, we set Bill's many albums and 45s in the center of each banquet table so guests could take home a few pieces of his vast and eclectic record collection—a small souvenir of his musical life. At the front of the room next to the bar, we set up a makeshift stage.

My band, Dan's band, our nephews, and a wide circle of musician friends played, swapping instruments and rotating players. Guitars and drums changed hands. Someone would step back, and another player would step in. The room was filled with friends and the many musicians Dan had encouraged and mentored when they were young, just as he had me and Bill.

To all of us, Dan was the rock star—the one we watched and learned from. The musicians filling the room were proof of that.

Over the years, he had given many young players space to learn and hone their chops, and they showed up for my family and Bill that night. The celebration of Bill's life unfolded in a way we all understood: music shared, passed along, and carried on.

When most of our guests had settled, we passed around a mic for guests to share their Bill recollections and stories. No surprise, each memory shared was full of humor, capturing his zany personality. As my family mingled with guests, their stories about Bill sparked forgotten memories of our own. We weren't only reminiscing about Bill, but trading Dorchester memories with friends. We laughed over moments we hadn't thought of in years, or hadn't heard at all, reliving the connections that tied us all together.

Dale took the mic. He shared his first impressions of Bill from when he first met our family in Savin Hill, embracing us in our weirdness as his second family.

"I remember when I first came to visit Marj for the weekend. Billy opened the door. He was all over me like a little kid with a hundred questions. Then he started asking me if I knew where he could get some weed."

"I cracked up. I said, 'Dude, what's up with you? I just met you! I don't have any weed. You must know plenty of people in this city you can call.'"

Bill's comfort level with Dale was solid early on.

Dale passed the mic to an old friend, Evan. "Oh, man! Where do I begin about good old Billy Boy? So many funny stories..." He paused to think.

"Okay, so in the '80s, I used to hang out with Billy and your family. He used to take me into Boston on the train. He'd show me all around the Boston Common and all those cool places. We'd walk around for hours. The first time he asked me to go, I was still in high school and I had no money for a train token. Billy winked and said, 'Follow me. We'll hop the turnstile at Savin Hill when the guy in the booth is making change.' I swear, that kid knew how to sneak into every T station in Boston. We didn't pay a dime to ride the trains all day!"

"Yup, sounds like Bill!" a guest shouted, echoed by others nodding and chuckling.

I shared a Billy memory—one of the many times when he didn't give me a fair warning on something, because he loved to "surprise" people.

"When we were young, we were too poor to afford skateboards. When I was ten, Billy built me a skateboard like his and Tommy's—he said Bobby taught him this hack—he nailed metal roller skate wheels to the bottom of a skinny picket fence post."

Friends clapped, thinking I was done with my story. I continued.

"So one day, he and Tommy took me to the Boston Common with our homemade skateboards, to the steep Freedom Trail path. The one with the red painted line."

Boston people nodded in recognition.

"Billy said, 'Start at the top, give it a little push, and wheeee— you'll be flying!'"

"Well, I flew, all right. The board rattled like the rickety Paragon Park roller coaster, and I couldn't stop it. I plowed into an unsuspecting group of tourists. No one was hurt except me. A kind man handed me McDonald's napkins for the blood, but my knee kept bleeding. On the train home from Park Street to Fields Corner, Billy said, 'Now you know why I call it Suicide Hill!'"

Marj shared a classic Billy memory.

"Bill detested cigarettes. He never smoked one and thought anyone who did was an idiot. When I was fifteen and he was fourteen, we were walking home one day and I asked him to hold my cigarettes so I wouldn't get caught with them if I smelled like cigarette smoke. He looked at me like I had ten heads. 'No way, man. I won't buy your cancer sticks, I won't hold them for you, and I definitely won't lie for you. Support your own dirty death wish.'"

She chuckled. "Then, in typical Bill style, he broke into the Ringo 'No No Song...'"

I chimed in, singing the lyric she meant: "No, No, No, No, you can't smoke it no more."

The crowd laughed. It was such a relatable Bill story.

Over the next half hour, people passed the mic, trading more Bill stories as my band set up. From the stage, I looked out at mostly laughing faces, with a few quietly tearing up. After my bands half-hour set, Dan's band moved in and began setting up their gear. In the corner, his guitarist, Bill, tuned his Wolfgang Special—an Eddie Van Halen signature model.

I'd met Bill the year before at a couple of Dan's gigs in New Hampshire. From those brief encounters, I found him attractive and easy to talk with—someone I'd have liked to know better. But he'd had a girlfriend then, and he still did, and she was sitting beside him. I said a quick hello to both of them, thinking, *What a lucky girl. Figures—all the good ones are taken. My life story.*

I joined a table where some of Billy's buddies were swapping stories about him and old cars.

"...Yeah, Bill said, 'Therapy? What do I need therapy for? I have a Delta 88.'"

I added a car memory. "When I was a senior in high school, Bill picked out my first car, a '72 Chevy Bel Air."

Bill's friend Rich perked up. "I remember that V8 guzzler! We called it the war wagon."

I grinned. "Yeah, it was a tank, alright. And it had more dents than a bargain-bin can of corn at B&M Market—but it ran great!"

I went out on a limb and confessed to an old Dot Rat move. "My Chevy only got eight miles to the gallon. So Billy taught me his 'fill up and flee' method at self-serve gas stations."

"Oh, man." Rich covered his mouth, stifling a laugh, embarrassed for me. "I remember him pulling that stunt a few times at the Gulf station on Columbia Road."

"Well, I did it a couple of times, too, I'm ashamed to admit." That got a laugh.

Glancing around, I noticed Bill's friend, Kevin, by the stage alone. In his trademark leather biker jacket, he sat in the corner, tinkering with Bill's old Gibson SG guitar. He and Bill had been bandmates and close friends back in the '90s. I made a beeline for the stage to say hello to him. I gave him a big hug. "I'm so glad you made it."

"Are you kidding? I wouldn't have missed this for anything. Bill was my brother from another mother, man." He turned back to the guitar in his hands. "Damn, this thing's ancient. The Seymour Duncan pickups he added years ago still sound great."

"Yup, and Dan's son, Dayne owns it now." I motioned in his direction. "He chose it when we divvied up Bill's remaining guitars. He's been learning to play and will jam with it tonight."

My voice started to crack thinking about how much I missed Bill. "I'm sure Margie's boys will play a little tonight. They each got a guitar from Bill's collection."

At a table with my bandmates, I shared how Bill still found ways to annoy me: a flicker of lights or an electrical glitch felt like he was saying hello, or how I dreamt about him. But most often, it was through the car radio. I'd flip the radio station just as a Who song started, and he'd come to mind instantly.

Most of my band members didn't know Bill well, but my good friend and drummer Rob did. He knew him from jams and parties at our old rehearsal studio.

"Rob, you'll appreciate this since we like the blues. I once said to Bill, 'rock and roll was born from the blues, so how can you hate the blues so much?' Without missing a beat, he shot back, ''Cause I ain't that bored, that's why!'"

Everyone chuckled, appreciating Bill's sarcastic, unfiltered response. Rob raised his beer in a toasting gesture. "Yeah, I can picture Billy saying that for sure."

Rich pulled me aside, away from the hum of conversation and music. He, Bill and I hung out a lot in the '90s.

"You know, when Bill found out he had cirrhosis and then Hep C, I saw a big change in him. I visited him a bunch of times, and he was calmer, more subdued. I could actually see his human side, which he always covered up with sarcasm... you know what I mean."

I nodded. "For sure."

Rich paused and glanced out at the roomful of friends, the absence of one person impossible to ignore. "He didn't want to die. He wanted to live so badly."

He then told me Bill was deeply sad about his estranged son. I hadn't realized how much it bothered him—he'd hidden it well when they lost many touch years before. Rich looked away and stared out toward the room again, his expression drawn.

"Bill didn't talk much about his feelings, but you could see it on his face how much he missed him. I never understood what happened there." Rich lowered his head before lifting his eyes to mine. "Such a shame."

"Yeah, I'm not sure what happened, either, Rich. We may never know. It's unfortunate."

I searched for something positive to say.

"But at the end of his life, Bill was surrounded by good friends like you and the others..." I winked. "I think he knew you were all there. That's what matters."

Chapter 53

Back Off, Boogaloo

After Dan's band finished up their forty-minute set of scorching rock classics, a few musician friends took the stage for an impromptu jam session. Kevin strapped on his beat-up Gibson and stepped up to the mic. "This one's for Bill. I think he came up with the title; it's a bit of a twist." He snickered to himself. "He called it 'Oh, What a Happy Day.'" Then, Kevin broke into a blistering punk anthem about despair.

I headed over to the table where Dan was telling a Billy story. A few people had known my father in the old days, while the rest had heard enough crazy stories about him to feel they knew him.

"...You know how big my old man was, right? Well, one time, timid little Billy stood up to him. I'll never forget it."

I pulled up a seat as Dan launched into a story I'd never heard before.

In the early '70s, Dan spent time around the Peewee Parksmen, the junior offshoot of the older Ronan Park-area Parksmen street gang. Some of the young boys carried knives in case of a "rumble" near First Parish Church or Ronan Park. Dan had amassed an impressive knife collection for such occasions, which he kept hidden in the top drawer of his bureau. The knives later came in handy on camping trips, or in the case of an unexpected attack walking around Dorchester.

Billy used to play baseball for Mill Stream Little League. He and a neighbor kid, Joey, used to practice catching back and forth across the street. Dad had warned Billy more than once, "Don't play catch near my car or you'll break my windshield."

In rare moments of carefree abandon, Billy forgot the warning. One day, his luck ran out. Joey's pitch was too fast, and Billy missed. The ball smashed into the windshield of Dad's Falcon, leaving a long, jagged crack.

"Oh, crap," Billy muttered, dread washing over him.

Joey crossed the street to assess the damage. He knew how things were in our house. "Man, sorry, Bill," he said, tracing his fingers over the crack. "I know your old man's gonna be rippin' mad."

Billy was already planning his next move. Knowing what was coming, he snuck into Danny's drawer and chose the biggest knife he could find—a Bowie knife with an eight-inch blade. He sat on the bottom bunk, gripping the handle with trembling hands, rehearsing what he would do and say when Dad came storming in.

Sure enough, a few minutes later, Dad appeared in the doorway, belt in hand. He started closing in on Billy.

"I told you not to throw baseballs in front of my goddamned car!" he bellowed.

Billy cowered on the bed, waving the knife with a shaking hand. "Don't come near me. Don't touch me. I'll stab you!"

This was odd. Dad wasn't used to being challenged, least of all by timid Billy.

"Billy, put the knife down," he commanded. Billy's grip tightened. He didn't budge.

Dad tried again. "Billy, give me the knife now."

But Billy held firm. Dad turned and left the room without a word and Billy escaped the beating. After the knife incident, Dad was heard to say, "Billy's a good egg. Soft as a grape, but a good egg."

Chapter 54

Passing the Audition

W**ITH** **SO** **MANY** musicians in the room at Bill's memorial jam, countless stories about bands and the parties they threw surfaced. At the bar, Rob and his wife Jane passed out a round of drinks to Dan, me, and a few other friends. I'd met Rob in 1994 by answering his classified ad in the *Boston Phoenix* newspaper, looking to form a band. He was from out of state, brand new to Boston and was glad to make a musician friend. Side note: Rob is a good guy I never dated. As he likes to remind me, "You said you only wanted to date Axl Rose-type guys." He, Jane, and I still joke about that one.

Rob looked around our circle. "I don't go as far back as you guys, but we had some great times down at the Ashmont studio. I first met Billy down there, in fact—when Ns & Vs ended."

When I was seventeen, I was in my first gigging band with Dan and a couple of his close friends. On my high school nights, we played late-night gigs at a Dorchester bar called the Pizza Factory. That's where performing live really started for me.

Years later, in 1990, Dan and I were in an original rock band called Ns & Vs. The band needed a singer but were against having

288

a female—especially a "bossy" one. They auditioned me, mostly so they'd have a singer to help work out a few new songs. I sang my adolescent lyrics and poems to a number of their original melodies, which fit perfectly. When rehearsal ended and I headed out through the bulkhead door, I turned to the guys and quoted Lennon from the famous The Beatles rooftop concert: "I hope I passed the audition." Turns out I did.

Things worked out well with Ns & Vs. We played a lot of great shows and threw parties that would've made 1999 jealous. After gigs at the Channel nightclub, opening for bands like Blue Öyster Cult, Foghat, and local favorites, the Fools and the Stompers, we crammed about thirty people into our trashy hang—a 300-square-foot basement of a law office on Ashmont Street in Dorchester, affectionately dubbed The Studio.

I sipped my wine. "Rob, I'm not sure if you remember, but when you and I met, five bands were sharing the studio. It was crazy, but it worked."

"Yeah. It did. The bands all rotated different rehearsal nights. That's why the rent was so cheap."

Dan's guitarist, Bill, joined our circle and I found myself edging a little closer to him. Another studio friend, John, joined our conversation, laughing. "Ugh! The avocado green shag rug! It was disgusting! People would sleep on that nasty, beer-stained floor. They didn't care about the broken glass and cigarette butts!"

With no windows, the studio never saw the light of day or got any fresh air. It was a rock and roll dungeon, our all-night speakeasy, like something out of New York's East Village punk era.

John was on a roll. "Remember the studio bathroom?"

Groans and laughter arose. Everyone remembered the "bathroom."

Many a night, a conversation at the studio would go something like this:

"Hey, man, where's the bathroom?"

"Oh, there's no bathroom, dude. You hafta go in there, behind the black curtain, in the slop sink." It was a balancing act for the women to sit on the edge.

Sometimes, a guest would pull one of us aside and whisper, "So, uhm... I gotta drop a deuce, man."

In this instance, the guest was literally shit outta luck. We'd tell them, "Well, you hafta hold it. Store 24 is on Dot Ave. Maybe if you buy a pack of gum, they'll let you use their bathroom. Sorry."

"Hey, Rob," I leaned toward him. "Remember when I offered up the studio to our first band? Those Quincy guys were horrified. They asked, 'Dorchester? Is it even safe?'"

Rob laughed. "Right, and then it ended up getting robbed, anyway! What a bummer."

A lot of good music was made at the old studio. I'm grateful to Dan for including me, for the friends I made there, and for the fun we all shared. Rob soon became part of our studio circle and my whole family, so he was no longer a stranger in a strange land.

I clinked wine glasses with Rob and Jane. "Here's to Billy."

"Here's to Billy," they echoed, and we all took a drink.

The night unfolded exactly as Bill would have wanted—a celebration of his life, filled with laughter, music, and fun memories. The love in the room made the weight of his loss a little easier to bear for my family and for everyone who gathered to celebrate him.

Chapter 55

Yesterday and Today

In the months after Bill's passing, I felt drawn to reconnect with my childhood. I decided to visit my early family homes, to see if I could get inside them and view them through adult eyes. I wondered what, if anything, might surface from those places— what new insights they might reveal about who we were and what made us who we were.

The first stop was to my earliest memory of home, Hancock Street, where we lived when I was age three to six. A young boy answered the door. He appeared to be Hispanic and didn't speak English. I struggled to communicate, relying on hand gestures and the few words I remembered from eighth-grade Spanish at the Grover—*casa* and *niña*. Cautiously, his grandparents let me in to look around the apartment.

I walked down the long, narrow hallway, the layout so familiar yet distant. The bedrooms branched off as they always had, but everything felt smaller than I remembered. I tried to picture my brothers' three sets of bunk beds crammed into the small back bedroom, my parents in their bedroom, but the impressions felt flat —just rooms, not memories.

In the dining room, I smiled at the clearest memory that surfaced: my family eating supper beside the bunk bed Margie and I shared, the dining room doubling as our bedroom. I glanced up and saw the beautiful stained-glass window I'd remembered, a familiar feature in many of Dorchester's triple-deckers. Marj used to wash it when she was little because she loved the way the sun shone through when it was clean. Maybe, in the midst of all the chaos, it had been her little beacon of joy and hope.

I stepped into the tiny kitchen. I knew I'd spent plenty of time there, but I couldn't summon a single memory of it. I tried to picture where my father assaulted my mother countless times, and where Dan said Johnny and Bobby had swung the ax at him—stories passed down, but not lived in my own mind. If one of my siblings had been with me on the day of my visit, their memories might have pulled a few of mine along with them. But alone, the apartment remained just another Dorchester triple-decker apartment. I felt at peace with my visit.

When I turned to leave, another Spanish word came to me: "Gracias."

From Hancock Street, I drove a mile and a half to the next home where we'd lived, on Bloomfield Street. Most of my memories of my father, from ages six to eleven, were rooted there. Miraculously, we lived there for five years, the longest stay in any home with him.

A teenager who looked to be Asian American was on the front porch. I introduced myself and explained I'd lived on the first floor as a little girl and I was curious to see the apartment again. He went inside and asked his grandmother if I could come in and look around. He came back out. "Sorry, she said no."

I fell back on my favorite mantra: "If you don't ask, the answer is always no." His grandmother, who didn't speak English, came to the front door. I tried explaining again. I told them my brother had recently died and how much it would mean to me to revisit the home I grew up in. The boy translated for his grandmother. I showed them my driver's license as reassurance of my intentions. As he translated, he handed my license back to me.

"Okay, she said you can come in, but only as far as the front room." I couldn't believe my luck. I stepped into the foyer, the place where my father had tried to kill Johnny with a baseball bat and had pulled a gun on him. Though I don't recall the events, I tried picturing them from hearing the stories but nothing came to me.

To the left was the parlor, where my father drank every night, listening to country records and sowing chaos. The woodwork and hardwood floors looked much as they had from years ago, but now the room seemed smaller, and foreign—like it were a neighbor's house I'd once played in, but not lived in. I looked up, half-expecting to see the many ceiling indentations my father had left with the baseball bat, pounding at the neighbors upstairs to quiet down. But the ceiling was smooth, the new drywall hiding any trace of his fury. I thought I'd recall more details of when Jimmy attacked my father with that same baseball bat, but it was a ghost of a moment I couldn't access.

The fireplace opening was still sealed, just as it had been when we lived there. But now, the mantle seemed minuscule. I smiled, remembering as a child begging Ma to hang my knee socks there at Christmastime because we couldn't afford store-bought stockings.

The grandmother sensed I wasn't a threat and said something to the boy in their language. He stepped ahead. "She said you can see the rest." I thought to myself, *I can't believe I got in. Bill's probably helping me with one of his loopholes right now.*

The boy led me through the foyer and down the long hall. Each room I peeked into now seemed tiny to me. It was hard to picture my five brothers in the small bedroom, which held two and a half bunk beds, since Bobby had never lived there. The dining room, with its ornate stained-glass window, which had once served as my parents' bedroom, was padlocked shut, so I didn't get to see inside.

He led me down the hallway toward the back of the house. The small kitchen, which I'd once thought huge as a kid, had the same layout, aside from updated cabinets and appliances. A coat of paint covered the grease and blood stains on the colonial-style wallpaper we'd left behind. Most of the assaults I remember happened there. Yet as I stood there, I felt nothing—no anger, no fear, not even a flicker of the past pressing in.

Off the kitchen, the tiny, narrow bathroom, once shared by nine of us, felt claustrophobic. Standing at the sink, all I could feel was how cramped it was, and I wondered how we'd ever made it work.

The bedroom Margie and I had shared, the one from the fire extinguisher incident, looked ordinary, as if nothing had ever happened there. I expected to feel something, maybe a trace of childhood trauma, but there was none. Shortly after the fire, a friend of Dad's covered the walls with cheerful flowered wallpaper, now long gone under many coats of paint. Maybe the fresh wallpaper had done its job back then, easing whatever bad memories I might have carried.

I asked to see the backyard where Billy, Tommy, and I had played. I wanted to remember us jumping into huge piles of leaves and digging in the sandbox Dad had got for us. The teen boy led me out back, and again, everything seemed much smaller than I remembered. Overgrown trees had replaced the rhubarb, blackberry, and raspberry bushes we'd ate from every summer. I showed the boy where a rose vine used to climb along the side property fence.

As we turned to leave, I looked back one last time. The yard felt empty, the past distant and unreachable. I thanked him, telling him he'd helped me fulfill a huge personal wish. I could tell he was pleased.

Driving away down the street, I glanced at the old Victorian houses I remembered. Some were painted new colors, some in disrepair, but mostly they looked about the same.

On the ride home, I thought about how being inside either childhood apartment stirred no emotion, only a dim recognition. Visiting those old homes was like visiting a loved one's grave—the body is there, but the person is not. They live in my heart and memory, not in the place itself. Dad, Johnny, Bobby, and Billy weren't there. Neither was I, my childhood, or the family we once were.

Instead of my usual guilt or self-judgment over feeling nothing, I smiled. I'd satisfied my insatiable curiosity and seen those apartments for what they were, and still are: places my family once lived, now homes for others to create their own memories and legacies.

As I neared the house I was renting, I remembered something I'd wondered about years earlier when Dad died: what his passing might change if anything. It occurred to me that it hadn't changed anything at all. Our lives had never depended on him. Ma was the glue holding everything together.

Chapter 56

Here Comes the Sun

In December 2017, encouraged by my women's group mentor, I took a bold step toward finding a meaningful relationship. She pushed me to step out on the skinny branch saying, "Let the universe know you mean business, Mary."

So I drafted a poem, "My Christmas Wish," listing the qualities I sought in a partner—kindness, healthy lifestyle, integrity, and a generous spirit. I slipped it in the Christmas cards of everyone I knew. I cringed at first, thinking some might have thought I was desperate or crazy, but I put it out there, anyway.

The poem didn't yield many suitors, but to my surprise, my brother Dan suggested someone—his guitarist Bill, the nice guy I'd admired since 2015.

"Bill's single again," Dan said.

"Oh, really? I've always liked Bill. I'd love to get to know him if he's interested too."

"Cool, I'll give him your number at our next band practice."

A week later, on Christmas morning, a snowstorm canceled my family gathering at Marj and Dale's. While tossing in a load of laundry in the basement, I heard my phone ring. I figured it was one of my friends calling to wish me a Merry Christmas. When I reached my phone, I saw a missed call from a New Hampshire number.

Hmmm. It's not Dan's number. Could it be Bill?

My heart leapt when I listened to the voicemail and heard his voice: "Merry Christmas, Mary! Dan said I should call you."

I called him back right away.

After some small talk, Bill asked me if I had any upcoming shows with my '60s & '70s acoustic band.

"Yes." I said. "In fact, I'm playing this Friday night at a coffee house in Dedham."

He took down the address. "Great, I'll be there. Can't wait!"

Bill braved icy roads from Candia, New Hampshire, a ninety-minute drive on a good day, and arrived early to see me—a refreshing change from the men I'd known. Before show time, we sat together, conversation flowing effortlessly, like we'd been friends for years. After the gig, our conversation carried over at a pub in West Roxbury. By the end of a beer, we had New Year's Eve plans together. Within a short period, we were seeing each other regularly and building a solid relationship.

Over the next few years, Bill and I grew closer in ways that felt steady and stable rather than dramatic and draining. We bonded over music, camping trips, and a shared commitment to living healthy and showing up for the people we loved. What mattered most to me, though, was his consistency. Bill kept his word. He had my back. He didn't disappear or deflect blame when things got heated. For once, I felt chosen and prioritized, without the constant second-guessing and melodrama of previous relationships I'd been in.

In 2019, Bill proposed on my fifty-third birthday. We got married in a small ceremony in 2021, opting to put our money toward a home instead of a wedding reception. It was the only home we liked and weren't outbid on in two years of home hunting during COVID. It felt meant to be.

Shortly after, Rob and Jane hosted a generous wedding celebration for us and fifty guests in their home. "My Christmas Wish" manifested. Even the Hallmark Channel couldn't have written such a great, sappy holiday movie as good as our love story!

Chapter 57

Lady "Ma" Donna

By her eighties, Ma's energy reflected her age. She lived independently for a while after Charlie died, but when she couldn't manage alone anymore, we moved her to a nursing home. Though the transition was difficult at first, she soon thrived, forming close friendships with other residents. For five years, frequent visitors surrounded her—her children and grandchildren, making her time there enjoyable.

At the nursing home, she used a wheelchair to get around, her conversations were simpler, and her memory had softened a bit. She started calling my husband Bill "Bob," which we all joked about. I was grateful she got to know him through our visits and through her beating him in their many games of checkers. She made it through the COVID lockdown without getting sick or depressed from isolation.

In April 2022, at eighty-seven, Ma's kidneys began failing from natural aging. Several times, she seemed as if she was rallying, talking and even singing along to old-time songs. Then, the next day, she would be unresponsive, her body shutting down a little more with each passing day. This went on for a couple of weeks. We knew she was nearing the end of her life. I visited her several times throughout April, my own knee surgery looming in early May, I didn't want to miss my chance to say goodbye.

Bill and I visited Ma on the last Sunday in April. With my surgery scheduled for the next day, I knew this would be our last visit. Resting in her bed with her eyes closed, she could hear me but couldn't respond verbally. Instead, she was speaking to me with her eyebrows. Each time I spoke, they lifted subtly, as if to acknowledge she'd heard.

Ma loved *The Wizard of Oz*, so I sang "Over the Rainbow" while brushing her hair. Her brows moved in a contented expression. I told her I loved her and I was sorry for being such a bossy, stubborn kid. In her forgiving way, her brows narrowed, as if to disagree, saying, "No, you weren't."

My last words to her were, "Ma, when you get to the other side, say hi to Billy, Johnny, and Bobby for me. Tell them I miss them."

The next morning, I went to my scheduled surgery. When I awoke groggy, I could sense the sadness on Bill's face. Through my post-anesthesia fog, I asked, "Is Ma still alive?"

"No, hon. Marj called. I'm sorry—your mom passed away a little while ago."

Lying in the recovery room, I felt sadness, but also the peace of having seen her and spoken to her the day before. I believe Ma's spirit was with me in the operating room, watching over her "baby," as she often called me. Her work on earth as a mother was done. It was time for her to reunite with her other five babies and, of course, her beloved Charlie and her parents.

At Ma's wake the following week, her cherished container with Bobby's ashes rested alongside her in the casket, her first baby with her, as she'd asked.

Ma lived far longer than her parents and two husbands. She lost three grown children and still found the strength to persevere.

She was a tough bird, as we say. She didn't die of a broken heart or a broken spirit. She passed away from natural causes, surrounded by the loving support of her children, their spouses, and her cherished grandsons Eric, Taylor and his wife Nicky, and Dayne.

Despite twenty-four brutal years with my father, my mother never turned to alcohol or drugs to cope. She never neglected us or allowed us to be separated or placed in foster care. She held us together when it would have been easy to fall apart.

Ma's resilience became our legacy. Each of us inherited her ability to bounce back in our own way. I feel her spirit with me every day when I cook. I learned by watching her create delicious meals. When Bill thanks me for a great meal, I say, "Thank Doris. She taught me all I know."

I hope Charlie, Johnny, Bobby, and Billy, and Ma's two infants —Billy #1 and her stillborn baby girl—are reunited with her.

After a life marked by torment in his own mind, I hope my father is enjoying Buck Owens songs with his parents and siblings, especially Uncle Bob.

I like to think my brothers are singing Beatles and Who songs.

Knowing Ma, she's singing Engelbert Humperdinck's "After the Lovin'" to Charlie in her Edith Bunker-like singing voice.

DURING MY RECOVERY from knee surgery, I had ample free time and grew more curious about our extended family, conducting extensive genealogy and public-records research on both sides. On my father's side, I'd learned two of his paternal uncles battled alcoholism and had spent time in Boston-area prisons. The apple hadn't fallen far from the family tree.

I'd also ordered a copy of my father's military discharge record. He served in Japan during the onset of the Korean War, assigned to a street peacekeeping guard role, not combat. His record listed two AW 107s (Articles of War 107): disciplinary actions resulting in lost pay. The discharge reason cited "CIR 39-PETS," an acronym for Personality, Emotional, Temperament, and Suitability issues. Many of his Army photos show him playing pool and goofing off with his barracks buddies, bottles of booze in hand. Dad looked like he was partying in the Army.

Dan pointed out that Dad was never promoted past the rank of private during his two years of service, a detail confirmed on his discharge form. We'd always thought he received a medical discharge due to a Jeep-accident–related back injury, but oddly, his discharge papers made no mention of either, only the "PETS" note. So when Dad's mother and her brother, Uncle Billy, said he came out of the Army "changed," it seemed possible to me that patterns might have already begun taking root and the habits he fell into in the Army only made things worse. I thought about how Ma's life might have gone if drinking hadn't been such a big part of my father's life. With his mental illness—if it could even have been recognized or treated back then—things perhaps could have been different. Our family might have taken a different course, especially Johnny.

A month after Ma passed, Bill and I hosted a summer cookout with my siblings. We sorted through her old photo albums and personal effects, each of us taking what we wanted to keep. As always, stories of our father surfaced.

Jim shared a memory, capturing how my mother endured life with Dickie for twenty-four years.

"In the mid-'70s, the old man had one of his outbursts, ranting and screaming from the parlor. Ma was in the pantry, putting dishes away, keeping her distance. I came around the corner to ask her something, and for a split second she froze, gripped with fear.

She thought I was the old man—coming after her in the pantry. The look of terror in her eyes was so sad to me. I told her, 'Ma, it's just me,' and she relaxed, letting out a huge sigh of relief."

It was a pivotal moment Jim never forgot, one of many during her tumultuous marriage.

I'm grateful that Margie and my brothers stepped in and urged Ma to divorce my father. Otherwise, she might never have met Charlie and had a second marriage built on stability, companionship, and support. They had twenty-five good years together.

In her twenty-four years married to my father, the farthest she'd ever traveled was fifty miles north to New Hampshire. Charlie took her places she'd never been—Quebec, Florida, Las Vegas, Arizona. They went to restaurants and concerts, plays and parties. She felt loved.

For her, finally, after all she had given, her love was reciprocated as the Beatles laid it out: "the love you take is equal to the love you make."

Chapter 58

My Long and Winding Road

REFLECTING on my Dorchester childhood has led me to look at how that upbringing carried me to where I am now, for better or worse.

After college, I grew a conscience and stopped stealing. Over the next twenty-five years, I worked with several animal shelters, rescuing and fostering homeless cats who couldn't pay me back. It was my way of making amends—with society, with God, and with myself for my rebellious, early life stealing.

Growing up in Dorchester and in my family, I developed a take-no-crap mentality. In a world feeling like every man for himself, I learned not to be a pushover. That toughness helped me survive, but over time it also hardened into rigidity. I saw a lot of things in black-and-white terms and felt compelled to have things be my way or the highway.

In 1999, the year my father and Johnny died, my body began falling apart—or so it felt. Neck pain, back pain, aching hips. Orthopedic specialists called my spine decrepit, which pushed me deeper into worry and fixation. I was only thirty-three. Why was my healthy body failing me? Doctors told me to quit working out and prescribed rest, injections, chiropractic care, and physical therapy. Nothing worked.

Like most people, I eventually got a "check-up from the neck up." Therapists traced my struggles back to childhood trauma, and some of it rang true. But the focus also kept me tethered to the past. What about the good things—music, close friends, and seven siblings who brought humor and fun into our house? At a certain point, it mattered more to move forward than to keep running on the hamster wheel.

One night in 2005, lying upside down on an inversion back-stretching table (spoiler alert: it didn't work), I watched *Chronicle* feature a segment on Dr. John Sarno's book *The Mindbody Prescription*. I straightened myself up—painfully—and bought the book.

It turns out my overactive mind had kept me in fight-or-flight mode long past its expiration date. GI upset, skin eruptions, and unexplained orthopedic pain still show up when my mind is churning, even when I don't consciously feel stressed. Understanding how the subconscious operates piqued my curiosity—not from a psychoanalytic angle, but from the experience of simply being human.

By my early forties, I began to see how the black-and-white attitude showed up in my dating life and the distance it created. Learning to pause, listen, and accept different views more didn't come easily. It took hard self-examination and a willingness to surrender old ways. I joined a women's group to help me with that, and to get my dating priorities in order. With their help, I stopped auditioning for men's approval and started choosing better. I valued integrity, personal generosity, a healthy lifestyle, and stable support, and I wouldn't accept anything less.

Over time, I learned to keep my own fiery spirit in check. I shifted from being straight-on pushy to direct; from tit-for-tat to letting things slide and handling conflict with more diplomacy. I'm not perfect; I'm a work in progress and will be until I'm dead and buried. In the meantime, *I'll follow the sun* and see where it takes me.

I'm not afraid to ask tough questions. But I've learned how you ask matters. I've also seen how humility and vulnerability mend hurts faster than righteousness. Not dwelling on past indignities helps me now—when I catch myself.

I came to see my parents were doing the best they could, with the minds they had and the hand they were dealt. The past, in all its ways, is long over, never to be lived again. I can remember the good without fixating on the bad. Like Ringo sang, *forget about the past and all your sorrows.*

I've come to learn that positive thinking doesn't settle a busy mind, less thinking does. Bad moods can overtake me but they aren't me; they're low-energy thoughts that eventually move on, reminding me of George's great song, "All Things Must Pass."

The sentiment, *everything has got to be just like you want it to* always hit home for me. Now, more often, I know I need to control less, accept more, and just *let it be.* I used to try to do my thinking "right" and force gratitude lists to feel lighter. Now I understand that when I don't take my thinking so seriously, gratitude seems to arrive on its own.

Life is all about perspective. I have a better appreciation of my parents' limitations and contributions. I can look back on my father's mental illness and addictions with understanding instead of thinking lowly of him. I can see my mother's choice to stay with him in terms of the times she lived in and her capacity to handle things, instead of the harsh judgment I held in my younger years. Motivational author Dr. Wayne Dyer (no relation) said, "Change the way you look at things, and the things you look at change." Some days I employ this attitude better than others. *Life goes on.*

Dan, Jim, Marj, Thom, and I stay in touch regularly. Though geographically scattered, we still gather for major holidays and birthdays, usually at my home now, after years of Marj and Dale opening theirs to all of us. Our gatherings still lead to reminiscing about the good and not-so-good old days. Despite everything we've been through, we mostly laugh, sharing our own versions of events and keeping our childhoods—and the family members we've lost—alive. Like many Dot Rats and Bostonians, we're still an opinionated, spirited bunch. Our aging memories spark lively debates, and we still enjoy the banter.

A year after we bought our home, my husband Bill and I fostered and adopted a sweet rescue dog, Chaqui (CHAH-kee). My little family now looks quite different from the one I grew up in, yet I wouldn't trade either for anything. Today, I live a peaceful life in a single-family home, with space to spread out and room to breathe. It's a far cry from the cramped triple-deckers of Dorchester, where the walls were thin and the streets never seemed to sleep.

Still, both places carry the heartbeat of home for me. Back then, my parents and eight kids filled those noisy apartments with chaos, music, and laughter. Now it's my husband, our dog, and quiet evenings reading or bingeing our favorite shows. Different worlds, different rhythms—but in both, what matters most is the love and the life lived inside them. And every so often, Bill and I keep the music alive, jamming with Dan, Rob, and other good friends.

Most of us still stay in touch with childhood friends from Dot, maintaining bonds to last a lifetime. We have each other's backs like family, never taking each other for granted. Whenever one of us siblings or a close friend needs help, we all know, *anytime at all, all you gotta do is call*, and we'll be there. Loyalty, love, and support are a legacy we learned from our parents and through growing up in Dorchester. It's what's always carried us through.

In the end, it comes down to what John and the Beatles sang—*Love is all you need*

O.F.D.

Epilogue

GROWING UP IN DORCHESTER, a pair of 140-foot-tall liquid natural gas tanks owned by Boston Gas Company were everyone's north star, a landmark for giving directions, and most importantly, a symbol of home.

Up until 1992, the two tanks stood side by side: one plain white tank stamped with the Boston Gas logo, the other transformed into a work of art by an artist and former nun, Corita Kent. She designed the tank's 'Rainbow Swash' design, a burst of color on the Boston Harbor horizon that could be spotted for miles on a clear day. The Rainbow tank still stands today, reminding Dorchester people of where they came from or where they still live. Traffic reporters still reference the iconic landmark: "93 south is snarled from the gas tank to the Braintree split." For Dorchester natives like me, hearing the phrase and seeing the live video feed is never just about traffic—it's about the place we proudly call home. Flying into Logan Airport, I know I'm home when I see the Rainbow tank below me in Boston Harbor, and get a little choked up.

When the COVID-19 lockdown hit in March 2020, I was

living in an apartment not far from Dorchester. I was looking for a distraction beyond adult coloring books and jigsaw puzzles. My husband Bill, a carpenter, had a truck bed full of scrap wood. Not a painter by any means, I grabbed a five-inch piece, thinking maybe I could paint something Boston-related on it. But what? My mind went straight to Dorchester—to home—to the gas tanks. I painted the two original gas tanks and the Savin Hill Bridge in the background, the shoreline of Malibu Beach where we swam as kids, and seagulls circling overhead in a Christmas-like snowfall. To my surprise, it came out okay. One piece led to another, and soon I was selling my gas tank paintings online, donating the proceeds to a homeless shelter and an animal rescue.

What started as a lockdown pastime turned into a passion and gave me a way to stay connected to my roots. I still paint those familiar landmarks—on plaques, mugs, even gas grill propane tanks, and a Gibson Les Paul shape guitar Dan built, which I painted in the Rainbow Swash design. Every December, my husband Bill cuts gas tank-shaped wood ornaments on his scroll saw, and I paint them for customers to hang on their Christmas trees, a little piece of Dot legacy proudly displayed. Some of my painted vases have served as urns, holding the ashes of people's loved ones. It's humbling, knowing what I paint carries both our neighborhood's landmark and the memory of a life once lived there.

The best part is always the conversations. Customers slip into Dot nostalgia right away. They ask, "What parish were you from?" because that's how many Bostonians place each other. My family marked homes by neighborhoods instead. "We lived everywhere—Uphams Corner, Fields Corner, Savin Hill, Andrew Square." It always sparks the familiar back-and-forth. "Fields Cohn-nuh, huh?" they'll say in their thick Boston accent. "Did you know the so-and-so family?" And depending on their age, somewhere in the list of my siblings' names, recognition usually emerges.

The tanks become more than paint and wood. They're conversation starters, memory keepers, reminders of how connected we all still are to each other. A hobby born out of lockdown keeps me rooted in the place I grew up. Thankfully, it was the only lockdown—or lock-up—I've ever had to live through. And every time I paint those Dorchester landmarks, childhood memories flood back —Billy or Danny playing their bass, Johnny's wild Dot Rat streak, Bobby's toughness, Margie's generosity and wisdom, Jimmy's phone pranks and music, Tommy's fearless fence hopping and tree climbing, and my parents holding it together the best they could. I think, too, of my Dorchester childhood friends who are still in touch.

With every brushstroke, I'm not just painting landmarks. I'm painting the life all Dot Rats lived—the streets we walked, the struggles we carried, the lessons learned, the pride we felt, the fun we had, and the losses we endured—from the place we will always call home.

Near or far, we'll always be O.F.D.

With a Lot of Help from My Friends

Acknowledgments

I have only sporadic recollections of my childhood, so my siblings' contributions were invaluable in helping me write this book.

My monumental and heartfelt gratitude to my living siblings: Dan, Jim, Marj, and Thom—for walking back through our shared past with me, and for trusting me with the memories that made this book possible.

To my late brothers, Bob, John, and Bill. I wish I could share this book with you, and I wish we could have had more time together. You will never be forgotten in our family. I miss you all tremendously.

And to all seven of my siblings, thank you for indulging me as your baby sister, for raising me well and street-smart, and for filling our childhood with seriously good music. I love you all.

With thanks to my mother, for giving my siblings and me a childhood filled with fun, despite the challenges you faced. You also taught me by example, how to forgive generously and move forward. Your resilience showed me how to get back up—again and again.

To my father, whose feisty spirit helped me grow a backbone instead of a wishbone and whose great American roots music filled our home. My path forward was shaped by what I took from our brief time together.

Warm thanks to extended family and friends who contributed memories, helping me to fill in the gaps.

Immense gratitude to author and mentor Mary Fenney, who

took a personal interest in my work and whose patient guidance helped me turn countless drafts into a coherent whole, allowing me to learn how to be a *paperback writer*. I'm indebted for the many video coaching calls and for talking me through eleventh-hour fine-tuning that had been missed along the way.

Warm appreciation to editor Abigail Degnan, for helping refine several drafts with care, insight and clarity.

Thank you Carolyn V. Hamilton for early memoir coaching. Thank you readers, Cheri Locke, Donna Marie West, Karen Kost-Rios, and Art Tagliaferri, for your time and thoughtful feedback. Thank you, Art, for giving countless ideas a place to be seen and supported on the Retro Dot Facebook page.

For my distant Quaker ancestor, Mary Barrett Dyer. I feel her quiet determination in me and hope to live up to the courage she modeled for the generations that followed.

Many thanks to Dot Rats everywhere, especially Cheryl and Joan. You helped make my formative years memorable and easier to weather.

Thank you to my canine companion, Chaqui, for your quiet company beside me through every written word of this book.

Utmost love and gratitude to my husband Bill for unwavering support, unconditional love, and tremendous patience throughout this project and in every corner of our life. You're the rock—and the roll.

I gratefully acknowledge the songs, music, and lyrics of John Lennon, Sir Paul McCartney, George Harrison, and Sir Ringo Starr (Richard Starkey). Their work, both as members of the Beatles and in their solo careers, has influenced my life and helped shape the emotional landscape of this book, including the following songs:

"A Day in the Life" - Lennon-McCartney

"All Those Years Ago" - G. Harrison

"Back Off Boogaloo" - R. Starkey, G. Harrison
"Beware of Darkness" - G. Harrison
"Carry That Weight" - Lennon-McCartney
"Crippled Inside" - J. Lennon
"Cry Baby Cry" - Lennon-McCartney
"Drive My Car" - Lennon-McCartney
"Getting Better" - Lennon-McCartney
"Hello, Goodbye" - Lennon-McCartney
"Help!" - Lennon McCartney
"Here Comes the Sun" - G. Harrison
"Here, There, and Everywhere" - Lennon-McCartney
"Hey Bulldog" - Lennon-McCartney
"Honey Pie" - Lennon-McCartney
"I've Just Seen a Face" - Lennon-McCartney
"It Don't Come Easy" - R. Starkey
"(Just Like) Starting Over" - J. Lennon
"Lady Madonna" - Lennon-McCartney
"Little Willow" – P. McCartney
"Love Comes to Everyone" - G. Harrison
"Not a Second Time" - Lennon-McCartney
"Nowhere Man" - Lennon-McCartney
"Photograph" - R. Starkey, G. Harrison
"Revolution" - Lennon-McCartney
"The End" - Lennon-McCartney
"The Long and Winding Road" - Lennon-McCartney
"This Song" - G. Harrison
"Two of Us" - Lennon-McCartney
"With a Little Help From My Friends" - Lennon-McCartney

I also thank Sir George Martin, whose brilliant production helped define the sound of The Beatles.

About the Author
Mary A. Dyer

Mary's love of writing began in fifth grade when she wrote and delivered a speech about the Beatles. In high school, a poem she wrote about John Lennon was published in her school newspaper, and she later won a statewide essay contest sponsored by a Boston newspaper.

Inspired by family friends who often said someone should tell the story of their turbulent yet unforgettable upbringing in Dorchester, Massachusetts, Mary decided to tell that story.

When she's not reading rock-star biographies, she refurbishes furniture, paints Dorchester landmarks, and sings in a '60s and '70s acoustic trio. Currently, She lives in New England with her husband, Bill, and their rescue dog, Chaqui.

www.facebook.com/marydyerauthor
www.marydyerauthor.com

www.ingramcontent.com/pod-product-compliance
Lightning Source LLC
Chambersburg PA
CBHW070849160726
48004CB00003B/990